Pioneers
of Psychology

Also by Raymond E. Fancher

Psychoanalytic Psychology:
The Development of Freud's Thought

Pioneers
of Psychology

Raymond E. Fancher

YORK UNIVERSITY

W · W · Norton & Company
New York

Library of Congress Cataloging in Publication Data

Fancher, Raymond E
   Pioneers of psychology.

   Includes bibliographies and index.
      1. Psychology—History. 2. Psychologists—
History. I. Title.
BF95.F3   1979   150'.92'2   78–10845
ISBN 0–393–01161–5
ISBN 0–393–09082–5 pbk.

1 2 3 4 5 6 7 8 9 0

For Joelle and Seth

Contents

Contents

Preface

This book is about the lives and works of some of the people who shaped the modern science of psychology. It attempts to illustrate how several fundamental ideas and theories actually came into being by presenting them in the contexts of the lives and perspectives of the individuals who first grappled with them. By blending the biographical with the theoretical, and showing how the early psychologists were driven to make their particular discoveries as much by their own personalities and life histories as by their dispassionate scientific analyses, it aims to lend vitality and interest to important ideas that otherwise might seem less compelling.

Psychology is such a vast and diversified field that it would be impossible for a single volume to cover its entire breadth in this manner. Accordingly, this book is representative rather than comprehensive in its coverage. As described below, chapter subjects were selected with an eye towards reasonably sampling the many topics covered in a typical introductory college course. Consistent with the format of most introductory psychology textbooks, the individual chapters are all self-contained, so they may be read in any sequence or combination.

The opening chapter presents some of the general foundations of modern psychology by taking the reclusive seventeenth-century philosopher, René Descartes, as its subject. Descartes was selected because of his pivotal and enormously influential role in the transition from the medieval to the modern view of psychological functioning. His conceptions of the brain, the reflex mechanism, the innate ideas of the mind, the passions, and the mind-body dichotomy were all partly rooted in medieval scholastic thought, but also became the starting points for major developments discussed in later chapters of this book.

Chapter Two focuses on a question from physiological psychology which has roots in Descartes's ideas, and which has been continuously and vigorously debated for the past two hundred years: namely, whether or to what extent specific psychological functions are localized in specific regions of the brain. This chapter tells how a whole series of individuals, from the phrenologist Franz Gall in the late 1700s to the neurosurgeon Wilder Penfield in the 1970s, have both disputed and built upon one another's work in trying to understand how the body's most mysterious and complicated organ works in controlling behavior.

The major subject of Chapter Three is the great all-around scientist of the nineteenth century, Hermann Helmholtz, chosen because he is generally regarded as the most important single figure in the development of modern theories of sensation and perception. Though most of the chapter is about Helmholtz himself, it opens with Immanuel Kant, whose philosophy framed Helmholtz's work, and closes with the Gestalt psychologists, whose perceptual theories followed in his wake.

Wilhelm Wundt and William James, the co-subjects of Chapter Four, were probably the two most important founders of psychology as an independent and popular discipline in the universities. Both men established experimental psychology laboratories in 1875, both were extremely learned generalists whose texts provided attractive overviews for the emerging field, and both drew large numbers of students to what had previously been a relatively minor branch of philosophy. A further spice is added to their pairing by the fact that they frequently disagreed, and did not care much for each other personally.

Chapter Five discusses several investigators of hypnotism and the social influence processes, beginning with Franz Mesmer's "animal magnetism" in the late 1700s and concluding a century later with Gustave Le Bon's provocative ideas about crowd behavior. This topic was selected because it attracted a host of colorful characters, while still raising many issues that are of continuing importance to students of social and abnormal psychology.

Chapter Six relates how Sigmund Freud drew upon his personal experiences as a doctor, as well as on his extremely rich intellectual background, to create psychoanalysis, arguably the most influential and controversial psychological theory of our time. Freud's ideas, of course, still dominate much of the discussion in abnormal psychology and personality theory, and have profoundly affected our entire intellectual climate.

The life and work of Francis Galton is the subject of Chapter Seven. This versatile and controversial Victorian gentleman —who made important contributions to African exploration, geography, meteorology, statistics, and fingerprint analysis, as well as to psychology—was the originator of the mental test, and an outspoken believer in the prepotency of heredity over environment in determining psychological attributes such as intelligence. His work laid the foundations for both the achievements and the still-unresolved disputes that characterize the modern fields of behavior genetics and mental measurement.

Chapter Eight is about two fathers of modern learning theory and behaviorism, the movement which for many years generally dominated American psychology. Beginning with the story of the Russian physiologist Ivan Pavlov, and his discovery of the conditioned reflex as a tool for studying the processes of the brain, the chapter goes on to tell how the American psychologist John B. Watson applied the conditioned reflex concept to a much wider range of human and animal behavior, making it the cornerstone of his behaviorist psychology.

Two of the most important of our contemporary psychologists, Jean Piaget and B. F. Skinner, are the subjects of the concluding chapter. Piaget's developmental-cognitive theory and Skinner's behavioristic theory of operant conditioning strongly contrast with one another in many respects, and thus illustrate psychology's continuing diversity. At the same time, the broad implications and practical applications following from both Piaget's and Skinner's work show that the creative traditions of psychology's earlier pioneers are still alive and well.

I suspect that few of my colleagues will quarrel with the inclusion of any of these individuals in the book, but that most will regret the omission of one or more favorite figures. In defense, I can simply repeat the relatively limited goals I have set for the book: to sample the field of psychology representatively rather than exhaustively, and to bring to life some important ideas and issues that run the risk of being buried in the more traditional textbook presentation. If anyone is stimulated to learn about psychology's other pioneers, or to seek out more extensive coverage of the history of psychology, the book will have been a success.

It was both entertaining and humbling to write this book. Entertaining, because I have been an addict of scientific biographies ever since my boyhood reading of Paul de Kruiff's *Microbe Hunters,* so my research into the lives of the early psychologists was more like recreation than work. But it was also humbling, because the further I got into the research, the more I realized how much I did not know. Inevitably, I was drawn into areas of psychological specialization in which I was little more than a layman, and I became very dependent upon the generous advice and criticism of colleagues who were expert in my weakest areas. I was extremely fortunate in enlisting such help, and acknowledge with deep thanks the assistance of Neil Agnew, Arthur Blumenthal, Kurt Danziger, Maureen Dennis, Norman Endler, Peter Kaiser, Bruno Kohn, Bernard Norton, Hiroshi Ono (and his entire graduate seminar on perception), and Malcolm Westcott. The errors in my

Preface

presentation will undoubtedly show that I failed to learn all that these colleagues tried to teach me, but the book is immeasurably better for their efforts.

I also wish to thank the people who assisted, in various ways, in the preparation of the final manuscript. Several of my York University classes suffered through, and helped me to improve, early versions of the material. Margery Adamson not only typed most of the manuscript, but also made valuable editorial suggestions. My students Michael Blacha and Catherine Gildiner helped to clarify several parts of the book, and my French "parents," Pierre and Esther Zarco, helped to locate the apartment in the south of France where the final revisions could be most agreeably completed. It has been a pleasure throughout to work with Donald Lamm, Donald Fusting, Mary Cunnane, and the editorial staff at Norton.

As usual, my wife Lynn was my first and best critic. My children Joelle and Seth tolerated with good humor many mealtime ramblings about the strange-looking men whose portraits decorated my study walls and whose lives preoccupied me for so long. I hope this book will one day help them to see why I found those men interesting.

Raymond E. Fancher

July, 1978

Pioneers
of Psychology

1

René Descartes and
the Foundations
of Modern Psychology

November 10, 1619 was St. Martin's Eve, and most of the residents of the south German city of Ulm were celebrating with drink and frivolity. René Descartes, a visiting twenty-three-year-old French soldier, was a notable exception. He spent the entire day inside a heated room engaged in almost obsessional meditation. Over and over again he mentally tested the surprising ideas that had recently occurred to him, sensing that they might resolve a tormenting personal conflict that had plagued him for years, but scarcely daring to hope so openly.

Finally, as a stormy night fell, he lay back exhausted on his bed and began to dream. At first all was fever, thunderstorms, and panic. Phantoms whirled about, and could not be driven away. Then he was in the street, caught in a terrifying wind that made him spin around three times on his left foot. He could not walk normally, and finally staggered to an open college gate. He wished to go to the college chapel and pray; on the way he passed several people who walked normally and spoke of a missing person and a melon from a foreign land. The wind blew Descartes violently against the chapel, then died down as he woke up.

After murmuring a prayer to exorcise the "evil genius" he was certain was plaguing him, Descartes fell back asleep. He saw a terrific lightning flash followed by sparks throughout the room, and again awoke, uncertain whether they had been real or dreamt. Reassured that he had been dreaming, he once again fell asleep and had another dream, much milder in tone than the others. He dreamed he opened a book of poetry on his table, and read the line "What path in life shall I follow?" A stranger appeared who conversed about another poem beginning with the words "Yes and no." The man and the book vanished, then the book reappeared newly decorated with engravings. As the night grew quiet Descartes gradually woke up, reflecting on his dreams. He quickly arrived at a personally compelling interpretation of the dreams that indicated his long crisis was over.

The first dream, he believed, was a clear warning that his old ways of life had been leading him into error. He had previously looked to the authorities for guidance in his thought and action. The terrifying wind in the dream represented an evil genius trying to drive him by force—that is, by mere authority—into a place (the chapel) where Descartes ought better to go under his own power. The lightning and sparks of the second dream represented the descent of the spirit of truth, which drove away the evil genius and inspired the mild third dream. That dream, with its obvious theme of vocational choice ("What path in life shall I follow?" "Yes and no.") seemed clearly to be a benediction on the new ideas. If Descartes devoted his life to their pursuit, he—acting alone and without the support of the authorities—could produce distinct improvements over previous modes of thought. These improvements were symbolized by the improved book at the end of the dream.

Whether or not Descartes's interpretations were literally true is inconsequential. The important point was that *he* believed them to be true, and thus they marked the end of a long crisis of indecision and doubt for him. Previously he had been a shy, reclusive, and perhaps mentally disturbed young man drifting aimlessly through life. Now he was a man with a mission, on his way to becoming the greatest philosopher of his time. Among many other contributions, he was to develop

1. René Decartes (1596–1650). *The National Library of Medicine, Bethesda, Maryland*

a general image of humanity that would dominate western thinking about the mind and body for centuries to come, and that would sow the seeds for a new science of psychology.

The ideas that occurred to Descartes at Ulm, and so changed his life, were the basis of a new *method* for obtaining knowledge. The new method was partly a reaction against the traditional scholastic philosophy in which Descartes had been trained, and partly a unique creation of his own remarkable personality. To appreciate the nature and significance of this revolutionary method, it will be helpful to review Descartes's early life and the times in which he grew up.

Descartes's Early Life and the Development of His Method

The details of Descartes's birth, like those of so many other parts of his life, are only vaguely known. He was an intensely private person as an adult, who tried to keep even the date of his birth secret lest he become the object of speculation by astrologers. Because an indiscreet artist wrote the date March 31, 1596 beneath Descartes's portrait, we now know he was born on that day in the small French town of La Haye. René's mother died shortly after his birth and he grew up on his grandmother's estate in La Haye. His father, a wealthy lawyer, practiced most of the year in Brittany, 150 miles away. The task of rearing him fell mainly to his grandmother, a nurse, and an older brother and sister. The exact circumstances of his childhood are unclear, but Descartes apparently grew up without close attachments to any of these early caretakers.

Young René was intellectually precocious, a fact which led his father to enroll him at the age of ten in the best and most progressive school in France, the College at La Flèche. The curriculum here, unusually comprehensive for the time, included the traditional subjects of literature, languages, philosophy, and theology, as well as a science that was still strongly connected with theology, and a mathematics that had not yet been integrated with science. Given the general state of early seventeenth-century knowledge, Descartes could say with only slight exaggeration that he learned everything to be learned from books during his stay there.

As in all schools of the time, the prevailing intellectual system at La Flèche was *scholasticism,* dating from the medieval teachings of Saints Anselm, Albertus Magnus, and Thomas Aquinas. According to scholastic doctrines, absolute truth had been revealed in the scriptures and the writings of Plato, Aristotle, and the early Christian fathers. The task of an academician was to provide logical proofs of these revealed truths. Though scholastic writings marked a great intellectual advance over the thought of the preceding Dark Ages, they often seem hollow from a modern perspective because they begin by assuming that the truth is already known, and merely attempt to prove it rationally.

The science taught at La Flèche was dominated by Aristotle, whose writings had been integrated into Christian thought by St. Thomas Aquinas. The Aristotelian view of the universe placed the earth at the center, surrounded by concentric crystalline spheres carrying the moon, sun, Mercury, Venus, Mars, Jupiter, Saturn, and the fixed stars. The outermost region of the universe was home to the "unmoved mover" —equated with God—who set all the spheres in motion about the earth. The hypothesis of Nicholas Copernicus (1473–1543), that the sun is at the center of the universe, had been published in 1543, but it was not taken seriously.

Biology was based on the Aristotlean notion of the *soul* as the supreme animating principle of the universe. Souls were believed to come in varying degrees of complexity, depending on their possessors' places in the hierarchy of nature. The simplest living organisms such as plants were said to possess a *vegetative soul,* which provided them with the ability to grow and reproduce. Higher organisms, such as animals, possessed in addition an *animal soul* (sometimes called *sensitive soul*) which provided the additional powers of locomotion, sensation, and imagination. Human beings alone among living creatures were said to possess *rational souls,* enabling them to

7

reason and take on all of the highest human virtues. Whereas the vegetative and animal souls were seen as perishable, the rational soul was immortal and potentially separable from the body. The functioning of the rational soul was thus more a matter of theology than of biology.

The Aristotelian doctrine of the soul contained a number of keen observations about biological and psychological functioning, but it suffered from a major scientific limitation. The functions of the soul were regarded as elemental explanatory factors in themselves, incapable of being explained in terms of more basic units. Living organisms grew, moved, or thought *because* they contained vegetative, animal, or rational souls. The analysis went no further. Progress in biology and psychology had to await the day when the soul itself became the object explained, rather than the explanatory factor.

In these, as well as in the more traditional philosophical and theological subjects, Descartes learned to construct, after the scholastic fashion, logical proofs of the preconceived conclusions. He was an apt pupil—so apt that he was soon granted the unusual privilege of remaining in bed in the morning (while the other students were up and doing their chores) and meditating on his subjects. Morning meditation beneath the bedcovers became a lifelong habit for Descartes, and he later reported that he did his most productive thinking there.

Following his graduation from La Flèche at age sixteen, Descartes dabbled in several different fields and soon went to Paris. Scholars disagree about the exact sequence of events there, but it seems that he entered upon a period of mild debauchery. As an independently wealthy young man with no adult supervision, he was attracted to the gaming table where his mathematical abilities reportedly made him a consistent winner. Soon, however, he came under the more uplifting influence of an older La Flèche alumnus, the Franciscan monk Marin Mersenne (1588–1648). A man of broad scholarly and philosophical interests, Mersenne took Descartes under his wing, sheltered him from much of Paris's temptation, and redirected his thought toward scholarly pursuits.

Unfortunately, Mersenne's beneficial influence did not last long at this time, because after a few months he was transferred away from Paris. Desolated at the loss of his closest friend, Descartes apparently took the extreme measure of retreating from society altogether. He took up residence in the Paris suburb of St. Germain, notifying no one—not even his family—of his whereabouts.

While Descartes left no exact record of his activities at St. Germain, the quiet country village's only unusual feature undoubtedly suggested to him one of his most important biological ideas. The Queen's fountaineers had constructed an intricate set of mechanical statues, activated by the flow of water through pipes in their interiors. These engineering masterpieces were located in six large and eerily lit grottoes cut into the banks of the Seine. The statues were secretly activated when spectators stepped on hidden floor plates. As one approached a statue of the goddess Diana bathing, for example, the statue retreated modestly into the recesses of the grotto. If the approach continued, a statue of Neptune was set in motion and came forward waving its trident menacingly. Though these statues were designed to be little more than diversions to amuse the Queen, they suggested the idea to the young Descartes that *real* animal bodies could be understood as hydraulically operated automata—an idea that he developed fully, and with great consequence, later in his life.

Another important event that probably coincided with Descartes's retreat to St. Germain was a particularly intense emotional and intellectual crisis. According to his autobiographical account, the essence of the problem was that all his hard-won academic knowledge suddenly seemed worthless. In a manner that must warm the heart of the most jaded university student of today, Descartes ticked off the deficiencies of all his academic subjects. The *classics* were sometimes interesting but always dangerous because "those who are too interested in things which occurred in past centuries are often remarkably ignorant of what is going on today." *Literature* was dangerous because it "makes us imagine a number of events as possible which are really impossible, and . . . those who regulate their behavior by the examples they find in books are apt to fall into the extravagances of the knights of romances." Great achievements in *poetry* and *theology* seemed primarily the results of natural gifts and divine inspiration, so those subjects could not really be studied profitably. *Mathematics* offered the pleasing certainty of its results, but seemed trivial because it had not yet been applied to the solution of any practical problems. And worst of all was *philosophy,* which had been studied for centuries by the most able of scholars, "without having produced anything which is not in dispute and consequently doubtful and uncertain. . . . When I noticed how many different opinions learned men may hold on the same subject, despite the fact that no more than one of them can ever be right, I resolved to consider almost as false any opinion which was merely plausible." [1]

These skeptical thoughts plunged Descartes into a deep depression because, as he wrote, "From my childhood I lived in a world of books, . . . taught that by their help I could gain a clear and assured understanding of everything useful in life. . . . But as soon as I had finished the course of studies which usually admits one to the ranks of the learned, . . . I found myself saddled with so many doubts and errors that I seemed to have gained nothing in trying to educate myself unless it was to discover more and more fully how ignorant I was." [2] Despite his intellectual brilliance and all his scholarly efforts, Descartes could not find certain knowledge from even the greatest of books. The foundations were cut from beneath him, and he entered a crisis of doubt.

From the evidence known, it is impossible to assess precisely the severity of Descartes's crisis. Certainly the feelings he described in his writings about the episode are not uncommon, and it is possible that his conflict was little more than a temporary "identity crisis" in an over-schooled young man who needed to broaden his horizons. His crisis may have been more than that, however. One recent commentator has suggested that his voluntary withdrawal into social isolation and private meditation, his lack of close emotional attachments, his tendency to "depersonalize" people by seeing them as analogous to mechanical statues, and his inclination to doubt the validity of commonly accepted knowledge are all features consistent with the mental disorder now known as schizophrenia.[3] Thus it is possible—though far from proved—that the young Descartes suffered from a severe mental breakdown.

Fortunately, it is unnecessary to establish a psychiatric diagnosis in order to understand and appreciate Descartes's accomplishments and their relation to his personality. It is sufficient merely to note that he was the kind of person who preferred solitude to society, his own ideas to those of others, and a skeptical to a credulous orientation toward the world. These attitudes inevitably led to some degree of conflict when he was young and untested, uncertain that his own ideas were any better than the conventional ones he distrusted so much. This conflict, in some form or other, preoccupied him during his retreat at St. Germain, and finally led him to seek a solution in the "real world" of experience rather than the private world of thought. In 1618, he enlisted in the army.

Though a Catholic himself, he volunteered for the Protestant forces of Prince Maurice of Nassau, on the eve of the Thirty Years War. No battles were being fought when Descartes enlisted, however, and he spent several months billeted in the Dutch city of Breda. To his disgust, he quickly found that soldiers possessed no more wisdom than scholars. "I found nothing there to satisfy me," he wrote, "and I noticed just about as much difference of opinion as I had previously remarked among scholars."[4] His intellectual crisis continued unabated.

A turning point occurred on November 10, 1618, when Descartes tried to read a mathematical problem posted on a public wall in Breda. Since it was written in Flemish he had trouble translating it, and asked the assistance of a bystander. The man, surprised and amused by a soldier with an interest in mathematics, engaged Descartes in a conversation that marked the beginning of an important friendship. The man was Isaac Beeckman (1588–1637), a Flemish doctor and mathematician of international reputation. Descartes was stimulated by this kind and learned man as he had never been before, and began spending several hours each day in serious intellectual conversation with him. Inspired to write his first original scholarly work, Descartes dedicated an essay on music to Beeckman. He showed a characteristic caution even here, however, admonishing Beeckman never to have the work published, or to show it to others. "Others would not overlook its imperfections, as I know you will," he wrote.[5]

Within a few weeks of their meeting, Beeckman had to leave Breda. The two maintained their relationship by letter, but this marked the end of their significant face-to-face friendship. Though brief, the relationship served as a major intellectual stimulant for Descartes, and his aspirations increased after their separation. But with Beeckman gone, and having no strong personal allegiance to Prince Maurice's cause, Descartes had little reason to stay in Breda. He still thought of himself as a soldier, however, so he switched sides to join the Catholic forces of Maximilian of Bavaria, several hundred miles away. Though the two armies were soon to become locked in the bitter combat of the Thirty Years War, his change of allegiance did not seem to trouble Descartes.

Rather than joining Maximilian directly, Descartes took a meandering journey through Poland and northern Germany. By the fall of 1619 he had reached the city of Ulm on the Danube. With winter coming on, Descartes decided to spend the cold season in the warmth and comfort of a heated room in a house near Ulm. There he gave himself up to several months of intensive meditation—much of it in the comfort of his bed—and as exciting new ideas occurred to him his military aspirations faded away.

One of Descartes's first accomplishments, perhaps occurring even before he reached Ulm, was his invention of the mathematical discipline of *analytic geometry*. According to one well-known story, the inspiration struck Descartes one morning as he was lying in bed, watching a fly buzzing in one of the corners of his room.[6] He suddenly realized that he could precisely define the position of the fly at any instant with just three numbers: the fly's perpendicular distances from the two walls and the ceiling. Generalizing from this, he realized that any points in space could be defined numerically by their distances from perpendicular lines or planes. (These reference lines—including the abscissa and ordinate so well known to mathematics students—have come to be called "Cartesian coordinates.") This meant that any geometric curve could be defined as a point moving in space with respect to the coordinates. Since the distances could be treated numerically, Descartes had provided a way that the previously separate disciplines of geometry (involving shapes) and algebra (involving numbers) could be integrated.

Analytic geometry had great practical repercussions, making it possible, for example, to represent with numbers astronomical phenomena such as planetary orbits. Since Descartes's earlier complaint about mathematics had concerned its lack of practical application, he had good reason to feel pleased with his invention. At Ulm, he began considering the question of whether the other branches of knowledge, already sufficiently practical in their implications, could not be given the same *certainty of results* as analytic geometry. His obsessional doubting reached extreme proportions once again, as he found that most supposed truths had no more foundation that the authority of those who stated them. This time, however, he conclusively resolved his crisis.

The first part of his resolution was the thought that the results of individual labor are usually superior to those of groups. As he described it, "One of the first [ideas] that occurred to me was that frequently there is less perfection in a work produced by several persons than in one produced by a single hand. Thus we notice that buildings conceived and completed by a single architect are usually more beautiful and better planned than those remodeled by several persons." [7] The same argument clearly applied to academic learning, which is normally acquired from an assortment of different teachers and books. How much better it would be if all knowledge were the result of systematic experience and reflection by a single person! Here was a perfect rationalization for Descartes's own tendencies toward solitary investigation, a justification for dismissing the supposed expertise of the academic authorities and for following his own inclinations instead. Descartes concluded, "As far as the opinions which I had been receiving since my birth were concerned, I could do no better than to reject them completely for once in my lifetime, and to resume them afterwards, or perhaps accept better ones in their place, when I had determined how they fitted into a rational scheme." [8]

These thoughts were soon followed by an even more exciting conception: the formulation of a *method* of solitary investigation that seemed to offer to all other sciences the certainty of geometry. The method consisted of just four rules, described by Descartes in one of his most famous passages:

The first rule was never to accept anything as true unless I recognized it to be certainly and evidently as such: that is, carefully to avoid all precipitation and prejudgment, and to include nothing in my conclusions unless it presented itself so clearly and distinctly to my mind that there was no reason or occasion to doubt.

The second was to divide each of the difficulties which I encountered into as many parts as possible, and as might be required for an easier solution.

The third was to think in an orderly fashion when concerned with the search for truth, beginning with the things which were simplest and easiest to understand, and gradually and by degrees reaching toward more complex knowledge, even treating, as though ordered, materials which were not necessarily so.

The last was, both in the process of searching and in reviewing when in difficulty, always to make enumerations so complete, and reviews so general, that I would be certain that nothing was omitted. [9]

The last three rules, requiring the division of subject matter into its simplest parts, the orderly building up of those parts into complex ideas, and the comprehensive coverage of all relevant details, were essentially a generalization from the geometrical mode of reasoning, where complex but certain conclusions may be reached by building upon simple axioms.

The first rule was the real key to the method, telling how "axioms" in non-mathematical fields may be arrived at. *Doubt everything,* said Descartes, and whatever proves itself incapable of being doubted may be taken as axiomatic.

Yet even as he conceived his promising new method based on doubt, he could not help being overcome by one final paroxysm of doubt. How could he be sure that his new method was correct? How could he know that if he gave himself over to systematic doubt his entire world would not dissolve completely? He tested the method in his mind over and over again, his feverish rumination finally reaching a climax on St. Martin's Eve, and giving way to his three dreams.

The dreams, and Descartes's interpretations of them, gave him the confidence he needed to end his crisis. Inspired by the thought that the ideas of individuals were superior to those of groups, he could go his solitary way with a clear conscience. And the act of doubting, previously his torment, could now be creatively employed in the search for truth. The dreams, whatever else they may have been, symbolized his final acceptance of these ideas, and indicated that he had made peace with his own nature. If he had previously tended toward emotional disturbance, he was now on the road to recovery, and secure in his vocation as a solitary philosopher. Furthermore, Descartes's method was perfectly suited to overcome the weaknesses of scholastic thought. Some of the most productive and influential thinking of the seventeenth century lay before him.

Physiological Thought: The "Treatise of Man"

Descartes worked in obscurity for nine years following his climactic experiences at Ulm. He spent some time in Paris, and travelled extensively throughout Europe as he worked to perfect and refine his method.

He set down some of his conclusions in an unfinished work entitled "Rules for the Direction of the Mind," which was published only posthumously. He gave directions there for dividing any subject into its most elementary and axiomatic units, or "simple natures." A simple nature was an impression or idea that was at once both *clear* and *distinct*. "Clear" meant immediately given in experience; "distinct" meant incapable of further analysis or doubt. The greatest temptation to error was posed by sensations that were clear but not distinct, that is, those sensations that had not been sufficiently doubted. An example was a stick partly immersed in water, which appeared to be bent. The image of the bent stick, like all immediate sensory impressions, was clear. It was not distinct, however, because further analysis, such as removing the stick from the water, could show it to be illusory.

When Descartes applied his method to an analysis of the physical world, he concluded that only two ideas passed his tests. These were the notions of *extension* (the dimensions occupied by a body in space) and *motion*. Thus all the phenomena of the physical world should be explainable as nothing more than material bodies in motion. Light, heat, sound, and all other physical characteristics must ultimately be derived from these simple natures. Further, since the idea had already occurred to Descartes that living bodies could be thought of as mechanical contrivances, the interactions of simple natures could be invoked to explain *physiological* as well as physical phenomena.

Though he was working and thinking in relative isolation, Descartes's theory of simple natures bore a remarkable resemblance to some concepts developed about the same time by the Italian scientist, Galileo Galilei (1564–1642). In 1623, Galileo published *The Assayer*, a work in which he distinguished between the *primary* and *secondary qualities* of matter. The primary qualities were shape, quantity, and motion, and were assumed to be inherent properties of matter itself. Secondary qualities did not reside in matter itself, but resulted when primary qualities impinged upon a sensing organism. Thus the sight, sound, smell, or feel of an object were its secondary qualities, while its primary qualities were the (abstractly considered) size, shape, and motion of the particles constituting it. Physics, for Galileo, was the analysis of primary qualities.

Obviously, Descartes's simple natures were almost identical with Galileo's primary qualities. It is not known whether Descartes read *The Assayer,* learned about it through correspondence, or developed his ideas independently because the idea of a physics based entirely on material particles in motion was generally in the air at the time. At any rate, he postulated a physical system very much in tune with the ideas of his most able scientific contemporaries, despite his penchant for intellectual isolation.

Only a few acquaintances, such as Mersenne, were aware of these developments in Descartes's thought until 1628, when a dramatic event in Paris brought him out of his self-imposed obscurity. A chemist named Chandoux delivered a public lecture attended by Descartes and the leading intellectual figures of the city. At the conclusion Chandoux was applauded heartily by everyone in the audience except Descartes, who was conspicuous for his lack of enthusiasm. Others in the audience demanded that he explain his objections to the lecture, so Descartes had no choice but to speak out publicly for the first time.

He praised the originality of Chandoux's arguments, but said they, like almost all the scientific ideas current at the time, were only plausible, not certain. Then he challenged members of the audience to state propositions they believed to be unquestionably either true or false. As a doubter of great virtuosity and experience, he was able to show how plausible arguments could make any true proposition seem false, and vice-versa. Next, he described the differences between clear and distinct ideas, and his own method for establishing certainty in knowledge. The audience was captivated by Descartes's intellectual mastery, and he emerged as the true champion of the meeting.*

One influential member of the audience, the Cardinal de

---

* The unfortunate Chandoux was apparently born under an unlucky star. Shortly after his humiliation by Descartes, he attempted to employ his scientific skills as a counterfeiter. He was unsuccessful, and hanged for his crime.

Bérule, was particularly impressed. He invited Descartes to his home for further discussion about the method. Descartes mentioned some of the progress he had made in physical analysis, and added the intriguing thought that physiology might be integrated with physics. The Cardinal was enthusiastic, and implored Descartes to publish his ideas. His enthusiasm was infectious, and Descartes set out with renewed vigor to systematize his physics and physiology, or, as he called them, his "mechanics" and his "medicine."

Even with the new motivation, however, published results were slow to follow. Predictably, the Parisian atmosphere was too distracting for Descartes and he fled once again to Holland, where he was to stay for twenty years. He preserved his anonymity there by moving twenty-four times, seldom leaving a forwarding address. It took several years of solitary labor to complete his mechanics and medicine, because not only did Descartes have to work out the physical details of light, heat, and gravity, but he also had to perfect his "'mechanical" analysis of the animal body. To this end he visited butcher shops to observe the slaughtering of animals, and to request particular organs which he could dissect himself at home. Though he occasionally consulted Andreas Vesalius's classic text on anatomy, he relied mainly on his own observations in trying to decide how the organs might work mechanically. He concluded that the animal body posed no mystery to one versed in physics.

In 1633 he completed a lengthy manuscript entitled *The World*, subdivided into a "Treatise of Light" and a "Treatise of Man." The first part described his physics, the second his physiology. Just as the cautious Descartes was about to give it to a printer, however, he received the staggering news that Galileo had been condemned by the Inquisition for suggesting that the earth is in motion around the sun. Previously, that idea had been acceptable to the Church if it was clearly labeled as hypothesis, and not presented as established truth. Suddenly it was heretical to express the idea at all. Descartes's

18

work employed this same heliocentric hypothesis, and, though he was personally in no danger in Protestant Holland, he was nevertheless concerned that his works should be acceptable in the Catholic universities of his native France. He withheld publication of *The World* completely, even its non-heretical parts. Fortunately for posterity, he preserved the original manuscript so his admirers were able to publish it shortly after his death.

One of the most outstanding features of *The World,* as of Descartes's thought generally, was the way it integrated several previously separate branches of science. From the time he had first conceived his method at Ulm, Descartes's goal had been the construction of a "universal science" that could connect all the arts and sciences within a single set of fundamental principles. This integrating quality made *The World* one of the first modern textbooks not only of physics and physiology, but of psychology as well. Descartes began by explaining the laws of the physical world and then applied them to an understanding of physiology. Then he went still further and tried to show how physiological processes could parallel certain psychological phenomena. Few of the specific physiological ideas are still accepted, and Descartes did not carry his psycho-physiological integration as far as psychologists do today. But *The World* clearly set the style for the future emergence of psychology as a member of the family of sciences.

Physics. The first part of *The World,* "Treatise of Light," presented Descartes's basic physics, the fundamental units of which were extended bodies in motion. As did Aristotle, Descartes believed there can be no void, so the *entire* universe must consist of different kinds of material particles in different kinds of motion. When a particle moves, according to this conception, it does not leave empty space behind it, but its place is instantaneously filled up by a different kind of particle. A good metaphor for this kind of universe is a fishpond which is completely filled with water, fish, and plants. As the fish swim or the plants sway beneath the water, they do not leave empty space behind them, nor do they disturb the overall tranquility of the pond. Nevertheless, their places are constantly and instantaneously filled by water.

Descartes believed the universe to be made up of three general kinds of particles, corresponding roughly to the classical elements of fire, water, and earth. The particles corresponding to fire or heat were supposedly so extremely tiny that they constituted "a virtually perfect fluid" capable of filling space of any shape. These particles filled up the interstices between other kinds of particles, and also because of their size tended to sift through to the center of the universe where they collected in pure concentration to form the sun. By placing the sun at the center of the universe, of course, Descartes endorsed the view that had brought Galileo to grief.

The largest category of the universe's particles were also imperceptibly small, but *spherical* in shape and thus larger than the heat particles. These were the "air" particles hypothesized to fill up the vast expanses of space. So small as to be transparent, they formed the physical basis of light rays.

The third element consisted of large and irregularly shaped particles, which were the only ones to strike the human senses as being solid. Corresponding to the classical element "earth", these particles were assumed to be the material basis of the earth, planets, and comets. All material bodies on earth were compounded out of these coarse particles.

As the treatise's title suggests, considerable attention was devoted to the subject of light. Light rays were conceptualized by Descartes as straight columns of contiguous but transparent "air" particles, extending between a perceived object and the eye. To the viewer, the sensation of light occurred when an object vibrated, and transmitted its vibration to the column of air extending between itself and the eye. Such a column would establish an identical pattern of vibrations in the material particles of the eye, from which they could be conveyed to the brain and perceived as a visual image. Descartes used the analogy of a blind man sensing the world by means of a stick. As he probes with his stick, signals are transmitted its length and perceived as pressure by the hand. The stick is analogous to a light ray, transmitting the motion of a stimulus from one end (the object) to the other (the eye). This theory obviously implied that the transmission of light was instantaneous, since both ends of the stick, or ray of light, must necessarily move simultaneously. Descartes candidly admitted that evidence showing the speed of light to be finite would discredit the theory. Such evidence was not forthcoming until 1676, however, and Descartes's theory remained plausible for many years.

This analysis of light suggests one of the fundamental points of contact between Descartes's physics and his physiology. The eye, like the entire animal body, was thought of as a system of material particles which itself was influenced or moved by the particles in motion that make up the physical world. The organs of the body, which Descartes so carefully dissected and analyzed, he saw as complex mechanical systems which followed the laws of natural science. This mechanistic view of the human body was developed fully in the second part of *The World,* the "Treatise of Man."

Physiology. Descartes was not the only person of his time to suggest a mechanistic view of the body. Galileo, for example, analyzed the bones and joints of the body as a mechanical system of levers. Santorio Santorio (1561–1636) showed how the thermometer, previously used only in the physical world, could be adapted to clinical purposes, and William Harvey (1578–1657) proved that the blood circulated throughout the body by analyzing the mechanical properties of the heart as a pump.

Thus the unique feature of "Treatise of Man" was not the idea of biological mechanism per se. Rather, it was the *scope* of the functions to which Descartes applied the idea. According to his own summary of the work, ten separate functions were given mechanistic explanations: the digestion of food, the circulation of the blood, the nourishment and growth of the body, respiration, sleeping and waking, sensation of the external world, imagination, memory, the appetites and passions, and the movements of the body. In short, Descartes completely obviated the necessity for the Aristotelian concepts of a "vegetative soul" or "animal soul" which he had been taught at La Flèche, and replaced them with a mechanistic analysis. He wrote that his ten functions

follow naturally in this machine entirely from the disposition of the organs—no more nor less than do the movements of a clock or other automaton, from the arrangement of its counterweights and wheels. Wherefore it is not necessary, on their account, to conceive of any vegetative or sensitive soul or any other principle of movement and life than its blood and its spirits, agitated by the heat of the fire which burns continually in its heart and which is of no other nature than all those fires that occur in inanimate bodies.[10]

The only animate function Descartes excluded from his mechanistic analysis was *reason*. After having replaced the vegetative and animal souls with new scientific concepts, he could not bring himself to do the same for the rational soul. Because of this, most of the "higher" psychological processes were not included in his machine, but were dealt with in a totally different and more old-fashioned way that will be described in detail later.

Despite his omission of the rational functions of the soul, Descartes dealt mechanistically in "Treatise of Man" with many activities that are regarded today as psychological. He saw these activities as being directly caused by the workings of the brain and nervous system, organs that he analyzed more thoroughly and with more sophistication than any of his predecessors. He thus began a general tradition of neuropsychological analysis that continues to the present day.

The physical features of the brain that seemed most important to Descartes were its cavities, or *ventricles*, that were filled with a fluid he referred to as the *animal spirits*. (This fluid now is commonly called the *cerebro-spinal fluid*.) He believed the animal spirits were constituted by the smallest and finest particles of the blood, which had undergone a sort of filtration through tiny arteries on their way to the brain. The coarser blood particles were presumably filtered out, leaving only this very pure, subtle fluid in the interior of the brain.

Descartes believed these "spirits" of the blood provided part of the mechanism for animate motion.

The structures most responsible for movement seemed to be the nerves, which radiated from the brain and spinal cord to muscle groups in all parts of the body. On the basis of dissections unaided by a microscope, Descartes convinced himself (falsely) that the nerve fibers were hollow. Inspired by the model of the St. Germain statues, he postulated a hydraulic mechanism for animal motion: animal spirits supposedly flowed through the nerves and into the muscles, causing them to swell and move. As Descartes wrote,

Now in the same measure that spirits enter the cavities of the brain they also leave them and enter the pores [or conduits] in its substance, and from these conduits they proceed to the nerves. And depending on their entering (or their mere tendency to enter) some nerves rather than others, they are able to change the shapes of the muscles into which these nerves are inserted and in this way to move all the members. Similarly you may have observed in the grottoes and fountains in the gardens of our kings that the force that makes the water leap from its source is able of itself to move divers machines and even to make them play certain instruments or pronounce certain words according to the various arrangements of the tubes through which the water is conducted.[11]

The brain, in this conception, was a complicated system of tubes and valves which could shunt the animal spirits into many different pathways and combinations to different nerves. *Memory* and *learning* occurred when repeated experiences caused certain pathways out of the multitude possible in the brain to become more open than others to the flow of spirits.

The Reflex. It was not sufficient merely to explain how the brain, nerves, and animal spirits caused the body to move. An equally important question concerned the *sources* of movement: What was it that turned the machine on, and started the animal spirits flowing in the first place? Part of Descartes's answer to this question was also suggested by St. Germain's hydraulic statues which were activated whenever a spectator stepped on certain floor plates. In other words, *pressure on a sensing device* triggered the flow of water through the tubes. Descartes imagined something directly analogous occurring in living bodies. Since his model of the physical world hypothesized that all physical phenomena were essentially material bodies in motion, the sensory stimuli impinging on a body could be thought of as pressures exerted by moving particles against a sense organ. Light, sound, and heat were columns of vibrating microscopic particles which pushed against the eye, ear, or skin. The movements of the sense organs were transmitted to the brain by the nerves, where they caused selected valves to open and to initiate movement in the body.

Though Descartes did not use these exact terms, he had formulated what is now called the *reflex,* where a specific motoric *response* is elicited in an organism by the application of a specific *stimulus* from the external world. All reflexive activity is caused by, or under the control of, stimuli that are external to the sensing organism.

Descartes believed his mechanical conception of the reflex to be supported by some further (also erroneous) observations of the fine structure of nerves. He thought that he saw extremely fine filaments running the length of nerves, inside the imaginary hollow places. He believed that these filaments transmitted the sensory pressures to the brain. Vibrations and pressures on the sense organs presumably created tugs and pulls on the filaments, which in turn pulled open valves in the brain to allow the flow of animal spirits back down the nerves to the muscles. This conception has recently been playfully labelled the "flush-toilet model" of the reflex, since the hypothetical mechanism so closely resembles that of a chain-operated water closet.[12]

Descartes's model of the brain enabled him to postulate two different kinds of reflexive responses. In one, the vital spirits flowed immediately down the same nerve whose fiber had been tugged. This resulted in an immediate and automatic movement, as when a hand is pulled away from a hot fire. In the second kind of response, the initial tug of the stimulus was assumed to start the animal spirits flowing through a maze of channels and pathways in the brain that had been laid down by "memory". Only after a certain amount of this activity in the brain would the spirits flow to the muscles via a nerve different from the one that was initially stimulated. This was equivalent to a *learned* response. The differentiation between innate and learned reflexive tendencies, with the latter entailing more activity within the brain itself, has been an influential and enduring idea in western psychology.

Emotion. Though Descartes saw the mechanical body as being set in motion by *external* stimulation, he also left a role for *internal* factors in determining the kind and intensity of the body's responses. He thought the responsiveness of the body was determined not only by the nerves, but also by the supply of animal spirits available to flow through them. If there was an abundant supply of the spirits, the pressure on the nerves' valves would be great and the tendency to respond even to very gentle stimulation would be increased. Similarly, local currents or "commotions" in isolated parts of the reservoir of spirits could alter the responsiveness of the nerves in contact with them. These variations in the supply of animal spirits were Descartes's physiological explanation of *emotion.* He provided the following specific examples:

When it is a question of forcefully avoiding some evil by overcoming it or by driving it away—as anger inclines us to do—then the spirits must be more unevenly agitated and stronger than they usually are. Whereas, when it is necessary to avoid harm with patience—as fear inclines us to do—then the spirits must be less abundant and weaker. For this purpose the heart must constrict at such a time, and must husband and save the blood against need.[13]

In general, then, the body's mechanical responses presumably occurred because of an interaction between the external stimulation impinging on the nerves, and the "emotional" preparedness of the animal spirits and nerves to respond. It should be emphasized that this emotional preparedness, while occurring inside the body, was just as mechanistically determined as sensory perception, since the state of the animal spirits was caused by the mechanical actions of the organs that created and circulated the blood. Emotions were no more a matter of the "will" than was the beating of the heart.

Variations in the supply of animal spirits accounted not only for emotions, but also for the difference between sleeping and waking. Descartes believed that the waking supply of animal spirits was ample and completely filled the cavities of the brain so that the brain tissue itself expanded somewhat. This expansion pulled all the nerve fibers to a state of tautness, so they were maximally sensitive to the tugs and pulls of external stimulation. Hence the body was highly responsive to the external world. In sleep, however, the brain became relatively devoid of animal spirits, its tissues became lax, and its nerve fibers slack. In this state they could not transmit vibrations to the brain, so the organism was unresponsive to stimulation. Only occasionally in sleep would random eddies in the spirits cause isolated parts of the brain to expand, with consequent temporary tightening of just a few fibers. Descartes used the analogy of a ship's sails in a weak, intermittent wind. A few of the ropes holding the sails are pulled taut for brief periods, but most remain slack. The disconnected experiences of *dreams* were supposed to occur in this state of random, low-level responsivity of the nerves.

Thus Descartes provided a mechanistic analysis for an extremely wide range of functions, including many that are "psychological" in the modern sense of the word. He believed, in fact, that animals could be understood completely in mechanistic terms as nothing more than automata. He granted that animal bodies might be more complicated than any man-made machine, containing more pipes which are more intricately interconnected with one another. But this was strictly a matter of degree, not of quality. As Descartes summarized his view in a letter to a friend, "The soul of beasts is nothing but their blood." [14]

Descartes was unable to go so far in his analysis of *human* experience, however. While human bodies unquestionably functioned in many machine-like ways, the *subjective* side of

26

experience—the facts of *consciousness* and *volition*—seemed to defy mechanistic analysis. It was self-evident to Descartes that many of his own responses occurred because he wanted them to, or because conscious reflection indicated that they were appropriate. Unable and unwilling to devise a mechanistic explanation for the facts of consciousness, Descartes asserted that they were the innately given attributes of a *soul* or *mind* that coexisted with the bodily machine. Consciousness, volition, and reason were uniquely human attributes, deriving from the unique human soul.

Descartes thus did not finish the revolution he began in "Treatise of Man." After dispensing with the lower functions of the soul by substituting mechanistic explanations, he could not do the same for the highest. He retained the traditional conception of the rational soul as an explanatory entity in itself, separate from the mechanical constraints of the physical world. People think, reason, and are conscious *because* they have souls. Accordingly, Descartes's analyses of the soul (or "mind," with which it is largely synonymous) followed a more metaphysical and less scientific pattern than his analyses of the body.

Descartes's philosophical speculations about the soul and its relation to the body preoccupied him increasingly after he finished *The World.* They resulted in a number of works he did see fit to publish, and which made him among the most famous of all European intellectuals. They also shaped the prevailing Western conception of the human mind and body as separate entities that interact with one another.

Philosophy of Mind

After suppressing publication of *The World,* Descartes began preparing a new volume that would be more certain to gain acceptance by the Church. He spent four years writing detailed treatises on optics, meteorology, and geometry—subjects he could deal with at some length while avoiding the heresy of a sun-centered universe. He also wrote a brief autobiographical "discourse" on his method, on how it came to be developed, and the primary conclusions to which it led. These conclusions included a brief summary of his view that the body is a machine, and the essence of his philosophical conception of the soul.

In 1637, all of these documents finally went to the printer to be published in a single volume bearing the lengthy title: *Discourse on the Method of Rightly Conducting the Reason and Seeking the Truth in the Field of Science; plus Dioptric, Meteorology, and Geometry, which are some of the Results of that Method*. Descartes showed his customary shyness even now, refusing to allow his name to appear on the book, and becoming greatly annoyed when Mersenne wrote an introduction to the Paris edition that made its authorship clear. Even so, he was eager to have it widely read, and as royalties asked only for 200 free copies, which he distributed to Europe's leading intellectual figures.

The book, unusual for its time by being written in an easily understandable French instead of the customary scholarly Latin, was generally well received. Contrary to Descartes's expectations, however, the brief autobiographical *Discourse on Method* was to be much more influential than the relatively ponderous scientific treatises, and to become a philosophical classic. Among its most important parts was a succinct analysis of the nature of the human soul.

Descartes began this analysis by describing what happened when he applied his first rule of systematic doubt to everything he could think of, even the most clear and distinct of sensory impressions. All sensory data were subject to at least some doubt, he found, because it was possible to imagine that they were illusory, as in a dream. Even the body itself could be doubted because it was possible to imagine that one has no body.

As Descartes continued to doubt, however, he at last came upon an idea that seemed absolutely certain, and that could form the bedrock of his philosophy of the mind. His description of this idea contains one of the most famous passages in Western philosophy:

As our senses deceive us at times, I was ready to suppose that nothing was at all the way our senses represented them to be. As there are men who make mistakes in reasoning even on the simplest topics in geometry, I judged that I was as liable to error as any other, and rejected as false all reasoning which I had previously accepted as valid demonstration. Finally, as the same percepts which we have when awake may come to us when asleep without their being true, I decided to suppose that nothing that had ever entered my mind was more real than the illusions of my dreams. But I soon noticed that while I thus wished to think everything false, it was necessarily true that I who thought so was something. Since this truth, *I think therefore I am, or exist,* was so firm and assured that all the most extravagant suppositions of the sceptics were unable to shake it, I judged that I could safely accept it as the first principle of the philosophy I was seeking.[15]

Paradoxically, Descartes discovered that the act of doubting gave direct evidence of the certainty he so much desired. He could doubt his senses and he could doubt the existence of his body and material world, but he could not doubt the reality of his act of doubting. Thus the one unquestionable reality was the activity of his own rational soul, or mind.

It followed logically from these reflections that the mind must stand in marked contrast to the body:

I concluded that I was a thing or substance whose whole essence or nature was only to think, and which, to exist, has no need of space nor of any material thing or body. Thus it follows that this ego, this mind, this soul, by which I am what I am, is entirely distinct from the body and is easier to know than the latter, and that even if the body were not, the soul would not cease to be all that it now is.[16]

The body, like all physical things, consisted entirely of extended material particles in motion. The soul, whose entire essence was to think, existed independently of material and spatial considerations.

One feature of the soul especially intrigued Descartes: it

never appeared directly or immediately as a conscious sensory experience. Though he was absolutely certain his soul existed, he never experienced the totality of his soul at once. On reflection, he developed a list of similar ideas which were incapable of being completely represented by a single sensory experience. Descartes believed that these ideas, such as "perfection," "unity," "infinity," and the geometrical axioms, must derive from the thinking soul itself. Though they may be alluded to or suggested by specific sensory experiences, their essential nature seemed independent of experience. Hence Descartes called them the *innate ideas* of the soul.

The innate ideas provided a foundation on which Descartes could anchor much of the rest of his philosophy. The innate idea of "perfection," combined with his certainty of the existence of his own mind, proved to Descartes the certain existence of a God who embodied all aspects of perfection. Supported by the assurance that he possessed an absolutely certain soul, and that there existed a perfect God, Descartes believed he could safely accept the conclusions of his method concerning the physical world. Thus knowledge derived from the senses could be trusted—not because it was inherently certain itself, but because the integrity of the mind that perceived it and the God that created it could not be questioned. And all of this was deduced by following a method whose cornerstone was doubt!

Because of his beliefs about the nature of the rational soul, two labels are commonly applied to Descartes. He is called a *rationalist*, because he believed that pure reason and intellect are more important than unvarnished sensory experience in attaining the highest knowledge. He is also called a *nativist* because he believed that the mind carries its most important ideas innately within it, independently of specific sensory experiences. Opponents of these positions (and there have been many of them), who believe that all ideas and knowledge come from sensory experience, are referred to as *empiricists*.

Still another label applied to Descartes is *dualist*, because of his sharp division of the human being into material body

and immaterial soul. The notion of dualism was scarcely original to Descartes, since theologians and philosophers for centuries had differentiated between a perishable, material body
and an immortal soul. Prior to Descartes, however, the predominant dualist view had been that the soul was much more
powerful than the body, controlling it in something like the
way a puppeteer controls his puppets. Descartes's relatively
higher valuation on the soul than the body was consistent
with this tradition, but he did not share the view that the soul
always dominated the body. The soul might be better and
more certain than the body, but so long as the two were
locked together in earthly existence it was not necessarily more
powerful. According to Descartes, the body and soul were
separate entities that *interacted* and mutually influenced
one another. Sometimes the conscious mind exerted clear control over the actions of the body, but at other times the body
could act independently or influence the conscious reactions
of mind.

Thus Descartes's dualism was an *interactive dualism,* and it
led to several important questions about the nature of mind-
body relationships. Descartes devoted considerable attention
to these questions in the years following *Discourse on
Method,* discussing them most completely in a *Treatise on the
Passions of the Soul* (1649). His resolution of the mind-body
issue has left many people unsatisfied, and made him a target
for the criticism of many modern philosophers. Nevertheless,
it has also been one of the most influential of all of his ideas.

Interactive Dualism

In principle, Descartes's conception of the relations between
body and soul was simple. Without a soul, the human body
would be an automaton responding to inner and outer stimulation according to the rules built into its mechanism. It
would be without consciousness, and completely under the
control of its emotions and external stimuli. Conversely, a
soul without a body would have consciousness, but only of the

innate ideas. It would lack the sensory impressions and ideas of substantial things that occupy human consciousness most of the time. Thus the body added richness to the contents of the soul's consciousness, while the soul added rationality and volition to the determinants of the body's behavior.

From a modern perspective, some of Descartes's strangest theorizing concerned the *location* of the mind-body interaction. He was faced with a logical dilemma here since the soul, as an immaterial entity, could not properly be said to be localized in any particular place. At the same time, however, it had to affect and be affected by the specific parts of the body, which did have definite locations in space. Descartes tried to resolve this problem by postulating a *localization of the interaction,* a particular place in the body where body and soul could influence each other even though the soul was not confined to that location. The *mechanics* of an interaction between a material and an immaterial entity were, and remain, an unsolvable problem.

From his physiological studies of the body, Descartes felt that the most logical point of interaction would be in the brain. The brain, after all, was the control center for all mechanical movement and sensation, and would surely be the most convenient place for the soul to interact with the body. He did not feel that the *entire* brain could be the locus of interaction, however, because he conceived of the soul as a unified, single entity, while the brain as a whole was physically divided into two symmetrical halves. He wrote,

I observe . . . the brain to be double, just as we have two eyes, two hands, two ears, and indeed, all the organs of our external senses double; and . . . since of any one thing at any one time we have only the single and simple thought, there must be some place where the two images which come from the two eyes, and where the two impressions which come from one single object by way of the double organs of the other senses, can unite before reaching the soul, and so prevent their representing to it two objects in place of one.[17]

From the purely mechanistic standpoint of the body, the double nature of the brain and the senses posed no problem.

Whether the mechanical signals sent to the brain were single, double, triple, or even resembled the exciting material stimulus, made no difference at all. All that was required was a specific signal of some kind that could mechanically trigger a specific response in the brain. The problem arose for Descartes only when *consciousness* entered the picture. Even though double signals were known to enter the double brain from the two eyes or two ears, the conscious mind perceived but a single object. Furthermore, Descartes assumed the conscious percept to be a perfect replica of the actual stimulating object; that is, the tree that we consciously see must be identical to a "real" tree existing in the external world and exciting our senses. Thus, Descartes believed there had to be a place where double sensory images could reassemble to form the unitary conscious percepts of the soul.

In Descartes's view this place had to be undivided, and the only undivided structure he found in the brain was the *pineal gland,* a small, roughly spherical structure located near the center. This structure had the further theoretical advantage of being surrounded by cerebrospinal fluid, and thus ideally situated to control the flow of animal spirits into the nerves. To clinch the case, Descartes erroneously believed the gland was a special feature of the human brain.* Here was surely the place where the uniquely human soul and the mechanical body could interact with one another.

Figure 1–1 illustrates Descartes's conception of how visual sensations are conveyed to the soul for rational consideration. The pineal gland is the structure marked *P,* located in the middle of the brain. In visual perception, light rays from an object are refracted by the eyes so that inverted images are created on the retinas. This is shown in the figure where rays from the top of the arrow terminate at the bottoms of the two retinas *(1),* while rays from the bottom of the arrow terminate

* Actually, the pineal gland (or *conarium* as it is called in Latin) was first discovered in an *ox's* brain, where its pine-cone shape gave rise to its name. Descartes apparently did not know this, illustrating one disadvantage of disregarding established authorities and texts.

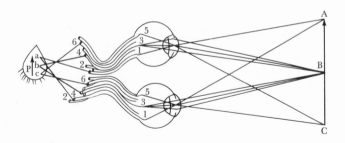

Figure 1–1 *Descartes's Conception of Visual Perception* [18]

at the tops of the retinas *(5)*. At the retinas, vibrations stimulate the ends of the nerve filaments, which are in turn set in motion and which open the valves in the brain at points *6, 4,* and *2.* At this point, an animal's processing of visual sensation stops. The flow of animal spirits within the brain and in the nerves can now begin, and produce responses according to Descartes's mechanistic principles.

In human beings the process goes farther, however, as the signals from the two images become re-inverted and fused into a single image on the pineal gland. Thus, the two signals from points *2* coalesce at *a,* the two from *4* at *b,* and the two from *6* at *c.* The soul, interacting with the body at *P,* is accordingly presented with a single, upright, and perfectly complete representation of the external reality. A conscious perception of the image by the soul follows.

By a necessarily undefined process, the soul may now play upon the various valves in the brain somewhat as a piano player plays upon the keys of his instrument. In light of its rational contemplation of the image, the soul may decide to inhibit, abet, or otherwise modify the reflexive responses that have been mechanically elicited in the body. In other words, the soul introduces reason into the mediation of behavior, making it conscious, deliberate, and freely willed.

According to Descartes, the *passions* were further important results of the body-soul interaction. Defined as the conscious experiences which accompany emotions, passions supposedly occurred when variations in the animal spirits caused movements in the pineal gland, which were then consciously detected by the soul. Descartes noted that the pineal gland, located as it was in the midst of a large pool of cerebrospinal fluid, was in an ideal position both to detect and to influence the flow of the animal spirits. Slight movements or currents in the spirits could cause the gland to move slightly and, conversely, slight movements of the gland could cause changes in the flow-patterns of the spirits.

Two principal effects supposedly followed these movements of the pineal gland. First, as the soul sensed the movements of the gland it had the conscious experience of a passion, such as love, hatred, wonder, fear, or desire. Second, the soul took a conscious attitude toward the passion and the situation in which it occurred. If the attitude were favorable, the soul could will the body to act in the same way it was mechanistically inclined by the emotion. In response to anger, the soul could *will* to attack the offending object, for example, and by manipulating the pineal gland it could direct the flow of spirits even more strongly into the nerves initiating an attack response.

At other times, however, the soul's rational faculties could perceive a passion as undesirable. The soul then exercised its free will and attempted to counteract the motivational effect of the emotion. But since the soul did not have complete control over the body, it was not always successful. Indeed, the soul's control over passions was seen as similar to its control over external sensory impressions. Sometimes, in the case of relatively mild passions, the soul could ignore their influences just as it could ignore slight noises from the external world while in a state of concentration. For very intense passions, however, the influence of the soul was ineffective. Descartes noted that people often strike out in anger or run away in panic, despite the fact that rational consideration would advise against these actions. In these cases he felt the "commotions" of the animal spirits were simply too strong to be counteracted by the soul's manipulation of the pineal gland.

Descartes was at pains to point out that these emotional conflicts were not the result of a division within the soul. The soul was perfectly unified and harmonious within itself; conflict arose only when the soul found itself at variance with the body. Descartes chided those who saw the soul as a divided entity:

> The error committed in representing [the soul] as displaying diverse personalities that ordinarily are at variance with one another arises from our failure to distinguish its function from those of the body, to which alone we must attribute whatever in us is observed to be repugnant to our reason. There is, therefore, no contest save that which takes place in the small gland which is in the center of the brain, when it is impelled to one side by the soul, and to another by the animal spirits.[19]

Nothing better epitomizes Descartes's interactive dualism than this description of conflict between the body and the soul. The soul was perfectly rational, consistent, and unified, but also limited in the power it could exert over the more unruly body. If the soul decided of its free will to augment the body's mechanical tendencies, all was well and harmonious. If it decided to oppose them, however, a struggle ensued which was played out with antagonistic pushes and pulls on the pineal gland. Neither body nor soul was presumed to have a consistent advantage in these struggles, but each had temporary periods of dominance. Accordingly, the competition between material body and immaterial soul, played out within the structures of the body, was the most crucial aspect of human existence.

Descartes's overall view of human beings, and his suggestions for how to study them, were thus curiously mixed. On the one hand, he taught that a person was a machine, capable of being studied by the methods of natural science. On the other hand, he taught that the most valuable and unique human attribute, the soul, was beyond the reach of scientific method and could be understood only by rational reflection. And then finally the interaction between body and soul was said to be deducible through a combination of anatomical inference, psychological introspection, and a peculiarly empty logical analysis. More than anything else in his works, his speculations about the mind-body interaction betrayed his medieval-scholastic background. His serious discussions of where an immaterial but unified agency like the soul could interact with a material but divided organ like the brain call to mind the debates of some scholastics over how many angels could dance on the head of a pin.

Despite the logical difficulties with parts of Descartes's position, however, minds and bodies still are spoken of in the same breath today. "Sound minds and strong bodies" continues to be a widely accepted ideal for human perfection, and current medical interest in "psychosomatic" problems suggests that the mind-body dichotomy is still a very real concept in scientific circles. For better or for worse, most people—at least in the West—continue to think of their minds and their bodies as separate but somehow interacting aspects of themselves. This is a tribute to the power of Descartes's theory. Whatever its faults, his interactive dualism captured the Western imagination to such an extent that it became accepted almost as a matter of course. Few theories, in any discipline, can claim equal success.

Descartes's Place in Modern Psychology

Descartes's theories were still evolving at his death, which occurred in 1650 under circumstances at once tragic and ironic. He had followed up the successful *Discourse on Method* with two more philosophical works, the *Meditations on First Philosophy* in 1641, and the *Principles of Philosophy* in 1644. These works brought him much recognition and, to his disgust, public controversy. After he had tried so hard to

make his writing acceptable to the Catholic Church, he suddenly found himself under attack by some of the Protestant
clergy in Holland. They argued that his writings led to athe-
ism, and succeeded for a time in having them banned from
Dutch universities. For Descartes, a man of genuine religious
tolerance who had been affiliated with both Protestant and
Catholic armies, and who had remained aloof from the
vicious Thirty Years War that so divided many Protestants
and Catholics, this was almost too much to bear.

In a characteristic response, he slowed down his rate of
publication rather than add more fuel to the fire. His only
new work to be published in his lifetime was *Passions of the
Soul* in 1649. He otherwise expressed his ideas privately in
unpublished manuscripts, or in long discursive letters to
trusted friends and a few highly-placed individuals who
sought instruction in his philosophy.

In the late 1640s he began such a correspondence with
Sweden's Queen Christina. Unfortunately, Christina immediately launched a campaign to persuade Descartes to come
to Sweden and be philosopher-in-residence at her court. For
some inexplicable reason he was tempted by this idea and in
1649 gave up his blessed Dutch anonymity in favor of the
fashionable life of a courtier.

The Swedish venture was disastrous from the beginning, as
he was willingly or unwillingly swept up in a wave of frivolity.
Among the tasks assigned him was the writing of verses to
accompany comedies and ballets celebrating Christina's accomplishments. His own vastly more important projects were
neglected. The cruelest irony of all, however, was the Queen's
determination to be tutored in philosophy at five o'clock in
the morning. Forced to travel to the palace before sunrise
during one of Sweden's most severe winters, Descartes contracted pneumonia. On February 11, 1650, less than six
months after his arrival in Sweden, he died at the age of
fifty-three.

Few men have ever left greater intellectual legacies. Besides leaving a philosophical view of humanity that continues to fascinate scholars after more than three centuries, as well as leaving the indispensible mathematical tool of analytic geometry, he also provided many ideas that helped form the foundations for a new science of psychology.

In assessing Descartes's psychological contributions, it is at once evident that he was more important for what he began that for what he completed. Like his physics, his psychological theories contained many incorrect elements that had to be set right by subsequent scholars. Descartes's conception of the bodily machinery was highly fanciful, for example, and was quickly superseded. Nerves are not hollow pipes, and they do not enclose filaments which transmit tugs and pulls to valves in the brain. The cerebrospinal fluid is not involved in the transmission of the neural impulse, does not cause the muscles to move by filling them up and making them swell, and does not cause passions by variations in its flow. In general, Descartes's conception of the body was excessively influenced by the scholastic tradition of explaining bodily functions as the result of "humors" and "spirits" flowing throughout the body, and by his chance observation of the hydraulic statues at St. Germain. He was also spectacularly wrong in his views about the pineal gland, which turns out not to be unique to human beings, and which does not play a major role in the rational control of behavior.

Such mistakes and misconceptions in Descartes's thought do not detract from his importance, however, because even though his ideas were wrong they were productive, and stimulated later researchers to correct them. The following psychological contributions, each of which will be taken up in more detail in later chapters of this book, are just a few examples.

One major contribution was Descartes's straightforward assertion that the brain is a pre-eminently important organ in the mediation of behavior. Before him, scholarly opinion about the brain had been mixed because of two peculiar facts. First, the blood drains rapidly from the brain following death, lending it a deceptively bloodless appearance upon post-mortem examination. Second, the physical penetration of a living brain by a spear or sword often caused no pain or other sensation in wounded soldiers. Many scholars had been unable to believe that such a "bloodless" and "insensitive" organ could have much importance in controlling behavior. Descartes, as we have seen, was guided by other facts to relate specific psychological functions to specific parts of the brain. His general idea was correct, even though the brain is actually more complicated than he imagined, and its functions are not localized in precisely the same places he suggested. Any current textbook of neuropsychology, which describes how different parts of the brain and nervous system influence different kinds of psychological functions, must accept "Treatise of Man" as its direct ancestor.

Another immensely productive idea was that of the reflex as an elementary unit of behavior. Reflexes may not have the precise filament and fluid mechanism that Descartes hypothesized for them, but the general idea of a stimulus-response sequence mediated by the nervous system is still a basic psychological concept. The analysis of behavior in terms of innate and acquired reflexes was raised to a high level by the Russian physiologist Ivan Pavlov, and it became the cornerstone of American *behaviorism*.

Descartes's conceptions of the forces that set the human machine in motion also laid the foundation for many later psychological analyses. He recognized that the sense organs are physical systems that respond in lawful, mechanistic ways to external physical forces such as light, heat, or sound, and that the sensory nerves somehow transmit signals from the sense organs to the brain, where they initiate conscious sensations of light, heat, or sound. The process by which the human nervous system converts external physical stimuli into conscious sensations has been of continuing interest to psychologists. Indeed, the analyses of sensation and perception conducted by the German scientist Hermann Helmholtz in the nineteenth century helped give psychologists their first clear idea of what a fully mechanistic "mind" might look like.

Descartes did not see the human body's reactions as completely determined by external stimulation impinging on its sense organs, of course. He also made important allowances for inner determinants of behavior such as the emotions or passions. Thus he was a precursor of the "dynamic psychologists," who stress the importance of temporally varying motivational factors on thought and behavior. Sigmund Freud's psychoanalytic view of man as a creature in conflict, impelled in one direction by his inner instincts and in another by the constraints of external reality, bears considerable resemblance to Descartes's notion of the body as a machine controlled by the combined and often conflicting influences of external stimulation, the animal spirits, and the rational soul.

Descartes's nativism and rationalism have also had major impacts on psychology, attracting both supporters and critics. The doctrine of innate ideas initially met with vigorous resistance from the English philosophers Thomas Hobbes, John Locke, and David Hume, who adopted the extreme empiricist position that *all* ideas must be the result of experience. Their empiricism in turn inspired a counter-reaction by the German, Immanuel Kant, who argued that the facts of human experience cannot be accounted for without postulating certain innate powers and functions of the mind. Few people today would accept Descartes's innate ideas as they originally stood, or even Kant's reformulation of them, but there is general agreement that certain innate organizing tendencies are present in the mind. As shall be seen, the teachings of Gestalt psychology have emphasized and documented many of these.

Finally, quite apart from these specific contributions, Descartes helped create the modern *general* attitude toward human psychology by partially replacing the Aristotelian-scholastic conception of the soul with a more precise mechanistic analysis. Even though he excluded the rational faculties from the new view, he set the wheels in motion so that after him, the development of an empirical science of the mind was just a matter of time.

Suggested Readings

An excellent discussion of the backgrounds of seventeenth-century science and of Descartes's role in the emergence of modern science is presented in Herbert Butterfield's *The Origins of Modern Science: 1300–1800* (London: G. Bell and Sons, 1957).

A good recent biography of Descartes is Jack Rochford Vrooman's *René Descartes: A Biography* (New York: G. P. Putnam's Sons, 1970). Readers proficient in French will enjoy dipping into the classic biography written by Descartes's admiring younger contemporary, Adrien Baillet: *La Vie de Monsieur Des-Cartes* (Paris, Horthemels, 1691). A scholarly updating of the Baillet biography, also in French, is included in the 13th volume of the Charles Adam and Paul Tannery edition of Descartes's *Oeuvres* (Paris: Cerf, 1897–1913). A lively though critical discussion of Descartes's personality, and its relation to his thought, is included in Julian Jaynes's paper, "The Problem of Animate Motion in the Seventeenth Century," included in Mary Henle, Julian Jaynes, and John J. Sullivan, eds., *Historical Conceptions of Psychology* (New York: Springer, 1973). A thorough and scholarly explication of Descartes's works is Norman Kemp Smith's *New Studies in the Philosophy of Descartes* (New York: Russell and Russell, 1963).

The best single introduction to Descartes is his own *Discourse on Method,* which is available in numerous inexpensive English translations. A good selection of several of his most popular works, including the *Discourse,* is *Descartes: Philosophical Writings* (New York: Modern Library, 1958). *The Treatise of Man* has recently been translated into English for the first time by Thomas Steele Hall (Cambridge, Massachusetts: Harvard University Press, 1972).

2

The Physiology of Mind:
Conceptions of the Brain
from Gall to Penfield

While Descartes clearly recognized the brain as the organ underlying such psychological functions as sensation, imagination, memory, and the initiation of movement, he did not believe that the rational faculties of the mind could be housed in so physically divided a structure. Indeed, he theorized that the rational mind was not localizable anywhere in space, but contented himself with the assertion that it interacts with the body at the small and symmetrical pineal gland in the center of the brain.

So influential was Descartes's conceptual separation of mind from body, that for years the idea of any physical basis for mind was anathema. Those few who dared raise such a possibility, like the French philosopher Julien Offray de La Mettrie (1709–1751), were reviled and persecuted. La Mettrie observed that while ill with fever his intellectual as well as his physical powers were diminished. This suggested to him that his mind as well as his body must be a machine whose efficiency can be impaired by the physical effects of illness. He extended Descartes's mechanistic analysis to its logical conclusion, and argued in his 1748 book, *The Human Machine*, that human beings as well as animals could be understood

43

completely as automata. The book was so repugnant to political and religious authorities that La Mettrie was banished
first from France and then even from the relatively tolerant
Holland, before finally finding refuge in the court of Frederick
the Great.

La Mettrie was too far ahead of his time to be accepted with
equanimity. It was simply not possible to overthrow the notion of an immaterial rational soul at a single blow. Accordingly, the first successful attempts to relate the brain to higher
mental functions did not deny the existence of the ineffable
soul, but asserted that the soul works through the entire brain
in effecting its results. "The brain is the organ of the mind"
became the tenet of a new group of scientists. Not so extreme
as "The brain *is* the mind," as La Mettrie would have had it,
the new credo nonetheless made it reasonable to look for correlations between specific psychological and neurophysiological functions. This was a major advance over Descartes's assertion that all mind-body interactions must take place within
the cramped confines of the pineal gland. The person most
responsible for establishing the new idea was a German physician named Franz Joseph Gall (1758–1828), one of the most
controversial scientific figures of the early nineteenth century.

Gall and the Phrenological Movement

For all the controversy Gall generated, everyone agreed he was
a brilliant brain anatomist. He examined the brains of humans
and animals alike, and introduced several new dissection techniques. He showed that the brain and spinal cord are composed of just two basic kinds of substance: the pulpy *gray
matter* which occupies the outer surface or cortex of the
brain, the inner part of the spinal cord, and several discrete
locations within the brain; and a *white matter* which consists of billions of fibers connecting the various gray areas.*

---

* It is now known that the brain and spinal cord are composed of billions of *neurons,* which are cell bodies interconnected with one another by
dendrites (which receive electrochemical stimulation from other cells) and

He also showed that the two halves of the brain are interconnected by stalks of white matter called *commissures,* and that the white fibers originating in the spinal cord cross over in the lower brain from one side to the other. This means that sensation ascending the spinal cord from one side of the body stimulates the brain on the opposite side, and that movement on one side of the body is initiated by brain activity on the opposite side. All of these fundamental facts about the nervous system are still taught today at the outset of any course on neurology.

More important for psychology were Gall's comparative studies of different kinds of brains. He examined the brains of different kinds of animals, children, elderly and brain damaged people, as well as normal adults. These studies showed, in a general but convincing way, that the higher mental functions of an organism were directly related to the size and intactness of its *cortex,* the mass of gray matter on the outer surface of the brain. Larger amounts of intact cortex were generally associated with more intelligent organisms. No one before Gall had shown so clearly that brain size paralleled mental development.

This demonstration of a relationship between mind and brain was accepted even by Gall's severest critics. Combined with his anatomical studies, it should have earned him a secure and respected place in the history of science. Unfortunately for his reputation, however, he embedded these non-controversial ideas within a larger theory that came to be called *phrenology.** Not content to stop with the bare assertion that the mind was localized somewhere and somehow in the brain, phrenology held that discrete psychological "facul-

---

axons (which transmit stimulation to other cells). The fibrous axons cluster together to form the white matter, while the cell bodies and dendrites constitute the gray.

* The actual word "phrenology" (literally, "science of the mind") was neither coined nor used by Gall, but by one of his students. The term has come to be so closely identified with Gall, however, that it will be used here to denote his general theory.

ties" were localized in specific small parts of the brain. Furthermore, Gall believed that bumps and indentations on the surface of the skull provided accurate measures of the underlying brain parts, and hence of the different faculties.

Phrenology was a curious mixture, combining some keen observations and insights with an inappropriate scientific procedure. Because of its transparent flaws, it quickly attracted the scorn of most of the scientific establishment. When Gall failed to win the respectful attention of professional scientists, he presented phrenology in spectacular lectures and demonstrations directed at laymen. These won him a wide popular following and a handsome income, but of course this only intensified the negative reaction among scientists. An English scientist typified this reaction when he called phrenology "that sinkhole of human folly and prating coxcombry." [1]

According to Gall's autobiography, the foundations of his curious science were laid by an observation he made as a schoolboy. He noticed a number of schoolfellows whom he did not believe to be as bright as himself, but who nevertheless got better grades because they were better memorizers. As he thought about each of these exasperating rivals, he realized that they all shared in common the feature of large, protuberant eyes.

This first observation of a correlation between a physical and a psychological characteristic took on theoretical significance for Gall many years later, as he was conducting his comparative anatomical studies of the brain.* Those studies

---

* The general idea that psychological characteristics may be reflected in physical features was not original to Gall, but was very popular in his time. The art of *physiognomy*—the reading of a person's character in his physical features—had been effectively advocated by the mystic Johann Kaspar Lavater (1741–1801) in the late eighteenth century, and remained influential through much of the nineteenth. In 1836, for example, the young student Charles Darwin was almost rejected for the post of naturalist aboard H.M.S. *Beagle* because the captain thought his nose was inappropriately shaped for a seafarer. Later in the century, the Italian criminologist Cesare Lombroso (1836–1901) published a highly influential physiognomic theory of the "criminal type," part of which still persists today in the myth that evil-doers must be shifty-eyed and sneering.

showed, of course, that behavioral differences between species were matched by differences in their brain structure. Since the most distinctive behavioral characteristic of humans was their higher mental functioning, and their most distinctive brain feature was their highly developed cortex, Gall concluded that the cortex was the seat of the higher functions. The non-cortical brain structures, which vary proportionately less than the cortex across species, were postulated to underlie the activities necessary for life itself, such as respiration, digestion, or locomotion.

Gall went further by noting that human beings differ not only from other species by virtue of their higher mental faculties, but also *within themselves* in the distribution of those faculties. Some people are more intelligent than others, more honest, more amorous, or have better memories. Since all of these personality characteristics are localized in the cortex, reasoned Gall, personality differences between human beings ought to be reflected by differences in their cortexes.

Here his childhood observation seemed relevant. Gall hypothesized that there must be a particular part of the cortex, lying directly behind the eyes, that is responsible for the faculty of "verbal memory." People whose brains are characterized by unusual development of this brain part must also have unusual memories for names and facts. Furthermore, their eyes will be pushed out by the highly developed brain tissue, thus accounting for their protuberance in people with good memories.

If the capacity for verbal memory were localized in one circumscribed region of the brain, it seemed reasonable to assign other higher faculties to other locations. Differences in personality endowment should be mirrored by differences in the development of the corresponding brain regions. Theoretically, a person's entire character could be mapped simply by noting the relative sizes of the different regions. This was the fundamental hypothesis of Gall's phrenology.

As he sought ways to confirm his basic hypothesis, Gall was faced with the problem of how to measure differences in brain configuration. X-rays had not yet been discovered, and the procedure of opening someone's skull was too drastic to be used except in extraordinary circumstances. Undaunted, Gall resorted to a secondary hypothesis. Just as the brain part responsible for verbal memory can cause the eyes to protrude, so highly developed regions in other parts of the cortex should cause measurable irregularities in the surrounding skull. *Craniometry,* or measurement of the physical dimensions of the skull, should lead to inferences about the dimensions of the underlying cortex. Gall's method of investigation was to seek correlations between skull measurements and personality traits.

Once embarked upon his program, Gall found it easy to develop hypotheses. Sometimes chance encounters helped, as when he "discovered" that the region determining sexual response is in the back of the neck. He was attending to one of his patients, whose habitual behavior earned her the posthumous title of "Gall's Passionate Widow." In the midst of an hysterical fit, she threw herself backwards with great force. Gall caught her to keep her from falling, and as he did so he supported the back of her neck with his hand. He immediately noticed that her neck was thick and hot, leading him to suspect that the structure at the base of her brain, the *cerebellum,* must be unusually well-developed and the source of her most prominent characteristic. Observations on other people satisfied Gall all too easily that well-developed necks were generally associated with heightened sexual motivation.

It is easy to laugh at such episodes, but it should be emphasized that there was nothing inherently improper about Gall's theory. In fact, it had a certain naive plausibility, and was testable by direct observation. Gall's major problems arose because of the slipshod way he made those observations, and because of his inability to modify his theory in accordance with data that did not confirm it.

Essentially, there were three crucial defects in his theory. First, the assumption that the shape of the skull accurately reflects the underlying brain was false. This obviously invalidated the phrenologists' claim that they could read character by measuring the skull. It did not invalidate the more basic hypothesis of a relationship between brain configuration and personality, however.

A second major defect lay in Gall's choice of psychological units to describe differences in personality. Since he wanted to account for psychological differences among people, he had to have a basic system of dimensions on which they could vary. The problem of describing variations in the physical characteristics of the brain was simple and straightforward compared with that of describing personality variations. Indeed, psychologists to the present day differ about the nature of the most basic dimensions of personality. Gall, however, unquestioningly adopted the view that all human variability in character can be accounted for by differing combinations of twenty-seven specific "faculties." The memory differences indicated by bulging eyes, for example, were reflections of differences in the "Faculty of attending to and distinguishing Words; Recollection of Words, or Verbal Memory." [2] The heightened sexuality of people with large cerebellums was due to the "Faculty of Amativeness." Other faculties in Gall's scheme included "acquisitiveness," "reverence," "benevolence," "secretiveness," and "mirthfulness." His phrenological program consisted of finding specific brain regions, or "organs," to correspond to the twenty-seven different faculties.

Of course the twenty-seven faculties Gall selected were completely arbitrary. He had no evidence that his list of faculties was any more basic than a list anyone else could devise. It is now generally recognized that personality characteristics such as "reverence" or "acquisitiveness" are not simple givens, but are the complex results of many factors interacting with one another. Several years after Gall's original formulation, his students found it necessary to add even more faculties to the list. One such typical phrenological configuration is given here in Figure 2–1. But no amount of manipulation could salvage the faculty approach to psychology, and so long as phrenology lacked an adequate system for describing psycho-

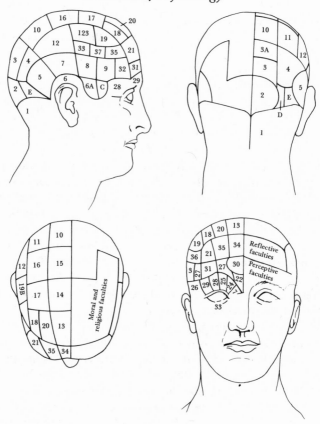

1. Amativeness.
2. Philoprogenitiveness.
3. Inhabitiveness.
3.A. Continuitiveness.
4. Adhesiveness.
D. Marriage or Union for Life.
5. Defensiveness.
E. The Centre of Energy.
6. Destructiveness.
6.A. Alimentiveness.
C. Bibativeness.
7. Secretiveness.
8. Acquisitiveness.
9. Constructiveness.
10. Self-Esteem.

11. Approbativeness.
12. Cautiousness.
13. Benevolence.
14. Reverence.
15. Firmness.
16. Conscientiousness.
17. Hope.
18. Marvellousness.
19. Love of the
    Picturesque.
19B. Sublimity.
20. Imitation.
21. Mirthfulness.
22. Individuality.
23. Form.

24. Size.
25. Weight.
26. Color.
27. Locality.
28. Number.
29. Order.
30. Eventuality.
31. Time.
32. Tune.
33. Verbal Memory
34. Comparison.
35. Causality.
36. Graveness.
37. Gayness.
38. Awe.

Figure 2–1 *A Typical Phrenological Configuration*

logical characteristics, it could never hope to account adequately for differences in human personality.

Even the inadequacy of its psychological assumptions did not discredit phrenology as much as its third fatal defect; the feckless methods by which its hypotheses were usually tested. Gall always maintained that his theory was grounded in observation, a statement that was literally true but that did not reflect the arbitrariness with which some observations were emphasized while others were conveniently ignored. Any positive evidence was unquestioningly and enthusiastically hailed; negative evidence was explained away.

Gall's treatment of the "organ of acquisitiveness" is a good case in point. He located this region after he had befriended a gang of lower class boys, who sometimes did errands for him. Having won their confidence, Gall noted that the boys varied greatly in their attitudes toward petty theft. Some openly admitted to thieving and bragged about their profits, while others were indifferent or expressed an active dislike of their larcenous companions. When Gall just happened to investigate the boys' heads he was astonished, he assures us, to find that the inveterate thieves had long prominences just above and to the front of the ears. The heads of the boys actively opposed to thievery were flat in that region, while the indifferent group had intermediate sized bumps there.

With little effort, Gall found other examples of people with large organs of acquisitiveness who also had marked inclinations to steal. One of the more memorable was a repeatedly-jailed young man who finally gained an almost psychotherapeutic—if somewhat slanderous—insight into his own nature, according to Gall: "As he felt incapable of resisting temptation, he wished to learn the trade of *tailor;* because, as he said, he might then indulge his inclination with impunity." [4] Another case was a mentally retarded young man with a small and unsymmetrical skull and retreating forehead, whose only well-developed feature was the organ of acquisitiveness. An incorrigible thief, this poor soul seemed to Gall to offer "conclusive proof" of his theory, since the activity of the boy's organ of acquisitiveness "was not balanced by the action of other parts," and the propensity to thievery was able to emerge with unmitigated strength.[5]

Though this case was conclusive proof to Gall, his mention of the potential "balancing action" of other brain parts highlights a dodge that he was only too quick to employ in other, less convenient cases. An individual with a huge organ of acquisitiveness but no thieving propensities could be explained away by invoking a large counteractive organ of "benevolence," for example. With twenty-seven or more independently varying faculties to work with, an almost infinitely large number of combinations existed to explain away any anomalous cases.

This was just one of the dubious strategies Gall employed in his analysis of two eminent Viennese gentlemen who led exemplary lives until middle age, despite large bulges of acquisitiveness. Then they both became insane, and when hospitalized, "they wandered all over the hospital, from morning till night, picking up whatever they could lay their hands on— straw, rags, clothes, wood," which they carefully concealed in their shared apartment. There, they stole from each other. Gall easily accounted for their changed behavior by asserting that up until their insanity, their acquisitive tendencies had been held in check by other well developed faculties of a more socialized nature. Then their insanity affected *just* the organs of those higher faculties, permitting the acquisitive tendencies to gain the upper hand. Gall summarized, "The case of these two persons proves, that a man, whose intellect is not quite too feeble, may, in health, overcome the unfortunate impulses of certain organs." [6] Between the counterbalancing effects of many faculties, and "illness" that arbitrarily interfered with some faculties but not with others, Gall could "prove" anything he chose.

If Gall himself was cavalier in his treatment of evidence, he attracted followers who raised such tendencies almost to an art form. When a cast of the right side of Napoleon's skull indicated a phrenological analysis markedly at variance with the emperor's known characteristics, the phrenologists unhesitatingly replied that his true personality was reflected on the left side—a cast of which was conveniently missing. When Descartes's skull was examined, it was found to be exceptionally small in the parts associated by phrenology with the rational faculties. The phrenologists retorted that Descartes's rationality had always been overrated.

Not surprisingly, such tactics made phrenologists the butt of many jokes in the scientific community. According to one story, a noted phrenologist was offered an opportunity to examine the preserved brain of the great physicist Laplace. When the brain of a recently deceased imbecile was secretly substituted for Laplace's, it had no effect on the phrenologist's glowing description of the brain's qualities. A widely circulated scientific joke had it that Gall's own skull, which was preserved following his death and placed on exhibition at the Musée de l'Homme in Paris, was twice as thick as the average.

The scientific establishment responded to phrenology with more than jokes, however. Several individuals recognized that phrenological hypotheses were potentially significant and scientifically testable, even if the phrenologists' own uncontrolled observations were inadequate tests. Foremost among these was a young Frenchman named Pierre Flourens (1794–1867), who conducted a series of experiments in the 1820s that appeared to settle the question of localization of functions in the brain for once and all. Actually, however, they merely presented one side of a classic scientific controversy that remains alive today.

Flourens and the Discrediting of Phrenology

It is difficult to think of two scientists working in the same area whose personalities and careers diverged more sharply than Gall and Flourens. Whereas Gall was always an outsider, never accepted by orthodox scientists, Flourens epitomized the man of the Establishment. A scientific prodigy who received his medical degree and published his first scientific paper at

2. Franz Joseph Gall (1758–1828), Pierre Flourens (1794–1867). Early opponents in the localization of function controversy. *The Bettman Archive, Inc. and The National Library of Medicine, Bethesda Maryland*

age nineteen, Flourens was the special protégé of Georges Cuvier (1769–1832), known as "The Dictator of Biology," and the most celebrated scientist in France. Cuvier's endorsement guaranteed that Flourens' work would be greeted enthusiastically, though it was good enough to stand out on its own.

Appalled by the shoddy methods of the phrenologists, Flourens determined to study the functions of the brain strictly by *experiment,* that is, by the systematic manipulation of the brains of animals, and the careful comparison of their behavior with that of control animals whose brains had not been altered. Experimental techniques promised much more precision and control over the variables than the simple naturalistic observation that Gall usually employed.

The specific technique Flourens employed was the *ablation,* or surgical removal, of certain small parts of the brain, followed by observation of the subject's behavior after recovery from the operation. Most brain tissue does not regenerate after removal. Thus if specific functions are observed to be permanently missing or altered following an ablation, then the ablated brain tissue may be assumed to be involved in the normal production of those functions.

Flourens did not invent the ablation technique, but he refined it to a new degree. His predecessors had failed to obtain conclusive results for two general reasons. First, they did not cleanly excise clear-cut brain regions, but merely pinched, pricked, or compressed parts of the brain. Since brain tissue is spongy in texture, it was seldom possible to determine precisely which parts of the brain were injured by these procedures, and to what extent. Thus any resulting behavior change could not be related to precisely localized brain lesions. Secondly, most of Flourens's predecessors were poor surgeons whose animals did not live long following their operations. It was often impossible to determine how much of their altered behavior was the result of specific ablations, and how much was caused by simple shock from the surgical trauma. Gall, who recognized the anti-phrenological bias of these early experimentalists, had some justification when he called them "mutilators" and dismissed their work as too sloppy to challenge his ideas. It was, of course, a case of the kettle calling the pot black.

Flourens was a much more formidable antagonist for Gall because of his extraordinary skill as a surgeon. Working on the small brains of birds and rabbits as well as dogs, he was able to ablate precisely determined, small portions of the brain. Rather than pinching or pricking the tissue, he completely removed thin slices from various locations. He carefully nursed his subjects following their operations, and so long as they were not missing a brain part necessary for life itself they usually survived. Flourens always waited until the animals had recovered as much as possible before drawing conclusions from his observations, making sure that the effects were the result of ablated brain tissue and not of post-operative complications.

Flourens set out to test Gall's hypotheses by ablating areas supposedly related to specific faculties. Since he worked with animals, he could not test those faculties that are uniquely human, such as verbal memory. But Gall had argued that many features of animal brains are similar to those of humans, including the "organ of amativeness," the cerebellum. Some of Flourens's earliest and most widely known studies involved ablation of this region. He found something quite different from what phrenology predicted, as evidenced by the following description of a dog whose cerebellum he had excised:

I removed the cerebellum in a young but vigorous dog by a series of deeper and deeper slices. The animal lost gradually the faculty of orderly and regular movement. Soon he could walk only by staggering in zig-zags. He fell back when he wanted to advance; when he wanted to turn to the right he turned to the left. As he made great efforts to move and could no longer moderate these efforts, he hurled himself impetuously forward, and did not fail to fall or roll over. If he found an object in his path, he was unable to avoid it, no matter what means he took; he hurled himself right and left; nevertheless he was perfectly well; when one irritated him he tried to bite; in fact, he bit any object one presented to him when he could reach it, but often he could no longer direct his movements with precision so as to reach the object. He had all his intellectual faculties, all his senses; he was only deprived of the faculty of co-ordinating and regularizing his movements.[7]

This is a classic description of a cerebellar lesion, scarcely to be improved upon even after years of further research. Flourens demonstrated conclusively that the function of the cerebellum is to organize and integrate the many small individual movements that must be combined in a flexible yet systematic way to constitute any purposive behavior. Even a simple act like walking requires the proper ordering of thousands of individual muscular movements. This integrating function of the cerebellum was a far cry from "amativeness," of course, and this disconfirmation of a specific phrenological localization was a severe blow to Gall's reputation.

Flourens also ablated tissue from the cortical lobes, the region implicated by Gall in the higher faculties. As sections were progressively removed, animals gradually lost the use of all their senses, and their capacity for voluntary action. Thus a totally decorticated pigeon was kept alive by force feeding and other ministrations by Flourens, but seemed totally insensitive to visual and auditory stimulation and never once initiated a movement that was not directly elicited by prodding. As Flourens concluded, "Picture to yourself an animal condemned to perpetual sleep, and deprived even of the faculty of dreaming during this sleep; such, almost exactly, had become the state of this pigeon whose cerebral hemispheres I had removed." [8] In his view, the animal had lost its *will* along with its cortex.

Flourens believed this finding disproved phrenology. It was true, of course, that he had shown positive evidence of a kind of brain localization. Cortical and cerebellar ablations yielded very different effects, indicating that the two brain parts serve different functions. But *within* the cortex or cerebellum, the functions seemed to Flourens to be evenly distributed. All of the various sensory and voluntary functions tended to disappear *together* as increasingly larger sections of cortex were ablated. If the functions were precisely localized in specific regions, as the phrenologists believed, one would have expected more specificity in the effects of small lesions—or at least so argued Flourens.

Actually, Flourens's logic on this point was far from unassailable, since it held good only if the dimensions of the small ablated regions corresponded precisely to the dimensions of a particular cerebral "organ." Flourens himself described the tissue he removed as "slices," however. Assuming phrenology to be correct, a "slice" could remove tissue from several cerebral organs at once, and result in a *general* lowering of functions as Flourens in fact observed. Gall eagerly seized upon this in his criticism of Flourens: "He mutilates all the organs at once, weakens them all, extirpates them all at the same time." [9] This was a cogent criticism, for Flourens did in fact miss important effects of cortical localization—though quite unlike those predicted by phrenology—because he removed tissue from several functionally distinct areas at once.

Flourens struck a somewhat more damaging blow to phrenology by his observation that animals sometimes recovered all or part of their lost functions with the passage of time. Phrenology held that the several organs covered the *entire* cortex and determined behavioral characteristics by their relative sizes. Accordingly, ablation ought to alter the relative sizes permanently, and there should be no return to the original condition following recovery. Flourens showed that there is much more plasticity to the brain than phrenology assumed, especially if the experimental animal was young and the original ablation relatively small. Researchers to the present day have been very interested in exploring the limits of this plasticity, in determining when and how recovery from brain damage is most likely to occur.

In summary, Flourens's experiments suggested conclusions about brain function that were quite different from phrenological theory. He had found evidence for a kind of localization of functions, but only of very general functions in the large anatomical divisions of the brain. Thus the cerebellum mediated motor coordination, while the cortex seemed the seat of "will." Within each division these specific functions— or *actions propres,* as Flourens called them—were evenly distributed, however. The *actions propres* bore scant similarity to the variegated faculties of the phrenologists.

Flourens's conception of the brain emphasized the integration among its separate parts. While each major part had its *action propre,* it also seemed functionally connected with the other parts. Injury to the cortex, for example, impaired the will and thus altered the kinds of movements that were voluntarily initiated; the cerebellum, which had to integrate the movements, was thus influenced as well. Conversely, deficiencies in motor coordination caused by injury to the cerebellum were perceived by the will, and influenced the volitional urges arising in the cortex. Thus, Flourens believed the separate brain parts were components of a single, harmonious, integrated system, manifesting an *action commune* that overrode and controlled their individual *actions propres.* In a conception more reminiscent of Descartes than of Gall, Flourens believed the brain and nervous system to be the seat of an integrated and harmonious soul.

His view was eagerly accepted by most of the scientific community. Phrenological hypotheses had been clearly repudiated by his findings on the cerebellum and the recovery of functions, and the cortex seemed to be the undifferentiated organ of a general "will." The question of localized functions within the cortex *seemed* conclusively answered in the negative.

But there was the one crucial flaw in Flourens's experiments. By taking undifferentiated slices from the cortexes of animals whose brains were relatively small to begin with, he had failed to discover the differentiations of function that were there. This error went undetected for many years, until brain researchers returned their attention to the highly developed human cortex and its relation to a uniquely human function, that of language.

Aphasia and the Discovery of Language Areas

Even in the wake of Flourens's success, the phrenological notion of cortical localization never quite died out because there remained one perplexing human condition that his theories could not explain. The condition was a malady now known as *motor aphasia,* in which an individual lost the ability to communicate by speech. Sometimes this was a highly circumscribed deficiency, involving no physical interference with the speech organs themselves, and no impairment of other intellective faculties. It usually followed an injury to the brain, often from a stroke.* Such a highly specific deficiency following brain injury was not consonant with a view of the brain as the organ of *generalized* mental faculties.

---

* A stroke, technically called a *cerebrovascular accident* or *CVA,* occurs when there is an interruption in the blood supply to part of the brain. Most often this occurs when a blood clot prevents blood from entering one of the cerebral arteries. Some brain neurons, deprived of blood, rapidly die. The major symptoms of stroke are the result of this localized destruction of cerebral tissue.

Cases of motor aphasia were quite well known in the eighteenth century. One well documented case was the famous English satirist Jonathan Swift (1667–1745), who was almost completely mute during the last year of his life despite the fact that he seemed to understand everything that was said to him. His only known utterances occurred in emotion-laden situations. Once, in a state of bitter agitation, he was overheard to say, "I am a fool." Another time he became angry at a servant who was trying to break up a large piece of coal. "That is a stone, you blockhead!" he shouted. Never once during his illness was Swift able to utter an ordinary declarative sentence.[10]

Another case was an autobiographical account by the French physician Jacques Lordat (1773–1870), who in 1825 suffered a temporary illness where he could not speak, write, or communicate in any verbal way, but who maintained his ability to think nonetheless. Lordat described the onset of his illness as follows: "I was informed that a person who had come to the house to enquire about my health had refrained from paying me a visit for fear of disturbing me. I tried to utter a few words to acknowledge this courtesy. My thoughts were ready, but the sounds that should convey them to my informant were no longer at my disposal. Turning away in dismay, I said to myself: *So it's true that I can no longer speak!*" [11] Lordat went on to report that subjectively his mental processes seemed completely unimpaired during the period of his illness. He was able to think, to recognize what was happening in the world, even to plan lectures in his head. It was only when he tried to communicate that his deficiency appeared. Finally, after many months of painstaking labor, he regained his capacity for language and was able to describe his illness in words.

Gall, who had been aware of cases like these, accounted for them as the result of specific injury to the "organ of verbal memory"—the area behind the eyes that had constituted his first phrenological discovery. He documented this explanation with a case of his own, a soldier who had been brought to him with a partial loss of the ability to name things or people. The patient had to resort to vague catch-all terms like "Mr. Such-a-one" in referring even to people he knew very well. The injury that had caused this partial aphasia was a sword injury to the head, with the sword point penetrating just beneath the left eye and extending into the organ of verbal memory. Gall's description of the case was the first specifically noted correlation of a speech deficit with injury to the left frontal lobe of the cortex. Though it was almost overlooked in the general devastation following Flourens's attack on phrenology, it was to be far from the last such case.

Gall's hypothesis was kept alive by a French physician named Jean Baptiste Bouillaud (1796–1881), who had once been his student. Bouillaud did not accept all phrenological doctrine, but felt there was at least a grain of truth to the notion of a "language center" in the frontal part of the cortex. He collected several reports in the medical literature that seemed to support the idea, though the evidence was very vague because no one had thought it important to preserve the relevant data. He then began speaking out in favor of the hypothesis at medical meetings, where he was always rebuffed. Once he became so exercised at the contemptuous treatment he received that he offered to pay five hundred francs to any-one who could show him a case of severe frontal lobe damage unaccompanied by speech disorders. No one regarded the issue seriously enough to take him up on his challenge.

Bouillaud's son-in-law, the neurologist Ernest Aubertin (1825–1893) could not ignore the question, however. He be-came convinced of his father-in-law's accuracy after locating a soldier whose gunshot wound had left a soft spot on the left frontal portion of his skull. The soldier recovered almost completely, and under normal conditions his speech was un-affected. When the soft spot was pressed with a spatula, how-ever, he immediately became aphasic. This case was not very convincing to skeptics, because of its obvious possibilities for conscious or unconscious dissimulation. Nevertheless, Auber-tin's subsequent advocacy of the localization hypothesis eventually precipitated a dramatic series of events at the Paris Society of Anthropology in 1861.

Broca's Area. The Society of Anthropology had been founded in 1859 by Paul Broca (1825–1880), a young surgeon with a strong side interest in physical anthropology. In particular, he was interested in comparing the head sizes of different cultural and racial groups, and he had devised a number of instruments for measuring the dimensions of skulls. Naturally, the society he founded attracted other people with special interests in the anatomy of the head and skull, including Aubertin.

Most members of the Society had been convinced by Flourens, and opposed Aubertin when he presented his views. After some months of purely verbal sparring, Aubertin finally issued a challenge in the tradition of his father-in-law: "I have studied for a long time a patient . . . who has lost his speech, who nevertheless understands all that is said to him, replying by signs in an intelligent manner to all questions put to him. . . . This man will die, without doubt, in a short time. In view of the symptoms which he presents, I have made a diagnosis of softening of the anterior lobes. If at autopsy the anterior lobes are found intact, then I shall renounce the ideas which I have sustained." [12]

Five days after this challenge a fortuitous event occurred that perhaps denied Aubertin a famous position in neurological history, but certainly made one for Broca. A new patient was transferred into Broca's surgical ward, terminally ill with advanced gangrene of the right leg. When Broca learned that he had been aphasic for twenty-one years, he asked Aubertin to conduct an examination. Aubertin found that he met the requirements perfectly for a test case, and unhesitatingly declared that he suffered from a lesion in the left front lobes of the cortex. Thus the opportunity passed to Broca to conduct the first deliberately planned test of the localization of speech hypothesis.

The fifty-one-year-old patient had suffered from epilepsy as a child but nevertheless had been able to acquire a skilled trade. He did not become aphasic until the age of thirty, under undetermined circumstances. Apart from his aphasia he remained healthy and intelligent at first. He could understand what was said to him, answering numerical questions by holding up fingers, and pointing correctly to objects that were named to him. When he wished to communicate he used gestures, accompanied by repeated utterance of a single syllable "tan." Because of this he became familiarly known in the hospital as "Tan." Tan's only other verbalization was the oath *"Sacre nom de Dieu!"* which he produced easily and frequently when he was frustrated.

Tan's illness remained confined to his speech for about ten years, after which he began to develop some new symptoms. The muscles of his right arm weakened, then became paralyzed. Progressive paralysis of the right leg began, until it became so difficult to move about that Tan took to bed almost constantly. By 1860 his vision began to disappear, and he became a pathetic figure passing his days alone and in darkness. He soon lost sensation as well as mobility on his right side, and thus did not notice an infection when it developed in his leg. By the time the hospital staff noticed the infection and transferred Tan to Broca's ward, the entire leg had become gangrenous.

Antibiotics were unknown in 1861, and Broca immediately recognized the case as hopeless. Thus he consulted Aubertin, and then began his own clinical examination of Tan's linguistic symptoms. Though very weak, Tan demonstrated that he had complete movement of his facial muscles; he could chew, whistle, and move his tongue at will. His hearing was unimpaired, as he could determine the ticking of a watch without difficulty. When asked how long he had been hospitalized, Tan raised an outspread hand four times and then added one finger, to indicate the correct answer of twenty-one years. Broca asked that same question on three successive days, receiving the same correct reply the first two times. The third time Tan apparently realized he was only being tested, and roused himself to a reasonably hearty *"Sacre nom de Dieu!"*—the only time he uttered his famous oath in Broca's presence.

Tan died within a few days, and Broca performed an

autopsy. He brought the brain with him to the next meeting of the Society of Anthropology, where his report created a sensation. An egg-sized portion of the left side of the brain had been destroyed. At the center of the lesion the brain tissue had literally liquefied, so there was almost nothing left; around the edges the brain tissue was merely softened. It seemed clear that Tan had suffered from a progressively spreading destruction of brain tissue, the symptoms of which had been first the speech loss and then the gradually increasing paralysis of his right side.

The key question for the audience, of course, concerned the location of the earliest part of the lesion, which must have been associated with the initial loss of speech. Though it was impossible to answer this question definitively, the center of the lesion seemed the most likely point of origin. This coincided with the lower part of the third convolution of the left frontal lobe—very close to where Gall, Bouillaud, and Aubertin had said the speech center must be. Broca himself reserved final judgment, but clearly inclined toward Aubertin's position in the debate.

Within a few months, Broca had an opportunity to confirm the findings with a second case. An eighty-four-year-old man had had a sudden and circumscribed speech loss a year and a half before his accidental death. Broca performed an autopsy, and found a small lesion in the third convolution of the left frontal lobe—exactly the same spot as the center of Tan's lesion. Now convinced that the localization of speech hypothesis truly had merit, Broca assembled several more confirming cases. The lesion accompanying speech loss was always in the same general part of the frontal lobe, and—a surprise finding—it was almost always in the *left* hemisphere. This left frontal area, shown in Figure 2–2, quickly became known as *Broca's Area.* The speech disorder Broca investigated came somewhat more gradually to be called aphasia, after the term used by Plato to denote the state of being at a loss for words.

Broca's demonstration of the speech area in the left frontal lobe was the first serious attack by an establishment figure on

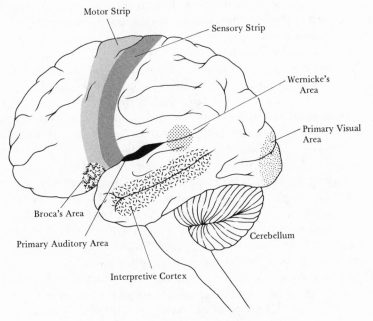

Figure 2–2 *Left Side of the Human Brain*

Flourens's concept of the cortex as an undifferentiated organ of the will. It was far from the last, however. The final third of the nineteenth century was marked by a resurgence of interest in the localization question that some called "the new phrenology." It became clearly apparent that Broca's area was not the only functionally distinct region of the cortex.

Sensory and Motor Areas. A landmark discovery was made in 1870, by two young German physiologists, Gustav Fritsch (1838–1927) and Eduard Hitzig (1838–1907). Employing a fashionable scientific technology of their time, they began experimenting on the effects of mild electrical stimulation applied by an electrode to different points on the cortex of a dog. Since the cortex was known to be insensitive to the pressure of touch, it came as something of a surprise when electrical stimulation of certain points on the cortex elicited movements on the opposite side of the body. Fritsch and Hitzig discovered a distinct region of the cortex now called the *motor strip,* whose stimulation always produced movement. Moreover, specific parts of the body were "projected" onto specific points in the motor strip, so that stimulation of a particular point always produced movement in the same part of the body. (See Figure 2–2 for the location of the motor strip.)

Between these findings and those of Broca, it became evident that localization of function *was* an important characteristic of the cortex, which the early ablation studies had failed to reveal. More refined techniques, employing both electrical stimulation and ablation of precisely delimited areas were devised to "map" the cortex much more finely than Flourens had done. Several people worked on this, but the most skillful was a young Scot named David Ferrier (1843–1928). In the early 1870s he demonstrated several distinct "'centers" in the cortex, to go along with Broca's area and the motor strip.

He discovered a portion of the occipital (rear) lobe, for example, which when stimulated electrically in monkeys resulted in fast movement of the eyeballs, as if the animals were seeing something. Moreover, when these same areas were completely ablated, the animals became blind but retained their other senses. It was clear that a "visual center" existed in the occipital cortex. Ferrier also discovered that the strip of cortex immediately behind the motor strip was a *sensory* area for the different parts of the body. Ablation of the motor strip removed voluntary *movement* in the various body parts, but did not affect *sensation;* that is, an animal could not voluntarily move its leg, but could still respond to stimulation of the leg. Ablation of the corresponding sensory areas had the opposite effect.

As this work was proceeding, brain anatomists were developing ever more precise methods, and showing that there were definite anatomical reasons for the locations of the various sensory and motor centers. Projections from the optic nerve, for example, passed through lower centers in the brain and finally terminated in the part of the occipital cortex that had been designated the visual center. Sensory and motor nerves from the different parts of the body connected with neural tracts that terminated in the sensory and motor strips. An anatomically distinct *auditory center* was hypothesized by tracing the projections of the auditory nerves to the temporal (side) regions of the cortex. Its existence was confirmed by subsequent stimulation and ablation studies. A center for the sense of smell was also discovered; it was relatively small in the human brain but proportionately much larger in the lower animals.

Though these newly found centers clearly confirmed the general principle of cortical localization, they certainly did not support phrenology. Apart from Broca's area, which bore a rough similarity to Gall's organ of verbal memory, the newly discovered centers were primarily *sensory* or *motor* in nature. Rather than the sites of highly developed faculties, they were the receiving points for different kinds of sensory information, or the initiating points for different kinds of movements.* Furthermore, there were large areas of cortex that were not part of demonstrably distinct centers. Neither stimulation nor ablation of these regions in experimental animals had any clear-cut observable effects.

All of these findings led to a new conception of the brain, according to which sensory information of different kinds was projected onto the cortex at the various sensory centers. The information from the centers was then permanently "stored" in brain tissue surrounding the areas. Thus visual "images," representing the memories of visual experiences, were presumably stored around the visual center, auditory images around the auditory center, and so on. Similarly, images representing the memories of specific motoric acts came to be stored in the front part of the cortex, near the motor strip.

---

* Even in Ferrier's time a few die-hard practicing phrenologists remained undaunted by the new discoveries. On learning that stimulation of the phrenologist's organ of pride and self-esteem produced leg movements, one ingenious practitioner retorted that they were actually rudimentary acts of *strutting*.

These storage areas took up some of the cortex that was not clearly a part of specific centers. The remaining brain parts were hypothesized to be *association areas*—tissue composed mainly of white matter which could be employed to interconnect the various images. These association fibers presumably enabled different images to be linked with one another, so that arousal could be communicated from one to another in sequence, producing *thought*. Circumstantial evidence supporting this interpretation came from the fact that the frontal lobes are especially rich in association fibers. Since highly developed frontal lobes are a distinguishing feature of the human brain, they would seem to provide an anatomical basis for human rational capacity.

Wernicke's Theory. In 1874, a young Breslau physician named Carl Wernicke (1848–1905) used this conception of the brain in an analysis of aphasia. Wernicke's theory set the style for aphasia research for many years to come. His first contribution was to provide an explanation for motor aphasia, by pointing out that Broca's area lay directly in front of the part of the motor strip associated with movement of the mouth, tongue, and face. According to the newly emerging conception of the brain, this was just where one should expect to find the stored "images" of various articulatory movements. When damage occurs to this area, then, the memory traces of the movements required to pronounce words must be completely or partially destroyed. The purely physical capacity for making the sounds remains as long as the motor strip is undamaged. But without the memory images linking specific movements to specific words, normal speech cannot be produced.*

Wernicke's theory went beyond motor aphasia and dealt

* Pure cases of motor aphasia like this are necessarily relatively infrequent. Accidental brain lesions follow a random pattern, and thus only occasionally fall entirely in one functional area without affecting neighboring ones as well. In most cases of motor aphasia, part of the motor strip is involved along with Broca's area. Thus there is disturbance in articulation and mouth movement in general, in addition to the specific language disturbance. The difficulty of finding "pure" cases of any kind of brain damage is one of the recurring frustrations of researchers in this field.

with other kinds of language disturbance as well. In motor aphasia, of course, it is primarily the capacity for speech that is impaired; the ability to understand words spoken by others is relatively unaffected. Wernicke discovered ten patients who manifested just the opposite syndrome, who were able to speak perfectly fluently, but whose comprehension of speech was severely impaired. In addition, their speech was marked by frequent mispronunciations and peculiar words even though its syntax was correct. The following dialogue from a more recent case illustrates this peculiar syndrome:

"What brings you to the hospital?" I asked the seventy-two year old retired butcher four weeks after his admission to the hospital.

"Boy, I'm sweating, I'm awful nervous, you know, once in a while I get caught up, I can't mention the tarripoi, a month ago, quite a little, I've done a lot well, I impose a lot, while on the other hand, you know what I mean, I have to run around, look it over, trebbin and all that sort of stuff."

I attempted several times to break in, but was unable to do so against this relentlessly steady and rapid outflow. Finally, I put up my hand, rested it on Gorgan's shoulder, and was able to gain a moment's reprieve.

"Thank you, Mr. Gorgan. I want to ask you a few—"

"Oh sure, go ahead, any old think you want. If I could I would. Oh, I'm taking the word the wrong way to say, all of the barbers here whenever they stop you it's going around and around, if you know what I mean, that is tying and tying for repucer, repuceration, well, we were trying the best that we could while another time it was with the beds over there the same thing . . ." [13]

Wernicke showed that the lesions causing this kind of aphasia were not in Broca's area, but in a region in the temporal lobe near the auditory area which has subsequently been named *Wernicke's area* in his honor (see Figure 2–2). Theoretically, this made very good sense because here was a very likely place for the auditory images of words to be stored. When a patient with a lesion in this area is spoken to, he "hears" the words (as he hears any sounds so long as his auditory center itself is intact) and knows he has been spoken to, and accordingly tries to respond. He does not understand what has been said to him, however, because his internal images of word sounds have been destroyed. When he begins to talk, in response to a message he has not understood, he possesses a full complement of the motor images for speech, and so he is able to articulate fluently. But since he has not understood what was said to him, his response is unconnected to it, and makes no sense to the listener. Wernicke pointed out that many patients of this type may be mistakenly diagnosed as psychotic if their brain injury has gone undetected. Indeed, if one did not know of the specific language deficit of these patients one would think them highly confused and irrational.

Wernicke also offered an explanation for the patients' *paraphasias,* as their mispronunciations and jumbled speech patterns were technically called. Normally, as a person speaks he listens to himself, and exerts a continuous monitoring and correction of his speech patterns as he goes along. If he hears himself mispronouncing a word, he can rapidly stop, correct himself, or start all over again with scarcely a break in his conversation. Aphasics of the type newly described by Wernicke lacked the auditory comprehension of their own words as well as those of others, and so also lacked this useful corrective ability.

Wernicke labelled this second kind of language disorder *sensory aphasia,* to distinguish it from the *motor aphasia* caused by destruction of Broca's area. In current terminology, sensory and motor aphasia are also frequently referred to as *Wernicke's aphasia* and *Broca's aphasia.*

Wernicke's theoretical conception of sensory and motor aphasia led him to predict that there must exist yet another kind of aphasic speech disorder. Since silent and automatic monitoring and correction of one's own speech can normally take place, this suggested that the intact brain must contain association fibers which connect the sensory images in Wernicke's area with the motor speech images in Broca's area. In the absence of such connections, specific word sounds could not be associated with specific motor responses, and the correction could not occur. Accordingly, Wernicke predicted the existence of an aphasia caused by destruction of just the association fibers, with Broca's and Wernicke's areas left intact. In such cases comprehension should be unimpaired, and speech should be fluent but marked by paraphasia. Wernicke called this circumscribed speech deficit *conduction aphasia*.

As far as Wernicke knew in 1874, no one had actually seen a pure case of conduction aphasia. He was not surprised at this, since theoretically such cases should be quite rare. Pure conduction aphasia required injury to a highly specific and small part of the brain, without accompanying damage to the nearby Broca's and Wernicke's areas. Furthermore, the predicted symptoms of conduction aphasia were neither as drastic or dramatic as those of the other aphasias, and it seemed possible that many cases of it might be simply overlooked.

With the publication of Wernicke's ideas, however, conduction aphasia took on a new theoretical significance, and investigators went on the lookout for it. In due course they located several cases which were marked by paraphasia, and, even more strikingly, by an inability to repeat aloud things that had been said to them. Though Wernicke had not specifically predicted this latter deficiency, it was clearly consistent with his theory. With no connections between the auditory images and the motor images of words, the patients could not guide their verbalizations on the basis of what they had just heard.

The discovery of pure cases of conduction aphasia was a remarkable vindication of Wernicke's theory, and a sign that brain localization was entering a new era of sophistication. Previously, efforts had been mainly descriptive and atheoretical in nature. One simply determined (or tried to determine) empirically where certain general functions were localized on the surface of the cortex. Apart from the trial and error procedure of repeated observations, there was no particular reason to look in one place ahead of another—that is, there was no logical model of the brain to guide the searches. The discovery of Broca's area had been a dramatic but largely circumstantial success following from an empirical but atheoretical approach to the brain.

A turning point in brain research had come with the discoveries of the sensory and motor centers in the cortex. These provided definite evidence of localization of elementary units of behavior, rather than the highly general faculties and functions posited by the phrenologists. The higher functions were not discrete entities each localized in its own place, but rather the complex results of the integration of many separate, more elemental units. Nothing illustrated this better than Wernicke's analysis of aphasia, which showed that language was not the single function of an isolated part of the brain, but a complex interaction among several different sensory, motor, and associative factors. Selective injury to one of the factors resulted in selective but incomplete impairment of language. Only when all of the areas were destroyed at once was there a complete loss of language.

Wernicke thus ushered in a new era in brain research. Human faculties were localizable, but not in the simplistic manner suggested by the phrenologists. Complex human behaviors would have to be analyzed in terms of their most basic sensory and motor tendencies, and then, given the knowledge of sensory and motor centers in the brain, one could begin to predict the effects of specific lesions on those behaviors.

Memory and the Equipotentiality of the Brain

Even with the new sophistication introduced by scientists such as Wernicke, hopes of developing a complete conception of the brain's role in higher mental functions were premature. Certain facts came to light even about language which, while not invalidating Wernicke's model, clearly indicated that the brain is not a pre-formed structure with ready-made slots for discrete entities such as "auditory word images," "motor word images," and the like.

One such fact was the usual left-side location of the language areas of the brain. Damage to the corresponding areas on the right may have interfered with other functions, but it did not cause aphasia. This unilaterality led some investigators from very early on to warn that Broca's and Wernicke's areas were not true "centers" like the auditory, visual, or sensori-motor areas which were always found on both sides of the brain. Furthermore, there were conditions under which the language areas could show more flexibility and plasticity than the bilateral centers. For example, if an infant suffered extensive damage to one of its sensory or motor centers, permanent deficits in the associated function inevitably occurred. There was no question but that elementary sensory and motor functions were inevitably and exclusively localized in those centers. If there were damage in infancy to the language areas, however, and the right side of the brain remained intact, language functions developed completely normally.* This suggested that language was not irrevocably destined for one and only one part of the left side of the brain, but that under certain conditions the other side could take over. Clearly, this was an indication of the brain's potential plasticity with respect to localization of a higher mental function.

Attempts to account for *memory* and *learning* have been even more indicative of the brain's plasticity. In Wernicke's time, the brain processes underlying memory seemed likely to be simple and straightforward. It was thought that images or "ideas" of specific events became "stored" in brain cells surrounding the sensory and motor areas, and were potentially interconnected with one another by the association fibers. Thus when one "idea" became aroused it could transmit its excitation to another with which it had been associated, thus exciting its memory. Learning presumably occurred when a

---

* It is still not known for certain whether such individuals suffer from any other defect. Preliminary data suggest that they may develop a relative weakness in tasks requiring *spatial orientation,* which seems to be the function normally associated with the right-side homologues of the language areas. This suggests, perhaps, that once the areas become "used-up" for the language functions in children with left-side damage they are no longer as available for the spatial tasks.

new connection was established between previously unassociated ideas. Thus, memories were held to be localized in specific brain cells and the association fibers interconnecting them.

One clinical fact did not quite fit with this simple conception of memory, however. When head injuries occurred memory was often affected, but not in the way this model suggested. If memories were truly localized in different parts of the brain, memory loss following brain damage should have depended on the specific part of the brain that was damaged. But, apart from the special sense in which "word memories" may be said to be lost in aphasia, no such relationship was commonly observed. Instead, the memory deficit almost always followed the same pattern, regardless of where the brain had been injured. *Recent* memories were lost most completely, and recovered most slowly. Well-ingrained memories of childhood or the distant past were least likely to be lost, and quickest to return. These results seemed difficult to reconcile with the localization of memory theory.

The doubts implanted by these observations grew in strength when supported by animal experiments conducted by the American psychologist Karl Spencer Lashley (1890–1959) in the 1920s. Lashley was the first doctoral student of John B. Watson (1878–1958), an almost legendary figure in American psychology and founder of the movement known as *behaviorism.** As behaviorists, both Watson and Lashley tried to restrict their studies to the analysis of objectively observable behavior. They ruled out, as unreliable and unverifiable, such methods as introspection and subjective reports of conscious states. Animals were particularly good subjects for behavioristic research because they could be easily and constantly observed, and their environments could be carefully and experimentally controlled; and, since they could not talk they were incapable of providing misleading subjective reports to the experimenter.

* See Chapter 8 for a detailed discussion of this movement.

A subject of particular interest to the behaviorists was *learning*—the acquisition of new responses as a result of experience. They devised a number of mazes and other problems that were difficult for animal subjects to solve at first, but that could be mastered over time. Laboratory animals such as white rats could learn to solve rather complicated mazes, for example, if they were rewarded with food pellets following each successful completion. Objective indices of their progress, or learning, were provided by the number of errors they made in the course of each succeeding trial.

According to Lashley's first hypothesis, learning the maze ought to be the result of specific reflex pathways becoming linked up in the brain; that is, the sensory image of one choice-point in the maze becomes linked in the rat's brain with a motor response of a right turn, another choice-point with a left turn, and so on. Lashley presumed these stimulus-response connections to be the result of neural connections being made between specific sensory and motor locations in the brain. According to this behavioristic variant of the localization of memory hypothesis, destruction of those specific brain locations ought to interfere with the learning, while destruction of other brain parts ought to have no effect on it. In other words, small lesions in the brain ought to have highly selective effects on learned behaviors, destroying some but leaving others intact.

Lashley undertook a massive research effort to test that hypothesis. He trained hundreds of animal subjects to run mazes of varying degrees of difficulty, ablated different amounts and parts of their brains, and then observed how much impairment there was on maze performance after recovery from the surgery. Contrary to expectations, he found that the most important determinants of learning loss were the difficulty of the task (there was much more learning loss on mazes that had been very difficult to learn successfully in the first place), and the absolute size of the ablation (a large ablation interfered with *all* tasks to a greater degree than a small one). The locations of the lesions seemed to make no difference, except in extreme cases where an entire sensory area happened to be removed. If a rat's entire visual center were ablated, for example, the animal became blind and could no longer employ the visual cues in the maze. These deficits were obviously not the same as a learning or memory loss, however, and so lent no support to the hypothesis that specific learned stimulus-response linkages were localized. Lashley's results are summarized in Figure 2–3, which shows the number of errors made by rats running mazes of three levels of difficulty, after six degrees of ablation.

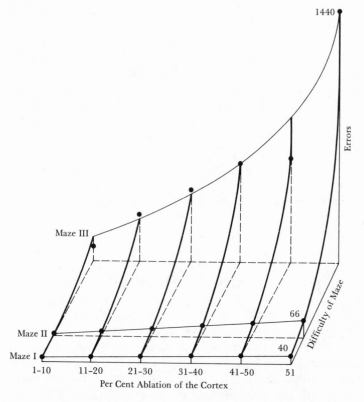

Figure 2–3 *Results of Lashley's Ablation Studies* [14]

The results, of course, hearkened back strongly to Flourens and his notion of the brain's *action commune*—though Lashley's findings suggested it is *memory* rather than the will that is evenly distributed. In another finding directly reminiscent of Flourens, Lashley discovered that his rats recovered from their learning deficits if their ablations had not been too extensive. Clearly, the same stimulus-response connections were capable of being mediated by physically different parts of the brain.

Lashley contributed two new terms to the brain scientists's lexicon when summarizing his results. In storing specific memories, he said, the brain tissues manifest *equipotentiality,* which he defined as "the apparent capacity of any intact part of a functional brain area to carry out . . . the functions which are lost by the destruction of the whole." Partially offsetting the rehabilitative capacity of equipotential brain tissue, however, was the *law of mass action,* "whereby the efficiency of performance of an entire complex function may be reduced in proportion to the extent of brain injury." [15]

Lashley's work dashed the hopes of discovering a simple and clear-cut brain mechanism for memory in which physically discrete sensory and motor images are physically connected by specific nerve tracts in the brain, much as two telephones are connected by wires on a switchboard. Lashley wryly expressed his own frustration toward the end of his life: "I sometimes feel in reviewing the evidence on the localization of the memory trace, that the necessary conclusion is learning just is not possible. It is difficult to conceive of a mechanism which can satisfy the conditions set for it." [16]

Lashley's negative verdict clearly holds good for any simple model of memory localization. Investigators have not yet completely given up on the problem, however, but have turned to rather more elaborate hypotheses. Some have pointed out that even the relatively simple maze-learning studied by Lashley involved much more than just the coupling of single sensations with single responses. The running of a maze involves various kinds of stimuli—visual, tactile, even auditory

77

and olfactory—and motor responses in many different parts of the body. Thus, many different parts of the sensory and motor cortex should be expected to be involved in numerous separate interconnections to create the physical basis of a single learned response. Damage to any small part of the brain might be expected to interfere with only a few of these interconnections, and to have a slight effect on learning. Damage to large areas, of course, should affect more of them, and produce a larger decrement. Following the same line of reasoning, complex learning tasks should involve more interconnections throughout the brain than simple tasks, and so be more likely to be impaired by any lesion that might develop.

A somewhat related explanation has been called the *redundancy hypothesis,* according to which every established memory is stored in *several* different locations scattered throughout the brain. Removal of an isolated brain area might then be expected to remove some, but not all, of the memory traces, with the percentage of intact traces determining the extent to which the memory or learning is retained. This hypothesis also has the virtue of accounting for human memory loss following head injury, if it is assumed that the redundancy of a memory trace increases over time. Old and well-established memories will thus have relatively numerous traces throughout the brain, and be relatively unaffected by injury. Recent memories, which have not yet been localized in many different places, are more susceptible to disruption.

Still another group of current brain researchers, led by the neurophysiologist Karl Pribram, have looked to the recently-discovered *hologram* as a plausible physical analogy for the brain processes involved in memory. It is beyond the scope of this chapter to describe the details of holograms, except to say that they are photographic plates on which visual information is evenly dispersed. A laser beam passed through the plate reveals a three-dimensional image of the object that has been holographed. If the plate is cut in pieces, each separate piece will yield the same image as the whole, but with less fidelity. The point is that each part of the plate contains the essentials of the whole image, and even if part of the plate is destroyed a somewhat inferior version of the whole image remains possible. Information is stored evenly throughout the plate, just as memory seems to be stored evenly throughout the brain tissue. Much remains to be done to demonstrate that the brain has actual physical properties similar to those of holograms and lasers, but the possibility is an intriguing one that is currently inspiring research and speculation.

It is obvious from these considerations that the mysteries of the brain, and the role that localization of function plays in it, are far from solved. Brain research is an exacting and difficult field that will challenge scientists for many years to come. One fact that seems certain, however, is that any final resolution will have to come to terms with the findings of some relatively recent experiments in which points in the conscious human brain are electrically stimulated. The implications of these findings are not yet completely understood, but they surely represent the latest and most exciting phase of the localization of function controversy.

The Stimulation of the Conscious Human Brain

Stimulation studies of the conscious human brain got off to a very poor start in 1874. In the wake of the revolutionary stimulation studies of animal brains by Fritsch and Hitzig, a Cincinnati physician named Roberts Bartholow seized an opportunity to follow up on a human brain. His subject was a thirty-year-old retarded woman who was hospitalized for a cancerous lesion of the scalp. Since part of her brain was visible through the opening in her skull, Bartholow, in his own words, "supposed that fine needles could be introduced without material injury to the cerebral matter." [17] Needles were forthwith made into electrodes, attached to a source of current, and inserted into the patient's brain. When mild stimulation was applied, muscles on the opposite side of the body contracted. When the needle was inserted deeper, the patient complained of an unpleasant tingling in the opposite arm. Then, "in order to develop more decided reactions, the strength of the current was increased," with the following results:

Her countenance exhibited great distress, and she began to cry. Very soon the left hand was extended as if taking hold of some object in front of her; the arm presently was agitated by clonic spasms; her eyes became fixed, with pupils widely dilated; lips were blue, and she frothed at the mouth; her breathing became stertorious; she lost consciousness, and was violently convulsed on the left side. The convulsion lasted five minutes, and was succeeded by coma.[18]

The patient's condition deteriorated rapidly after this experience, and a planned repetition of the experiment had to be cancelled. Three days later she died. Bartholow performed an autopsy on her brain and concluded that "although it is obvious that even fine needles cannot be introduced into the cerebral substance without doing mischief, yet the fatal result in this case must be attributed to the extension of the [original disease]." [19] Bartholow's reassurance notwithstanding, his publication of this grisly experiment created such an outcry in Cincinnati that he was forced to leave town.

It is gratifying to report that more recent stimulation studies on humans have been performed under much more ethical and humane conditions, and have yielded much more valuable scientific results. They were carried out primarily by the Canadian neurosurgeon Wilder Penfield (1891–1976) and his colleagues.

Penfield began in the 1930s by seeking new surgical treatments for the disease *epilepsy*. The major symptoms of epilepsy are seizures brought on by a massive activation of cerebral neurons, often beginning at a small diseased "focus" in the brain and then spreading out into larger and larger areas. If the spread of activation becomes large enough, loss of consciousness and convulsions result.

Such epileptic seizures are frequently preceded by a peculiar subjective sensation known as an *aura*, which the patient recognizes as a warning sign that a seizure is imminent. Auras differ greatly from one patient to another, but may be such sensations as a particular smell, a tingling or some other feeling in a particular part of the body, an intense feeling of familiarity or *déjà vu,* or the inexplicable appearances of an emotion such as rage, guilt, depression, or elation. The Russian writer Dostoyevsky was an epileptic who frequently experienced an aura of irrational guilt, the feeling that he had committed some unknown but unspeakable crime. On other occasions he had quite a different aura, "a feeling of happiness such as it is quite impossible to imagine in a normal state . . . for a few seconds of such bliss, one would gladly give up ten years of one's life." [20]

In most cases today, epilepsy is sufficiently controlled by routine medical procedures, so patients can lead normal lives. In a very few cases it proves intractable, however, and it was these people that Penfield sought to help. He thought that perhaps if he could surgically remove the diseased focus from the brain, seizures could be prevented. The problem was to discover where each focus was, so it could be removed.

Penfield thought there might be a relationship between the location of the focus and the nature of the aura. Perhaps the aura was the conscious result of the neural discharges at the focus, before the activation spread to surrounding areas. If so, it appeared logical that auras would vary as a function of the location of the focus, given what was known about the localization of function in the brain.

This speculation led to a daring surgical strategy, employed only on severely epileptic patients who gave their fully informed consent to undergo an experimental procedure. In the surgery, the surface of the brain was carefully exposed while the patient remained fully conscious. Penfield then stimulated different points on the cortex with an electrode, to see if he could artificially re-create each patient's aura. In many cases he could, and when he removed the suspect brain tissue the patient's epilepsy was often cured or improved.

A fringe benefit of this remarkable therapeutic procedure was the information it provided about artificial brain stimulation and the localization of function. In the course of probing for aura-producing locations in many patients, Penfield stimulated virtually all exposable areas of the cortex, and observed the responses in fully conscious, intelligent, and cooperative individuals. Many of these responses were predictable in advance, given the earlier localization studies. Stimulation of the motor region, for example, produced involuntary movements in the opposite side of the body. The patients were surprised to see themselves making these movements, because they had no awareness of willing to do so. When the adjacent sensory strip was stimulated, patients reported subjective sensations of tingling, quivering, or pressure in the corresponding body parts. Stimulation of the visual area produced lights, colors, flashes, and abstract patterns; the auditory area yielded clicks, buzzes, chirps, rumbles and other sounds.

There were many surprises as well. Penfield discovered that when the regions immediately surrounding the primary visual and auditory areas were stimulated, patients experienced fullfledged hallucinations that were replete with meaning. While stimulation of the primary visual area produced "contentless" sensations like flashes of light or color, the newly discovered *secondary visual region* yielded lifelike visual perceptions. Upon stimulation of this area, one patient immediately said, "Oh, Gee, Gosh, robbers are coming at me with guns." He reported that he actually *saw* the robbers coming, from behind him and to the left. Stimulation of a second nearby point resulted in the hallucination of the patient's brother coming toward him with a rifle in his hand.[21]

A comparable division occurred between primary and secondary auditory areas. Whereas stimulation of the primary area yielded abstract sounds, the surrounding secondary area produced organized auditory experiences such as the voice of a mother calling a child, or a Beethoven symphony. So real and surprising were these effects that some patients accused Penfield of secretly turning on a radio.

Penfield's most surprising results of all occurred when he

stimulated areas throughout the temporal lobe, the side area of the cortex near the ear. Apart from the auditory area, no part of the temporal lobe had previously been strongly implicated in localization of function studies. Penfield found, however, that most of the temporal lobe constituted what he called *the interpretive cortex,* and yielded specific *psychical responses* when stimulated. (See Figure 2–2 for the location of the interpretive cortex.) These responses were of two general types. First, there were "interpretive responses," in which the patient's immediate situation was suddenly seen in a new light. Depending on the point of stimulation, these interpretations included sudden feelings of *déjà vu,* the opposite sensation that everything was suddenly strange or absurd, senses of foreboding and fear, or inexplicable exhilaration. Many of these interpretive sensations were like epileptic auras, of course, which suddenly became explicable as the result of focal discharges in these locations of the temporal lobe. Here, also, was the first indication that highly specific emotional and orienting attitudes were localized in the brain, just as sensations and movements were.

The second class of responses to stimulation of the interpretive cortex were "experiential responses." Many patients described these experiences as "dreams" or "flashbacks" to events that had occurred to them in the past, and they seemed to be hallucinatory re-creations of events from their past lives. All of the details of the original experiences were there, the sights, sounds, and other sensory impressions that had been part of the first experience. The hallucinated experiences were usually unremarkable in content, and seemed to be ordinary everyday impressions. One patient, for example, reported, "Oh, a familiar memory—in an office somewhere. I could see the desks. I was there and someone was calling to me—a man leaning on a desk with a pencil in his hand." Other typical responses were, "A scene from a play. They were talking and I could see it," and "A familiar memory—the place where I hang my coat up—where I go to work." [22]

These exciting findings currently raise more questions than

they answer. Certainly they demonstrate more localization than had previously been shown. But what specifically is it that is localized in the interpretive cortex and the secondary sensory areas? On the one hand it is tempting to speculate that Penfield has provided the long awaited evidence for localization of memory. The vivid detail of the hallucinated responses suggests that even the most inconsequential of experiences may become permanently recorded in specific cerebral tissues, and made potentially available for future use in memory. But any such interpretation must be made very cautiously and tentatively.

One reason for caution is that Penfield's patients' "experiential responses" were quite different from normal "memories." The patients themselves were very clear in describing their responses as much more vivid than normal memories, more on the order of dreams than ordinary recollections or thoughts. Since the stimulations did not produce normal memories, it is clear that the usual functioning of memory must involve something different from the mere electrical excitation of specific neurons in the interpretive cortex. Penfield himself thought that his temporal stimulations initiated a "scanning" of the experiences recorded in the brain that is part but not all of the regular memory process.

Another reason for caution is that the exact effects of artificial electrical stimulation on the cerebral neurons are unknown. Penfield believed that electrical stimulations and epileptic discharges *inhibit* rather than activate the normal functions of the neurons affected. Thus experiential and interpretive responses may really be caused by activation of some as yet unknown part of the brain whose function is normally *opposed* by the interpretive cortex. The whole question of what is localized where thus becomes very complicated for brain researchers.

Even if these questions are answered and it turns out that memories and emotions, as well as sensations, are localized in specifiable cerebral areas, the task of understanding the brain will have just begun. After brain scientists learn *where* psychological functions take place they will still have to determine *how* they occur. Penfield noted that his patients' experiential responses were much more like videotape playbacks than like still pictures. Thus, the cerebral neurons must somehow represent the *flow* of experience and not just stationary impressions of it. Much more is involved than the simple storage of one "'idea'' in a single neural cell. It will be a problem of the future to determine specifically how the circuitry of the brain can accomplish such a marvelous feat of engineering.

As these and other puzzles about the relationships between brain and behavior are resolved in the years ahead, one fact is certain: the localization of function question will continue to be relevant. The question has changed in form since the days when Gall and Flourens were antagonists, shaped by increasingly sophisticated conceptions both of the physical brain itself and of the psychological "mind" the brain subserves. But there will continue to be some findings which emphasize the differentiation among the specific parts of the brain, and others which emphasize the integrity and unity of the brain's overall functioning. As in the past, scientists on both sides will have something valid to say.

Suggested Readings

For good general accounts of the history of the localization of function controversy see David Kretch's "Cortical Localization of Function" in Leo Postman, ed., *Psychology in the Making* (New York: Knopf, 1962), and Robert M. Young's *Mind, Brain and Adaptation in the Nineteenth Century* (Oxford: Clarendon Press, 1970).

For an account of Gall's contributions see "Gall and the Phrenological Movement" by Owsei Temkin in *Bulletin of the History of Medicine* (21:275–321, 1947). On Flourens, see J. M. D. Olmstead's "Pierre Flourens" in E. A. Underwood, ed., *Science, Medicine, and History* (New York: Oxford University Press, 1953). An interesting account of the events leading up to Broca's discovery is in Byron Stookey's "A Note on the Early History of Cerebral Localization," *Bulletin of the New York Academy of Medicine* (*30*:559–578, 1954). For a detailed and informed appreciation of Wernicke see "Wernicke's Contribution to the Study of Aphasia," by Norman Geschwind, in *Cortex* (*3*:449–463, 1967). Karl Lashley summarized his own findings in *Brain Mechanisms and Intelligence* (Chicago: University of Chicago Press, 1929), as did Penfield in Wilder Penfield and Lamar Roberts, *Speech and Brain-Mechanisms* (Princeton: Princeton University Press, 1959).

Highly readable up-to-date accounts of brain function and pathology are Howard Gardner's *The Shattered Mind* (New York: Knopf, 1975) and Steven Rose's *The Conscious Brain* (New York: Knopf, 1973).

3

The Sensing and Perceiving Mind:
Kant, Helmholtz, and the Gestalt Psychologsists

At some point in the early 1770s, the German philosopher Immanuel Kant (1724–1804) was, in his own words, "aroused from my dogmatic slumber." Previously he had been a respected but unspectacular scholar, turning out essays on such philosophical subjects as the existence of God, or the difference between absolute and relative space. Now, well into middle-age, he embarked on a program of theorizing that would revitalize the entire philosophical world, and permanently refashion the German view of humanity and nature. Among the results was a climate of opinion in which the scientific study of the mind could develop and prosper.

The stimulus that aroused Kant with such great consequences was the skeptical philosophy of the Englishman, David Hume (1711–1776). Hume had called into question the logical status of a number of cherished human concepts, including the notion of *causality*. People are in the habit of perceiving certain events as "caused by" preceding events. When one billiard ball strikes another, for example, the movement in the second is perceived as having been caused by the impact of the first. Scientific theories are based on the assumption that specific antecedent conditions cause specific consequences. These common but naive uses of the term "cause" suggest that there exists a necessary sequential relationship between certain events, and that the necessity is somehow immediately apprehended when we perceive causality.

Hume called into question the necessity of causal relations. All we can ever know, he argued, is that certain regular sequences have occurred in the past, and we expect that they will be repeated in the future. "Causality" is nothing more than that. The conviction that a billiard ball's motion is caused by its impact with another is nothing more than the recollection that all previous impacts led to similar motion. Causality—the *necessity* of a connection between two events—is thus never directly perceived, and it has only a probabilistic rather than an absolute basis. Hume summarized his position as follows: " 'Tis not, therefore, reason, which is the guide of life, but custom. That alone determines the mind, in all instances, to suppose the future conformable to the past." [1]

To practical people, these qualifications made no difference. They continued to base their actions on suppositions of causality, and whether those suppositions derived directly from the actual external world or only indirectly from their own experience was inconsequential. But to a philosopher like Kant, concerned with discovering the ultimate truths of the universe, the issue was crucial. If one could not actually "see" causality in nature, then the logical underpinnings of the entire structure of knowledge were challenged.

Kant's response to the challenge was simple but revolutionary. Since causality (along with several other compelling impressions) cannot be proven to exist in the external natural world, he said, it must exist instead in the human mind. He asserted that there are two separate domains of reality, one completely inside the mind, the other completely outside. The external, or *noumenal* world consists of "things-in-themselves" —objects in a "pure" state independent of human reason. Though presumed to exist, and to interact in some way with human consciousness, the noumenal world can never be known directly. For once it encounters and interacts with the human mind, it becomes converted by the mind into the inner, *phenomenal* world. The word "phenomenal" is derived from the Greek *phainomenon,* or "appearance," and suggests the nature of the inner world. What human beings actually experience is not the objective reality of things-in-themselves, but a series of "appearances" or phenomena that are the creations of an active mind encountering the noumenal world. The mind is thus not just a passive reflector of external reality, as Hume's analysis would have it, but a *creator* in its own right of phenomenal reality.

According to Kant, the mind follows certain specifiable rules as it creates phenomena. All experiences must be localized in time and space, and organized in terms of twelve *categories* defining quality, quantity, relation, and mode. Among the quantitative categories are the foundations of the mathematical axioms; among the relational categories is the concept of causality. This means that human beings cannot help but experience the world as organized in time and space, and as following the mathematical and causal laws—not because the noumenal world is "really" that way, but because the human mind must structure experience that way. Here was a return to Descartes's innate ideas, with a new twist.

The most important psychological feature of Kant's theory was not the absolute correctness of his list of categories, but its suggestion of a new general picture of the human mind and its relationship to nature. Previously it had been believed that conscious sensations of the external world were direct copies of real objects. Aristotle, for example, had assumed that the sense organs take on the forms of perceived objects much as soft wax takes on the form of an object impressed upon it. Descartes's position almost two thousand years later was essentially the same. He believed that vibrations from external objects are transmitted directly to the sense organs, which in turn convey them to the pineal gland where they may be directly perceived by the soul. When the visual patterns of vibrations become inverted on the retina, they must be re-inverted before reaching the pineal gland, so the soul can have a perfect, upright image to deal with. Both Aristotle and Descartes assumed a perfect one-to-one relationship between objects in the external world and the sensations of those objects in the inner world of consciousness.

The Kantian view suggested something quite different, however. According to it, human sensory experience has already been filtered through the categories of the mind, and so is as much a function of the perceiving mind itself as of the external world it records. To understand experience, it is as necessary to analyze the mind as it is to analyze the natural world. Thus Kant created a climate in which the study of the mind took on new complexity and importance.

Kant's formulation was strictly philosophical. He did not specify *how* the mind creates its phenomena, nor did he locate the mind in specific structures of the body. With the definitive localization of mental functions in the brain and nervous system in the early nineteenth century, however, it was only a matter of time before others would do so. Their efforts were further stimulated by a major neurophysiological discovery made in England, but first appreciated in Germany because of its obvious relevance to Kantian theory.

The discovery was that each sensory nerve has its own *specific nerve energy;* that is, that it conveys one and only one kind of sensory stimulation. Traditionally, it had been believed that any sensory nerve could transmit any kind of sensory information to the brain, much as a hollow tube can transmit many different kinds of substances from one end to the other. According to this view, a given nerve would convey visual sensations to the brain when stimulated by light, and auditory sensations when stimulated by sound. However, by the early nineteenth century it was clear that this was not true. Certain sensory nerves were strictly visual in nature, and no matter how they were stimulated they always conveyed visual stimulation. For example, the optic nerve extending from the back of the eyeball always conveyed sensations of light regardless of whether it was stimulated by electrical excitation, pressure on the eyeball,* or by light actually falling on the retina. Other nerves were strictly auditory, and conveyed sensations of sound no matter how they were stimulated; still other nerves were specific to the other senses.

Because of this nerve specificity, of course, conscious sensations were not necessarily infallible representations of external stimulation. Seeing a particular pattern of light only meant that particular optical nerves were being stimulated. And while the stimulation *may* have originated in a real external object, there could be no assurance of the fact. The immediate source of sensory impressions was thus not the external world itself, but a nervous system which interacted with the external world while making its own contribution to sensation. This was directly equivalent to the Kantian assertion that phenomenal reality is the creation of a mind that is influenced by the noumenal world, but contributes independent categories and dimensions of its own.

The first systematic studies of sensation and perception—and by implication of the mind itself—were carried out within this matrix of neurophysiology and Kantian philosophy. The strongest proponent of the doctrine of specific nerve energies was the German physiologist Johannes Müller (1801–1858), a brilliant teacher and administrator who established the world's first institute for experimental physiology in Berlin. Among the many exceptionally gifted students Müller attracted to his institute was Hermann Helmholtz (1821–1894), who would carry the doctrine of specific nerve energies to its most far-reaching conclusions, and become one of the greatest scientists of the nineteenth century.

---

* You can demonstrate this yourself by turning your eyes as far to the right as possible, closing the eyelids, and pressing gently on the left side of the left eyeball. The pressure excites the optic nerve at the back of the eyeball, and results in a sensation of colored light in the right hand side of the visual field.

Hermann Helmholtz: Early Life

Hermann Helmholtz was born on August 31, 1821, in the German town of Potsdam. His father was an intellectually ambitious high school teacher of philology, who strongly encouraged his son's early-demonstrated academic bent. Kantian philosophy was a major interest of the father, though the son was more attracted to scientific subjects. Physics became his consuming passion from the moment he discovered some old textbooks on his father's library shelves. Young Helmholtz worked on optics diagrams beneath his school desk when he should have been studying Latin, spoiled the family linen with his chemical experiments, and in due course became the most promising young scientist in town.

The early 1800s were heady times for those interested and gifted in science. The monumental theories of Isaac Newton were more than a century old, and from the perspective of the times it seemed they would soon provide a rational explanation for all the physical phenomena of the universe. Despite Helmholtz's ability in this exciting field, however, a career as a physicist was ruled out for him. Pure science was at that time largely the prerogative of the rich, and financial considerations made Helmholtz seek a more practical vocation. Fortunately, the Prussian government had established a program by which poor but talented students could receive free medical training at Berlin's Royal Friedrich-Wilhelm Institute for Medicine and Surgery, in exchange for eight years' service as army surgeons. Though medicine was not physics it at least involved scientific training, so Helmholtz applied and was accepted as a seventeen-year-old. He was a model student, spending most of his time studying his medical subjects. Occasionally, however, he relaxed by playing the piano, reading Goethe and Byron, or (as he put it in a letter home) "sometimes for a change the integral calculus."

While in his second year of medical school Helmholtz began his study of physiology at Müller's institute. Among his fellow students there were Émile du Bois-Reymond (1819–1892), who

3. Herman Helmholtz (1821–1895). *The National Library of Medicine, Bethesda, Maryland*

later collaborated with Helmholtz and gained fame by establishing the electro-chemical nature of the nervous impulse; Rudolf Virchow (1821–1902), who later pioneered the cellular theory of pathology; and Ernst Brücke (1819–1893), who later became the most influential teacher of Sigmund Freud.

At the institute, Helmholtz shone even among this exceptional group of students because of his expertise in physics.

Müller was a progressive scientist for his day, quick to use the principles of physical science in the explanation of physiological phenomena. For example, he noted that the eye is like a camera, projecting an inverted image on the retina through a convex lens in full accordance with the laws of physical optics. He also employed physical knowledge about the transmission of sound waves through solid and liquid media in his analysis of the functions of the middle and outer ear.

Helmholtz and his friends greatly respected their teacher, and accepted almost everything he had to say. But on one important point they found themselves in disagreement with him. Müller, for all the modernity of most of his views, still clung to an old physiological doctrine known as *vitalism*. According to this doctrine, all living organisms were imbued with an immaterial and ineffable "life force" which was responsible for the phenomena of life, and which was ultimately unanalyzable by scientific methods. Müller did not deny that ordinary physical and chemical processes took place in a living organism; his willingness to employ physical principles in his analyses was testimony to that. But he also believed that all of these processes were somehow harnessed and controlled by the vital force. In its absence the processes presumably ran amok, leading to the putrefaction and decay of the body rather than to its health. Death was the result of the withdrawal of the vital force. Müller's belief in vitalism implied that there was a limit to the extent of possible scientific understanding of physiological processes. Useful as scientific analysis might be, he held that the ultimate mystery of the life force, and thus of life itself, could never be analyzed.

Helmholtz and his friends were reluctant to accept this limitation on science. For his own part, Helmholtz was uncomfortable with vitalism because it seemed peculiarly analogous to a gravity-driven perpetual motion machine, which he knew to be a physical impossibility. If such a machine were possible, it would have to operate in principle something like the following. A weight must be acted upon by gravity so that it falls a certain distance. Then the force of gravity must be temporarily suspended so the weight can be raised to its original position without the exertion of any additional force. Then gravity is re-instituted, the weight falls again, and the whole process is repeated perpetually. The problem, of course, is that for such a machine to work, the force of gravity must be temporarily and arbitrarily suspended. This is impossible, since Newtonian physics teaches that the force of gravity is universal and permanent.

To Helmholtz's mind, the vitalists' conception of the organic body seemed analogous to such a perpetual motion machine. Sometimes the vital force acted, causing organs to function so as to promote life. But then, for some arbitrary reason, the force was suspended, allowing the organs to decay according to a completely different set of laws. Helmholtz could not prove that such an arbitrary and capricious force was impossible, but since it differed so much from the grand and universal force of gravitation, he believed it to be vaguely "contrary to nature."

The belief Helmholtz and his friends adopted in place of vitalism was *mechanism,* an extension of Newtonian analysis into the whole of physiology. According to mechanism *all* organic and physiological processes were potentially understandable in terms of ordinary physical and chemical principles, which in turn were reducible to forces of attraction and repulsion among material bodies. The processes occurring in a living body were perhaps very complex, but they were nonetheless subject to the same universal laws as inanimate processes. The essence of this view was clearly and dramatically expressed by a solemn article of faith that some of the mechanistically oriented students composed. "No other forces than the common physical-chemical ones are active within the organism," they affirmed. "In those cases which cannot at the time be explained by these forces one has either to find the specific way or form of their action by means of the physical mathematical method, or to assume new forces equal in dignity to the physical-chemical forces inherent in matter, reducible to the force of attraction and repulsion." [2]

The students' avowal of mechanism did not necessarily cause them to practice physiology in a manner different from Müller's. The difference was one of emphasis and attitude, rather than physiological doctrine per se. No "ultimate experiment" was possible to enable one to choose between the two doctrines, and Müller was ready to apply physical principles to physiology just as far as they could go. He differed from his students only in his certitude that at some point a limit would be reached when the vital principle entered the picture.

The difference in emphasis and attitude did subtly influence the kinds of problems chosen for investigation, however, even though the methods were similar once research was started. Thus Müller was reasonably certain that the deepest mysteries of neurological functioning involved the life force and were probably insusceptible to physical analysis. He believed the nervous impulse to travel with infinite or near infinite speed along the nerve fiber, probably because of its close involvement with the life force. Accordingly, he did not even contemplate doing research to study the physico-chemical properties of the nervous impulse. The mechanistically oriented, students believed *all* physiological problems were potentially susceptible to physical analysis, and so operated under no such constraint. In time, their optimism would pay enormous dividends.

The Triumph of Mechanism in Physiology

Helmholtz completed his doctoral dissertation—a microscopic study of the nerve structure of invertebrates—under Müller's direction, and was awarded his medical degree at the age of twenty-one. Immediately ahead lay his eight-year military obligation. He became an army surgeon in his home town of Potsdam, and settled into barracks life. Like many another inducted into the peace-time military, he found his duties tedious but scarcely all-consuming of his time. He managed to construct a small laboratory in his barracks where he conducted physiological experiments on frogs in his spare time.

Conceived within the mechanist framework, his experiments investigated relationships between metabolic body processes and the heat generated by muscles. They showed that muscular activity by the frog led to measurable chemical changes within the muscles which could be accounted for as chemical reactions involving the oxidation of nutrients consumed by the animal. Then, in a series of detailed mathematical calculations, Helmholtz tied everything together. He showed that, if one measured the total food and oxygen consumed by an organism over a given period of time, and then calculated the total physical energy potentially releasable by their chemical combination, that energy was sufficient to produce all of the muscular work produced by the organism, as well as the heat it generated. Thus he demonstrated that ordinary chemical reactions were capable of producing (thought not necessarily that they *did* produce) all of the physical activity and heat generated by a living organism. Consistent with mechanist doctrine, he showed that it was feasible to analyze a living body as if it were a machine, in terms of fuel input, work output, and overall efficiency.

A more remarkable achievement marked 1847, Helmholtz's fifth year in the army. During the 1840s, several scientists in Europe had been developing the idea of the *conservation of energy*. According to this notion, all the different kinds of physical force in the universe—heat, light, gravity, electricity, etc.—were potentially interchangeable forms of a single huge but finite reservoir of energy. Energy was never created or destroyed, but only transformed from one state to another.

Under the conservation of energy hypothesis, a machine was simply a device that transformed energy from a less useful to a more useful form. A steam engine, for example, transformed the heat from a fire into the motion of steam molecules, whose energy was transformed into the motion of pistons, which in turn activated the moving parts of the engine. Helmholtz had assumed the conservation of energy in his discussion of muscular metabolism, showing that the energy output of a muscle (measured in terms of heat and physical work produced) was identical in magnitude to its energy input (measured in terms of the potential chemical energy stored in food and oxygen).

While the idea of conservation of energy was very much in the air, no one had systematically raised it to a high level of generalization. Helmholtz accomplished this in his 1847 paper, "The Conservation of Force," which began by showing that a successful perpetual motion machine would violate the conservation of energy. He then proved mathematically the impossibility of constructing perpetual motion machines driven by gravity, heat, electricity, magnetism, or electromagnetism, thus suggesting that the conservation of energy must hold in each of those fields. After linking together these formerly diverse fields of physics, Helmholtz concluded by pointing out that all *organic* processes studied so far had seemed similarly ruled by the conservation of energy. Indeed, though Helmholtz did not say so explicitly, one of his major purposes was to demonstrate indirectly the "contrariness" of the vitalist position. The vital force, capable of being arbitrarily introduced or suspended, did *not* obey the law of conservation of energy. Thus, its disparity from every other known force was implicitly emphasized, and it was shown to be even more implausible than it had seemed before. Physiology was nudged just a bit closer to physics.

This paper was unusual in style and Helmholtz had to publish it at his own expense, but its merits were soon appreciated. The Prussian government, unusually progressive when it came to educational matters, recognized his talent and excused him from further military obligation as soon as a suitable academic post became available. Helmholtz was appointed lecturer on anatomy at Berlin's Academy of Arts in 1848, and the next year was given an even better job as professor of physiology at the ancient and highly respected East Prussian university at Königsberg. Coincidentally, this was the place where Kant had spent his entire life.

The change brought two welcome improvements to Helmholtz's life. He was now financially able to marry his fiancée of several years, Olga von Velten, and he was at last able to devote himself totally to scientific pursuits. When he completed his six-year tenure at Königsberg in 1855, he was one of the most highly regarded scientists in the world.

While preparing an optics lecture during his first year at Königsberg, Helmholtz suddenly realized that a partially silvered mirror could be aligned in such a way as to allow an observer to look directly at the retina of a living subject's eye. He immediately realized the potential medical and scientific value of his discovery, and constructed his first *ophthalmoscope*. Though someone else (unknown to Helmholtz) had invented a similar instrument several years before, Helmholtz was a much better publicist. He demonstrated his ophthalmoscope at most of Europe's leading laboratories, and it was quickly adopted as a valuable medical tool. It also served as a sort of ticket of introduction for Helmholtz to the eminent scientists of the day, and enabled him to establish a wide circle of professional friends and acquaintances.

The ophthalmoscope was just a temporary diversion for Helmholtz, however. His major preoccupation during the early Königsberg years was the measurement of the speed with which a nervous impulse travels along a nerve fiber. Müller, in accordance with his vitalist leanings, had taught that the speed was instantaneous or so fast as to be unmeasurable. But in the 1840s, Helmholtz's friend du Bois-Reymond had studied the chemical structure of nerve fibers, and concluded that the nervous impulse could well be an electrochemical phenomenon. He constructed a theory about the nature of the nervous impulse that suggested to Helmholtz that its speed might be much slower than anyone had previously imagined—perhaps even slow enough to be measured in a laboratory. He tested this startling assumption in one of the most influential experiments of the century.

To perform his research, Helmholtz needed an instrument capable of measuring very small fractions of seconds—smaller than could be reliably detected by any existing timepiece.

99

He devised it from a simple laboratory galvanometer, an instrument that detects the presence and strength of an electric current in a wire. The current causes a needle to deflect, with the amount of deflection corresponding to the strength of the current. Helmholtz knew that when the current was first turned on it took a short but measurable amount of time to reach its maximum level, and hence for the needle to reach its maximum deflection. If the current were turned off before it reached its maximum level, the proportion of needle deflection achieved was an accurate measure of the very small amount of time the current had been on.

Armed with this galvanometric stopwatch, Helmholtz measured the speed of the neural impulse in a severed frog's leg. He knew that the mild electrical stimulation of the motor nerve, which ran the length of the leg, would cause a twitch in the foot muscle attached to the end of the nerve. With great delicacy and ingenuity Helmholtz attached a switch to the foot, so that twitching of the muscle could turn *off* the electrical current. The electrical circuit passed through a time-calibrated galvonometer. When the current was turned on, the galvanometer needle was set in motion, but as soon as the foot twitched the current was cut off and the needle deflection ceased. Its maximum reading provided a measure of the time the current had flowed. Now Helmholtz could compare the times required when electrical stimulation was applied to various locations on the nerve fiber. He found that the farther the stimulation point was from the foot muscle, the longer the total reaction time. Since the only difference between these conditions was the distance the impulse had to travel along the nerve fiber before activating the muscle, the speed of the impulse itself could be measured. To his delight, Helmholtz discovered that a point four inches from the muscle required .003 seconds longer than one only one inch away. This indicated that the average speed of the impulse through the extra three inches must have been about eighty-three feet per second.

After establishing the rate of speed in a frog's leg, Helmholtz turned to human subjects whom he trained to make a specific response such as pushing a button whenever a stimulus was applied to the leg. His results were highly variable, but reaction times tended to be longer when the stimulus was applied to the toe than when the thigh was stimulated. This enabled a rough estimate of the speed of the impulse in human sensory nerves: between 165 and 330 feet per second, according to Helmholtz's calculations. He could not regard these results with the certainty of those from the frog's leg, because of the extreme variability both within and between individual subjects. The studies were highly significant nonetheless, both because they were generally consistent with the frog studies, and because they helped introduce the "reaction time" method of experimentation which was to become very important in future psychological research. Helmholtz himself soon abandoned the technique, however.

It took a few years before the significance of Helmholtz's experiments registered with the scientific world at large, in part because the published descriptions were written in an exceptionally turgid style, not immediately comprehensible to those unfamiliar with the work.* A more important reason, however, was that the results were simply too astonishing to be readily believed. Mental processes are subjectively experienced as occurring instantaneously, and physiologists believed

---

* When du Bois-Reymond received the first written report of Helmholtz's experiments, he responded with a candor that could only have been sustained by true friendship: "Your work, I say with pride and grief, is understood and recognized by myself alone. You have, begging your pardon, expressed the subject so obscurely that your report could at best only be an introduction to the discovery of method." Helmholtz's father, an ever watchful critic, fully concurred in the negative evaluation of his son's ability to express himself. Commenting on a public lecture Helmholtz had delivered, he wrote, "He is so little able to escape from his scientific rigidity of expression, . . . that I am filled with respect for an audience that could understand and thank him for it." [3]
Helmholtz evidently took these criticisms to heart. He began to take great pains over his writing style, and later became an acknowledged master of popular scientific writing.

the neurological events paralleling them should be instantaneous also. Yet Helmholtz's results suggested something very different. According to them, a whale receiving a wound to its tail would not even become conscious of its injury until a full second had elapsed to permit an impulse to travel from the tail to the brain. It would be another full second before a motor impulse initiating defensive action in the tail could be sent back. Though long reaction times are in fact characteristic of large animals, most scientists found them hard to believe at first.

Helmholtz and du Bois-Reymond ushered in a new phase in the life sciences with their studies of the neural impulse. They clearly demonstrated the advantages of adopting a mechanistic view of the nervous system. As Helmholtz's biographer has noted, "The unexpectedly low rate of propagation in the nervous system . . . [was] incompatible with the older view of an immaterial or imponderable principle as the nervous agent, but quite in harmony with the theory of the motion of material particles in the nerve substance." [4] The results did not *prove* the complete validity of mechanism, because such proof was impossible as long as there remained any unanswered physiological questions. But they did show that the mechanist point of view was more productive than vitalism, by suggesting important experiments that vitalism discouraged. Had Helmholtz and du Bois-Reymond not been mechanists, they would never have thought to try their experiments.

The implications of this work extended far beyond the realm of pure physiology. Brain localizationists since Gall had recognized that the brain and central nervous system were responsible for mental phenomena, and now that neurological processes were shown to be capable of mechanistic explanation it became more plausible to regard mental processes in the same way. The mind could be conceptualized as a complicated system of interacting neural units, with all of its processes potentially capable of mechanical explanation. The process of mechanizing the soul, begun by Descartes, seemed capable of being completed.

Studies of Sensation and Perception

Helmholtz's experiments on the speed of nervous transmission were sufficient by themselves to earn him a place in the history of psychology. But he was shortly to make even more important contributions to the new science with an extensive series of studies of vision and audition. He always refused to consider himself a "psychologist," since the term had certain negative connotations in the nineteenth century much as "metaphysician" does today. Nevertheless, this work still stands as the foundation of the modern psychology of sensaton and perception.

Helmholtz's study of vision and hearing was carried out between 1853 and 1868 at the universities of Königsberg, Bonn, and Heidelberg, and was reported in two monumental works. The studies of vision appeared in the *Handbook of Physiological Optics,* published in three volumes between 1856 and 1867. The ponderously titled book on hearing, *The Theory of the Sensation of Tone as a Physiological Basis for the Theory of Music,* was published in 1863. Helmholtz tried and nearly succeeded in these books to offer complete coverage of the major thought on vision and hearing, even going so far as to teach himself Dutch so he could read an important article in the original. To ensure the reliability of his volumes, he personally replicated in his own laboratory all the major studies of other scientists.

Helmholtz used similar strategies in approaching both vision and audition. Only the work on vision will be discussed here, as representative of his general style. He began by dividing his work into primarily *physical, physiological,* or *psychological* categories, although all three were closely interrelated in his thinking. The physical part sought an understanding of the eye as an optical instrument, analyzing the processes by which light from the external world comes to be transformed into a focused image on the retina. The physiological analyses took up the problem of how the image on the retina conveys signals to the brain, and results in conscious *sensations* of light. The psychological analyses went one step farther, and asked how it is that sensations of light become converted into meaningful *perceptions* of objects and events in the external world.

Helmholtz's distinction between sensation and perception is perhaps best explained by an example. Sensations are the raw elements of conscious experience. In vision, they are the spatially organized patches of colored light that make up the visual field, quite independent of any meaning that might be attached to them. The perceptions, on the other hand, are the meaningful interpretations that are imposed on the sensations. When you view a landscape, your sensations are discontinuous patches of green, blue, brown and yellow light. Your perceptions, however, are of grass, trees, sky, and sunlight. The conversion of an image on the retina into sensations of color is a physiological process, mediated by the neurological apparatus between the eye and the brain. The conversion of sensation into perception is a psychological process, mediated by activities in the brain but also dependent upon the learning and experience of the individual. Sensation and perception both transform input of one kind into conscious output of another. As such, they are both creative processes performed on external stimulation by an agency that may be thought of as similar to the Kantian "mind."

Optical Properties of the Eye. Now consider some of Helmholtz's specific points. In his physical analyses, Helmholtz showed how the optical properties of the eye could be described just as if it were a camera or other optical instrument. As is shown in Figure 3–1, the eye has a curved, transparent surface, called the *cornea,* in front of a transparent, elliptically-shaped *lens.* Because of its curvature, the cornea-lens system refracts (bends) incoming light rays in such a way that a miniature, inverted image of the external scene is projected to the back of the eye and onto the highly neurologically sensitive area known as the *retina.* The retina is analogous to the light-sensitive film in a camera.

Like many cameras, though using a different mechanism,

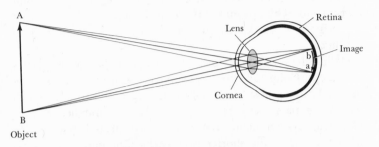

Figure 3–1 *Optical Properties of the Eye*

the eye can adjust the focus of the image on the retina, permitting a sharp image of near-by objects at one moment, distant ones at another. The eye's mechanism for this is the lens, which by minute muscular adjustments may be made to assume a flat shape and bring distant objects into focus, or to bulge in the middle for sharply-focused near objects. Helmholtz himself devised several ingenious instruments for measuring these alterations in the lens's shape, which are referred to as *accommodation*.

Helmholtz noted that when the eye was compared with other optical devices, virtually every one of its features had at least one defect that would be considered unacceptable in a camera, telescope, or other man-made system. The eye's field of maximum acuity is extremely small, for example, consisting only of that part of the image that falls on a tiny section of the retina known as the *fovea*. Helmholtz said the fovea's size can be estimated by extending an arm straight out in front, and focusing on the nail of the forefinger. The image of the nail completely fills the fovea. Visual acuity within the fovea is extremely good, as an observer can distinguish images there separated by no more than one-sixtieth of the diameter of the nail. With increasing distance from the fovea, acuity decreases rapidly, and at the edges of the visual field images are very imprecise indeed. A photograph providing an image like that recorded by the eye would be very unsatisfactory, because so much of it would be blurred beyond recognition. The eye makes up for this, of course, by shifting its focus very quickly from one part of the visual field to another.

Helmholtz noted many other "deficiencies" in the properties of the eye. Colors are not perfectly reproduced in the retinal image, both because the fluid in the eyeball through which light must pass is not perfectly transparent, and because the refracting system bends the longer rays of red light somewhat more than the shorter rays at the blue end of the spectrum. The defect known as *astigmatism* also occurs in all eyes, though to varying degrees. It results from an imperfect alignment of the various parts of the refractive surfaces of the eye. Perhaps the best known visual defect of all is the *blind spot,* a portion of the visual field where no image appears at all. This occurs because the small part of the retina where the optic nerve is attached contains no light-sensitive receptor cells.*

Helmholtz's descriptions of these and other defects in the eye did more than just provide important practical information for eye specialists: they also were the opening wedge for a Kantian philosophical argument concerning the nature of experienced reality. Helmholtz demonstrated that even at the level of the eye itself, the registered image was not a perfect reproduction of the external stimulus. Light underwent a certain amount of distortion and transformation before it ever became registered on the retina. As it was processed further, and became a series of conscious *sensations* of light, the distortions and transformations became even more accentuated. Visual sensory experience was far from an exact duplication of the light rays that constituted the visual stimu-

* For a demonstration of the blind spot, draw two X's side by side on a sheet of paper, two inches apart. Hold the paper at arm's length, close the left eye, and focus on the left-hand X. Bring the paper slowly toward the eye. At a certain distance the right-hand X will suddenly "disappear" as its image falls upon the blind spot.

lus, and nothing made this clearer than Helmholtz's analysis of *color vision*.

Color Vision. In 1672, Isaac Newton reported his famous discovery that the white light emanating from the sun was really much more complicated than it seemed. He showed that if a narrow band of sunlight were passed through a transparent triangular prism, as shown in Fig. 3–2, it emerged as the multi-colored band of light known as the *spectrum*. One end of the spectrum was red, and the other colors passed successively through orange, yellow, green, and blue, to violet at the other end.

Newton explained this striking phenomenon by suggesting that each of the different spectral colors was a light of a particular wave length, and that the white light of the sun was composed of all the different wave lengths combined. When sunlight passed through a prism the different wave lengths became separated because the longer waves at the red end were refracted or bent more than the shorter ones at the violet end. Differences in the wave length of this light were experienced by the human sense as differences in color. On the basis of Newton's early experiments alone, it seemed that color sensation might be a simple reflection of a quantitatively varying physical stimulus, with a different color for each separate wave length, and with the sensation of white indicating a mixture of all the different wave lengths.

Newton himself recognized that this was not true, however—

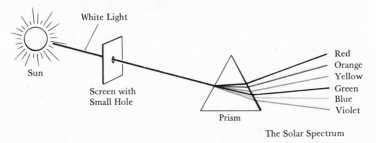

White Light

Sun

Screen with
Small Hole

Prism

Red
Orange
Yellow
Green
Blue
Violet

The Solar Spectrum

Figure 3–2 *The Solar Spectrum*

that the property of color does not belong to the light waves themselves. This was made clear by experiments in *color mixing*. For example, if pure red and pure yellow light were mixed, the result was a sensation of orange. If a certain shade of red were combined with a certain blue-green, the result was white, and so on. These results were puzzling theoretically, because they indicated that the same sensation of color could result from widely varying physical stimuli. When one sees the color white, for example, the senses do not distinguish between a white made up of all the wave lengths combined, as in sunlight, and a white that is a mixture of only two wave lengths such as the red and blue-green cited above. Similarly, the sense of vision does not distinguish between the spectral orange of a single wave length and a compound orange composed of a mixture of red and yellow. Thus, the visual sense does not provide a perfect indication of the combinations of light rays constituting the physical environment, but sometimes renders widely divergent patterns of physical stimulation as subjectively equal.

The details of color mixing were determined with great precision in the nineteenth century, and Helmholtz set himself to postulate a physiological mechanism that could account for them. His solution was a modification of Müller's specific nerve energy hypothesis. The experiments had indicated that by mixing the proper combinations of colored lights, almost any pure spectral hue could be duplicated. Furthermore, three specific colors were found—a certain hue of red, a certain blue-violet, and a certain green—which, if mixed in the proper proportions, could reproduce any other color. These three colors could be viewed as the building blocks from which all other colors could be created, and they were called the *primary colors.* *

---

* Most children learn from experiences with paint boxes that the three primary colors are red, blue, and *yellow,* rather than red, blue, and green. The discrepancy arises because paint boxes contain pigments, which absorb as well as reflect light. The absorbing powers of the pigments give them different results when mixed, compared to the mixture of pure light.

Having determined that human vision detects three primary colors, Helmholtz hypothesized that the retina was equipped with three different kinds of receptor cells, each responding most strongly to one of the three primary colors. The nerve attached to each receptor presumably transmitted a message to the brain whenever it was excited by the appropriately colored light. This was a refinement of Müller's specific energy theory, suggesting that individual nerves transmitted sensory messages not only of a specific *kind* (visual, auditory, tactile, etc.), but also of a specific *quality* (for example, the visual nerves were further subdivided into the three basic sub-types for color).

Helmholtz knew that a similar theory of color vision had been suggested earlier by the versatile English scientist Thomas Young (1773–1829). Although Young's theory was without extensive experimental support, Helmholtz always acknowledged Young's priority for what has come to be known as the *Young-Helmholtz theory*. Other names frequently applied to it by researchers are the *trichromatic theory* and the *component theory*, because it regards color sensation as resulting from different combinations of just three basic components.

With his component theory, Helmholtz was able to account for many of the facts of color vision. When spectral red, green, or blue-violet light strikes the retina, only one kind of receptor is strongly stimulated and the resulting sensation is of a pure primary color. Light from the non-primary colors, or from some combination of primary colors, results in the stimulation of some combination of the three receptors. The consequent subjective sensation is of a non-primary color. Thus when the red and blue receptors are simultaneously stimulated, the result is a sensation of purple. If all three kinds of receptor are equally and simultaneously stimulated, the resulting sensation is of white light. White sunlight, consisting of light of all wave lengths, naturally produces this sensation by stimulating all three receptors equally. White-producing *pairs* of colors, referred to as *complementary colors,* are two colors which in combination stimulate all three receptor types. For the complementary pair of red and bluish-green, for example, the red light stimulates the red receptors, and the bluish-green light excites both the green and blue; thus all three are simultaneously excited and a subjective sensation of white occurs.

This theory explained the laws of color mixture as contributions of the human visual apparatus itself, having little to do with the objective physical properties of light waves. As Helmholtz summarized his position: "The inaccuracies and imperfections of the eye as an optical instrument, and the deficiencies of the image on the retina, now appear insignificant in comparison with the incongruities we have met with in the field of sensation. One might almost believe that Nature had here contradicted herself on purpose in order to destroy any dream of a pre-existing harmony between the outer and the inner world." [5] The sensory apparatus, and by implication the mind as well, was not a passive instrument that merely reproduced everything that happened to it, but instead was an active agency that transformed and sometimes rearranged incoming stimulation. Helmholtz clearly recognized the consistency of this basic point of view with Kantian philosophy and wrote, "That the character of our perceptions is conditioned just as much by the nature of our senses as by the external things . . . is of the greatest importance for the theory of our faculty of perception. What the physiology of the senses has demonstrated experimentally in more recent times, Kant earlier tried to do . . . for the ideas of the human mind in general." [6]

Visual Perception. Though the Kantian point of view was completely consistent with Helmholtz's analyses of visual *sensation,* it was only partially so for visual *perception.* First, the point of agreement: Helmholtz realized that as sensations were responded to and given meaning by the perceptual processes, they underwent further creative transformations worthy of the Kantian "mind." The content of a perception was quite different from both the physical stimulus that initiated it and the pure sensations that immediately underlay it. This fact was most clearly illustrated by the occurence of *optical illusions*. In the illusion of Figure 3–3, for example, the two parallel lines are of absolutely equal length, and the images they cast on the retina are of equal length as well. Nevertheless, the lines are *perceived* as unequal in length. The mind, in this case, makes a mistake in its interpretation of its visual sensations.

Helmholtz's major disagreement with Kant arose over the *origins* of certain perceptual processes. Kant had attributed a relatively large number of innate categories and intuitions to the mind, including notions of time and space, and the basic axioms underlying mathematics. Since perception often involved the interpretation of sensations in terms of these ideas, Kant's theory was *nativistic*.

Helmholtz agreed that sensation was the result of innate and inalterable physiological processes, and that perception tended to occur instantaneously, automatically, and irresistably, without any impression of conscious control by the perceiver. But he was also impressed with the influence of experience on perception, and accordingly chose to regard perception as a mainly learned rather than an innate phenomenon. Thus Helmholtz's theory of perception was relatively *empiricist,* in opposition to Kant's nativism.

No one could deny that some perceptual processes were acquired only after experience, a fact dramatically illustrated by individuals born blind, but granted sight by surgical pro-

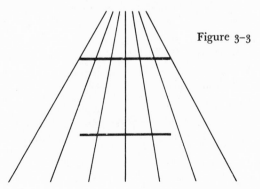

Figure 3–3

cedures in adulthood. Such individuals always reported that their first responses to visual sensations were bewilderment and confusion. The simplest geometrical shapes were not recognized visually, even though the patients may have had extensive tactile experiences with such shapes before their operations. Clearly, such individuals had to *learn* to "see" the objects of the physical world. The question separating empiricist from nativist—Helmholtz from Kant—then, was not one of whether *any* perceptual processes were acquired by experience, but of *how many*.

Conceding that nativism could not be conclusively or completely disproved, Helmholtz chose as a matter of strategy— much as he had earlier chosen to adopt mechanism as a strategy—to regard all perception as an acquired phenomenon. He distinguished between sensation and perception by asserting that sensation was dependent upon the physiology of the nerves, and thus innate, while perception depended upon the experience of the individual, and was acquired. In his writings on perception, Helmholtz tried to show that many of Kant's presumably innate phenomena could be accounted for by empiricist principles.

In one series of classic experiments, Helmholtz showed how space perception could be altered by experience. This did not prove that space perception *arose* from experience, but demonstrated that it was not an inherently immutable process. Helmholtz had subjects wear spectacles with prismatic lenses that distorted the visual field in some systematic way, such as by making objects look as if they were several inches to the right of their actual location. Subjects were first asked to look at an object placed before them, then close their eyes and reach out to touch the object. Invariably, they reached to the right of the object, toward the apparent rather than the real position. Next, subjects were given several minutes to handle the objects while looking at them through the spectacles. At first this seemed strange, and the subjects had to instruct themselves consciously to place their hands to the left of where it seemed they ought to be. Soon, however, something Helmholtz called *perceptual adaptation* occurred, and the subjects were able to handle the objects easily and naturally, without even thinking about it. As proof, they could now easily perform the task on which they had initially failed; after closing their eyes, they immediately and unerringly touched the objects. Even more dramatically, they removed the spectacles and began making mistakes again, but this time to the left instead of the right. So complete and automatic had their adaptation become that it took a minute or two for them to resume their normal spatial orientation.

Helmholtz speculated that perceptual adaptation, and the origin of spatial perception as well, resulted from a process he called *unconscious inference.* As the result of experience—such as the manipulation of objects while wearing distorting glasses —rules were learned that operated much like the major premise in a syllogism. Perceptions were the conclusions drawn from the syllogisms. Consider the following simplified example of how depth perception might result from such a process.

A person without depth perception sees two apples, the image of one being larger than the other. When he reaches for the apples, trial and error shows that he must reach farther to grasp the small one. Through this and similar experiences he learns that objects casting small retinal images are, on the average, farther away than those casting large ones. Soon a general rule is learned, to the effect that the size of an object's retinal image is inversely related to the distance between the object and the eye. After this has been learned, a syllogistic reasoning process can occur whenever an object is sensed whose retinal image becomes progressively smaller:

Major premise: The size of an object's retinal image varies inversely with the object's distance from the eye.

Minor premise: The retinal image of object X, currently in view, is now getting smaller.

Conclusion: Object X is moving farther away.

A major difference between a perception and a syllogism, of course, was that a perception occurred instantaneously and effortlessly while a syllogism was a time-consuming and often laborious exercise. Helmholtz accounted for this difference by assuming that the major premise governing a perception has been so well learned as to become automatic and unconscious. Such learning would not be unique to perceptual processes, since it also occurs in the acquisition of language. When we learn as children what a "chair" is, for example, we have repeated experiences where the sound of the word "chair" is paired with our action of sitting down in one. Soon we develop an idea of what a chair is from these experiences, and use the word properly in speech. When we use the word, however, we do not, and probably cannot, remember the specific instances from the training period when the word was associated with the experiences. Whenever we use the word "chair" we implicitly make use of a long series of training experiences, the exact memories of which have disappeared.

Helmholtz argued that a similar process must occur with the major premise in an unconscious inference: "[Perceptual] inferences are unconscious insofar as their major premise is not necessarily expressed in the form of a proposition; it is formed from a series of experiences whose individual members have entered consciousness only in the form of sense impressions which have long since disappeared from memory. Some fresh impression forms the minor premise, to which the rule impressed on us by previous observation is applied." [7] Such empirically derived but unconscious major premises could form the basis of all perception, including space perception, according to Helmholtz.

Just as syllogisms could lead to false conclusions if based on false premises, so could unconscious inferences sometimes lead to faulty perceptions such as optical illusions. In the illusion illustrated in Figure 3–3, for example, the error may be attributed to the faulty premise that converging straight lines are indicative of depth. In *three* dimensions this premise is in fact valid, because the retinal images of parallel lines do converge with increasing distance from the eye. In two dimensions, however, the convergence of the lines gives the false impression that the top line is farther away than the bottom one—a fact that artists take advantage of when trying to create a two-dimensional illusion of depth. Since the retinal images of the two lines are the same, but the top one is perceived as farther away, the top line is also perceived as being of greater real length. All of these inferences are unconscious, so the perceived difference in length comes directly and irresistibly to consciousness, more like an intuition than a rational thought.

Helmholtz's Place in Psychology

Throughout his entire academic life, Helmholtz retained his passion for physics. Even while concentrating on physiology and psychology, he found time to write occasional articles on such topics as vortex motion in liquids, friction in liquids, and the motion of air waves in open-ended tubes. His fame increased, and in 1871 his lifelong ambition was finally achieved when he was appointed professor of physics at the University of Berlin. From then on his physiology and psychology were restricted primarily to revising his earlier works. He became a full-time physicist, and made outstanding contributions to thermodynamics, meteorology, and the newly developing electromagnetic theory.

In 1882, Helmholtz's achievements were officially noted by the German emperor, who raised him to the rank of hereditary nobility; Hermann *von* Helmholtz became his new legal name. In the same year, the government established a research institute expressly for him, where he pursued his work in physics until he died in 1894. At his death he was mourned throughout the world. The emperor had a monument erected to his honor in Berlin, and in Britain a heartfelt if unclassical "Ode to Helmholtz" appeared in the press along with glowing obituaries.*

Though he won his greatest honors as a physicist and never considered himself a psychologist, Helmholtz nevertheless holds an enormously important position in the history of psychology for two major reasons. First, he helped show that the neurological processes underlying mental functions, previously assumed to be ineffable, were subject to rigorous laboratory experimentation. Second, he helped to develop a scientific conception of the Kantian mind with his integrated physical, physiological, and psychological analyses of vision and audition. The sensing and perceiving mind was no longer a metaphysical entity, but a real system of organs operating by lawful mechanistic principles.

Many of Helmholtz's specific psychological ideas and theories have stood the test of time extremely well. The Young-Helmholtz theory of color vision, for example, continues to be amply confirmed by modern research. Indeed, it has recently been shown that the color receptor cells in the retina—the *cones*—come in three different varieties, each containing a pigment that maximally absorbs one of the three primary colors. The absence of one or more of these pigments, or anomalies in their distribution and composition, cause the visual defects popularly known as color blindness.**

The part of Helmholtz's work that has been most modified is his theory of perception. The term "unconscious inference" is no longer used, having given way to a variegated set of

---

* The ode began with the lines, "What matter titles? HELMHOLTZ is a name/ That challenges, alone, the award of fame!/ When Emperors, Kings, Pretenders, shadows all,/ Leave not a dust-trace on our whirling ball,/ Thy work, oh grave-eyed searcher, shall endure,/ Unmarred by faction, from low passion pure." [8]

** It is recognized today that the trichromatic theory does not account for all the phenomena of color vision, and that certain structures in the brain modify some impulses from the retina. This does not invalidate the trichromatic theory, however, but simply indicates that the processing of color does not stop at the retina.

concepts such as "apperception," "set," and the recent ideas of the "information processing" approach. Probably the most controversial of Helmholtz's views on perception has been his extreme empiricism. While no one denies that many aspects of perception are learned, it has not been proved that they all are. In fact, evidence strongly supportive of the nativist interpretation of depth perception has been provided by the "visual cliff" experiments performed in the late 1950s by Cornell University's Eleanor Gibson and colleagues. These experiments showed that visually inexperienced animals and human infants systematically avoided walking or crawling on parts of a glass platform with no visible surface directly below. If they had been unable to use the cues of ordinary depth perception, they should not have avoided these areas; and since they seemed too young to have learned depth perception by experience, the ability must have been innate.

Despite these partial contradictions, Helmholtz's perceptual theory has had a continuous influence on later scientists' choices of experiments to perform. Perceptionists still study the phenomena of perceptual adaptation, and they still employ distorting spectacles much like Helmholtz's originals. Though the modern studies of adaptation receive somewhat more refined interpretations than Helmholtz gave his, he nonetheless would feel at home in the laboratories that carry them out.

Even students of perception whose theories differ markedly from Helmholtz's in detail have proceeded according to the same general Kantian assumptions that guided his work. That is, they have begun by noting discrepancies between the objective properties of external stimulation and the subjective qualities of conscious perception, and concluded by accounting for the discrepancies in terms of neurological function. Among such scientists were the *Gestalt psychologists,* who strongly influenced perceptual theory in the years following Helmholtz's death.

Gestalt Psychology: A Brief Overview

The word *Gestalt* is German, and though its meaning is roughly equivalent to the English "form" or "shape," it is generally used in untranslated form by English–speaking psychologists. The term made its first appearance in psychological vocabularies in 1890, when it was used to denote certain perceptual "form qualities"—*Gestaltqualitäten*—that could not be broken down into separate elements, but instead resided in the overall configurations of perceived objects. Two good examples of these qualities were the "squareness" of a square, or the melody of a musical piece. In both cases, the quality did not inhere in the separate parts of the percepts, but in their total configurations. Thus a square could be made up of any group of four equal straight lines, so long as they bore the proper relationships to one another. "Squareness" resided not in the particular lines used, but in the relationships of the four lines to one another. Similarly, a melody retained its distinctive quality regardless of the key in which it was played, or the timbre of its specific notes. "Yankee Doodle" was recognizable whether played in the highest register of the piccolo or the lowest of the tuba. Its particular melody was independent of the specific notes that made it up, residing instead in the relationships among the notes.

Though the Gestalt qualities were pointed out and named in 1890, they were not generally regarded as having major psychological importance until 1910. Then, a young German psychologist named Max Wertheimer (1880–1943) had a sudden inspiration for a research project. He abandoned his summer vacation to carry it out, with the assistance of Kurt Koffka (1886–1941) and Wolfgang Köhler (1887–1967), younger colleagues at the University of Frankfurt. The outcome of the research was the founding of the movement known as Gestalt psychology.

Wertheimer's idea was to carry out systematic study of an optical illusion that was attracting wide popular notice in the early 1900s, the *apparent movement* produced by a rapid succession of still images in devices like stroboscopes or the primitive movie projectors in nickelodeons. Wertheimer and his colleagues carried out the first systematic studies of this illusion by employing very simple stimuli. With a tachisto-scope—a device that projects light on a screen for measured fractions of a second—they flashed light alternately through two slits, one vertical and the other tilted by some thirty degrees. If the interval between the flashes was relatively long (more than one-fifth of a second) an observer saw the "true" state of affairs: two rapidly alternating lights. If the interval was very short (less than one one-hundredth of a second), both slits appeared to be illuminated constantly. Apparent movement appeared when the alternation times were in the intermediate ranges, with the strongest effect at about one-twentieth of a second between flashes. The observer then had a very distinct perception of the light "falling over" from the vertical to the inclined position, and then rising back to the vertical, over and over again. Wertheimer named this apparent movement—a simplified version of a motion picture—the *phi phenomenon.*

Wertheimer went on to show that an observer, presented with randomly distributed examples of real movement and comparable apparent movement, could not distinguish the one type from the other. Furthermore, both real and apparent movement produced identical *negative after-images*—the tendency to see still objects as moving in a direction opposite to that of a moving object that has been observed immediately before. Here was a perceptual situation similar in some ways to color vision, where widely differing physical stimuli gave rise to subjectively identical conscious experiences. In real movement, light swept across the retina and fell on all the receptors lying in its swath. In the phi phenomenon, only the receptors at the two separate end points became illuminated. Since such widely varying retinal events led to identical perceptions of movement, at least some of the processes underlying the perception of motion must have taken place at a neurological level higher than the retina. That is, movement was an attribute that could be imposed upon stationary images by the higher brain processes.

In the years following their work on apparent movement, Wertheimer, Koffka, and Köhler became aware of many other instances where the perceiving mind imposed its own structure and organization upon its objects. Perception, it became clear, was much more than the simple addition of sensory elements, or the unconscious inferring of logical relationships among elements. In particular, the three psychologists were impressed with the extent to which the mind tended to organize experience into *wholes* whose significance exceeded the sum of their individual parts. The earlier described Gestalt qualities were important here as examples. Just as the phi phenomenon was more than the sum of the individual light flashes on the retina, so was a square more than the sum of its four sides, and a melody more than a particular sequence of tones. The new Gestalt psychologists' great contribution was the realization that these wholes, or Gestalts, were perceptual requirements imposed by the perceiving mind itself. The tendency to see the world in terms of indivisible wholes was no more avoidable than was the tendency to experience it in terms of colors, sounds, or smells.

The Gestalt psychologists were not content to rest with the bare assertion that perception occurs in terms of wholes, but also specified some of the conditions under which different kinds of wholes tend to be perceived. Their work in this area was extensive, and can only be sampled here.

They noted that the perceptual field must always be divided into the *figure* and the *ground*, the figure being the whole percept attended to in consciousness, and the ground the backdrop against which the figure must define itself. There can be no figure without a ground, just as the printed words on this page cannot be perceived (as figure) except against the background of the white page. Figure and ground may never both be in consciousness simultaneously—they would both be part of the figure in that case—but they may reverse. One of the classic examples of figure-ground reversal is provided in

Figure 3–4

Figure 3–4, where the illustration may be seen as a white vase against a black ground, or as black profiled faces against a white ground. The vase and the faces may not be seen at the same time, however, because that would constitute a figure with no ground. Thus the Gestalts in a particular visual field may change constantly, but they always appear as only part of the entire field, standing out against a background.

Another important characteristic of perceived Gestalts is that they tend to *simplify* the perceptual fields in which they occur. Relatively complicated aggregates of stimuli become organized into simpler groups according to such principles as contiguity or similarity. In the left-hand portion of Figure 3–5, for example, variations in the spacing of the circles lead

Figure 3–5

to a perception of "three groups of circles," rather than to "seventeen circles." In observing the right-hand portion, most people employ the similarity cues and see "alternating rows of circles and dots" rather than the more complicated "columns of mixed circles and dots."

While many of their examples were drawn from visual perception, the Gestalt psychologists noted that their principles applied to other sense modalities as well. Perceived *sounds,* for example, must always be heard against a relatively neutral background. There can also be auditory figure-ground reversals, as when anxious airplane passengers "listen" for the ominous periods of silence that may punctuate the droning of a faulty engine. Temporal sequences of sounds may also be organized into contiguous groups, as in the perceived regularity of a drum cadence; or into similar groups, as when the violin part is clearly perceived above the background of the rest of an orchestra.

In general, then, the Gestalt psychologists significantly expanded the list of known situations in which the human mind imposes an order of its own making on the objects of its perception. Though they came long after Kant and did not consider themselves to be "Kantians," they extended and clarified the Kantian notion of a creative, transforming mind to an even greater extent than Helmholtz had, and supported their arguments with impressive empirical evidence. In most respects their work complemented rather than contradicted Helmholtz's, though it suggested a nativistic element in certain perceptual processes that Helmholtz regarded as acquired.

The Gestalt psychologists, especially Köhler, followed Helmholtz's pattern further by trying to integrate their psychological findings with current physics and neurophysiology. For Helmholtz, the most basic physical metaphor had been the Newtonian universe of material particles attracting and repelling one another mechanistically. For Köhler, it was the newer idea of the *force field.* Toward the end of the nineteenth century it became clear to physicists that many phenomena, particularly of an electrical or magnetic nature, could not be explained as the result of isolated bodies acting upon one another. Instead, whole distributions of forces, or "fields," had to be taken into consideration. To take a very simple example, the fate of a single charged particle could not be predicted in isolation; what happened to it depended on the entire electrical environment, or field, in which it happened to be. Köhler contrasted the methods of the new field theorists with those of traditional physics as follows: "[The field theorist] begins with a given 'whole' and only then arrives at the parts by analysis, while the ordinary procedures are founded on the principle of beginning with the parts and building up the wholes by synthesis." [9] The emphasis on wholes as the *starting points* for physical analysis naturally appealed to the Gestalt psychologists, who had independently arrived at much the same strategy for psychological analysis.

Köhler was struck by yet another similarity. The field theorists had noted that physical fields tend over time to organize themselves into increasingly simple configurations. An electric charge upon a condenser, for example, quickly distributes itself evenly on the entire surface, so that differences of electrical potential exist nowhere on the surface. In general, forces in a field tend to even themselves out as much as possible, so that the final organization is simpler than the original one. This tendency of physical fields to simplify themselves seemed to Köhler to be directly analogous to events in the perceptual field that he and his colleagues had observed. The grouping of stimulus elements into Gestalts by similarity or contiguity, the perception of continuous movement instead of discontinuous visual stimuli, and many other perceptual effects all involved the simplification of originally more complex stimuli.

After noting these similarities, Köhler reflected that the organ of perception, the brain, was itself a physical system that distributed and processed electrical charges. He thought that perhaps the similarities between physical and perceptual fields were more than coincidental, and that the phenomena of perception were the direct result of field effects occurring within the brain. These considerations suggested the hypothesis of *psychophysical isomorphism,* according to which "psychological facts and the underlying events in the brain resemble each other in all their structural characteristics." [10] The hypothesis did not suggest that perceptual and brain processes were identical with one another, but only that they shared the same structural properties in something like the way a map shares the structural properties of the terrain it charts. Obviously, according to this hypothesis one can learn something about the way the brain functions from studying the facts of perception, and vice versa. The brain ought to be studied as an organized whole system, and not merely in terms of its separate components. As a functional unit, the brain might best be understood as an overall configuration, or field, of electrical charges.

Psychophysical isomorphism was a highly speculative hypothesis when it was first suggested, and it remains so today. It has a certain plausibility, and does not actively violate established knowledge about the brain. But no one has yet come close to being able to map the entire field of electrical forces in the brain, so it has not yet been determined if it, in fact, directly parallels perceptual or other psychological experiences. This remains an intriguing research problem for the future.

Obviously, the hypothesis of psychophysical isomorphism and all the rest of the details of the Gestalt analysis of perception differed markedly from Helmholtz's analyses. These differences should not obscure several important lines of continuity, however. Both Helmholtz and the Gestalt psychologists saw sensation and perception as the creations of an active mind. Both began to specify the characteristics of the mind by noting discrepancies between the "objective" properties of external stimulation, and the resulting conscious experiences. By describing these discrepancies in precise ways, both Helmholtz and the Gestaltists helped provide lawful descriptions of the mind itself, and thus specified a subject matter for scientific psychology. Finally, both Helmholtz and the Gestaltists believed that psychological phenomena were closely related to underlying physical and physiological processes, so that some psychological hypotheses were potentially testable by non-psychological means.

These same lines of continuity link Kant, Helmholtz and the Gestalt psychologists with most modern researchers in the fields of sensation and perception. The further specification and elaboration of the perceiving mind, and its explanation in terms of physical processes occurring in the nervous system, remain as principal goals of psychology.

Suggested Readings

For a good discussion of Kant's influence on the development of psychology, see Chapter 15, "The Kantian Background " in D. B. Klein's *A History of Scientific Psychology* (New York: Basic Books, 1970). The development of the law of specific nerve energies is described in Chapters 2 and 5 of Edwin G. Boring's *A History of Experimental Psychology* (New York: Appleton-Century-Crofts, 1957).

An excellent sampling of Helmholtz's writings have been translated and edited by Russell Kahl, in *Selected Writings of Hermann von Helmholtz* (Middletown, Connecticut: Wesleyan University Press, 1971). Included in the volume are Helmholtz's paper on the conservation of energy, a brief autobiographical sketch, and popularized accounts of his theories of vision and hearing. The standard biography of Helmholtz is Leo Koenigsberger's *Hermann von Helmholtz,* translated by F. A. Welby (New York: Dover, 1965).

A lucid, engaging, and brief introduction to Gestalt psychology is provided by Wolfgang Köhler's *The Task of Gestalt Psychology* (Princeton, New Jersey: Princeton University Press, 1969). For a more extended account, see Köhler's *Gestalt Psychology* (New York: Liveright, 1947).

4

Psychology in the University
Wilhelm Wundt and William James

Psychology is so well entrenched in the university today that it is difficult to realize how new it is as a major academic subject. Little more than a century ago, psychology per se was a relatively minor branch of philosophy, and there were no laboratories explicitly devoted to psychological research. Then, in the 1870s, university courses in scientific psychology began to be taught. In 1875, two laboratories for psychology were established, one in Germany and the other in the United States. By the turn of the century there were more than a hundred, concentrated mainly in those two countries. Psychology was well on its way to becoming the major academic discipline it is today.

The two professors who set up the first two laboratories deserve much of the credit for the development of academic psychology. The German was Wilhelm Wundt (1832–1920), who is generally remembered as the "founder" of the new science of experimental psychology. As he wrote in his 1874 textbook, *Principles of Physiological Psychology,* "The work I here present to the public is an attempt to mark out a new domain of science." [1] He followed through on the new science in 1879 by converting his laboratory, which had been originally established only for demonstration purposes, into the first institute for research in experimental psychology. Here was a place where students could come explicitly for the purpose of studying psychology and conducting psychological research. At first the institute was small and maintained partly at Wundt's own expense, but it soon began attracting students from all over the world who returned home to establish their own laboratories and institutes, modelled after Wundt's.

The American professor was William James (1842–1910), perhaps the greatest writer and teacher psychology has ever had. James never founded an institute, or even carried out much research himself, but used his laboratory to enrich his classroom presentations. He had a thorough grasp of the psychological literature in French and German as well as English, and a capacity to illuminate this extensive information with his own remarkable personality. His courses and his classic 1890 textbook, *The Principles of Psychology,* were tremendous popular successes because they made psychology seem interesting and personally relevant.

4. Wilhelm Wundt (1832–1920), William James (1842–1910). Pioneers of academic psychology. *Wide World Photo, Inc. and The National Library of Medicine, Bethesda, Maryland*

Ironically, these two great pioneers of academic psychology did not care particularly for each other's work. Wundt found little that was original in James, and reportedly warned his students against spending too much time on such a "second rate philosopher." After reading James's *The Principles of Psychology,* Wundt remarked, "It is literature, it is beautiful, but it is not psychology." [2]

James, for his part, found much of Wundt's work to be plodding and without human interest. After praising the innovative features of Wundt's experimental psychology, James went on in his textbook to write that it "could hardly have arisen in a country whose natives could be *bored.* . . . There is little of the grand style about these new prism, pendulum, and chronograph-philosophers. They mean business, not chivalry." [3] He was even more outspoken in a private letter to a friend:

Since there must be professors in the world, Wundt is the most praiseworthy and never-too-much-to-be-respected type of the species. He isn't a genius, he is a professor—a being whose duty is to know everything, and have his own opinion about everything, connected with his [department or specialty]. . . . He says of each possible subject, "Here I must have an opinion. Let's see! What shall it be? How many possible opinions are there? three? four? Yes! just four! Shall I take one of these? It will seem more original to take a higher opinion, a sort of *Vermittelungsansicht* [mediating attitude] between them all. That I will do, etc., etc." So he acquires a complete assortment of opinions of his own; and, as his memory is so good, he seldom forgets which they are! . . . He has utilized to the uttermost fibre every gift that Heaven endowed him with at his birth, and made of it all that mortal pertinacity could make. He is the finished example of how much mere *education* can do for a man.[4]

For all of their differences and animosities, however, Wundt and James complemented one another in their effects on the historical development of their new science. Wundt made experimental psychology a concrete reality, giving students a place to work and genuine psychological problems to work on. James interpreted the new science and gave it wide meaning for an entire generation of students. Between the two of them they got scientific psychology off to a rousing start in the universities.

Wilhelm Wundt: Early Life and Education

Wilhelm Wundt was born on August 16, 1832 near the German city of Mannheim. His father was a pastor, and both parents' families had histories of intellectual achievement. He was the fourth and last child in the family, though his only sibling to survive infancy was a brother eight years older. This brother was sent away to school, so young Wilhelm lived much the life of an only child. He was very lonely as a child, his only like-aged playmate being a retarded boy who could barely speak. His favorite companion was a lame bookbinder who told him adventure stories and tall tales. Not surprisingly in such an environment, the boy developed a strong and academically debilitating tendency toward daydreaming. It was to be many years before he could break himself of the habit.

When he was about eight, Wilhelm's education was entrusted to a young vicar who worked for his father. This happy relationship lasted for four years, until Wilhelm had to cease his private education and attend a high school. His first year, spent in a small village, was disastrous. His daydreaming kept him in constant academic difficulty, and he had brutal teachers who often slapped him in the face. His schoolmates for the most part were farm boys whose highest intellectual aspirations were to become country priests. Wundt made no friends, and finally failed.

The next year he started high school over again in the more cosmopolitan university town of Heidelberg. This was a much happier situation. His older brother and a cousin were university students there, and for the first time in his life he made friends of his own age who shared his interests. Wilhelm's intellectual interests began to develop strongly, and even though his overall academic record was not outstanding, he found teachers who recognized his promise and encouraged his efforts. In this more stimulating environment, he finally gained control over his daydreaming.

After graduation from high school, Wundt enrolled in the pre-medical program at the University of Tübingen, where his uncle was a professor. Though he enjoyed the life of a university student there, his academic interests never really caught hold and the whole first year was something of a false start. At the end of the year Wundt was forced to do some hard thinking about his future. His father had died, leaving only enough money for him to complete three more years of university. He had just wasted one year, and so would have to work extremely hard if he were to complete his medical education.

With these thoughts as an incentive, he transferred to the University of Heidelberg where he became the top medical student in his class and, even more importantly, developed his first real interests in research and writing. He did his first empirical research under the supervision of Robert Bunsen (1811–1899), then a famous chemist and now remembered as inventor of the laboratory burner that bears his name. Using himself as a research subject, Wundt eliminated salt from his diet and studied changes in the salt concentration of his urine. When Wundt published the results of this small study in 1853, it marked the beginning of one of the most extraordinary publication records ever established. He went on to publish almost five hundred more articles and books over the next sixty-seven years, totalling close to 60,000 printed pages.*

---

* Reading fifty pages a day, it would take almost three years to get through the works of Wundt. Not surprisingly, this prodigious productivity irritated Wundt's opponents greatly. William James privately complained that when critics "make mincemeat of some one of his views by their criticism, he is meanwhile writing a book on an entirely different subject. Cut him up like a worm, and each fragment crawls; there is no *noeud vital* in his mental medulla oblongata, so that you can't kill him all at once." [5] When James McKeen Cattell, Wundt's first laboratory assistant, presented him with an American typewriter, a rival German psychologist grumbled that it was an evil gift, enabling Wundt to write twice as many books as would have been possible without it.

Psychology in the University

After taking his medical degree *summa cum laude* in late 1855, Wundt went to Berlin to study for a few months with Johannes Müller and Émile du Bois-Reymond at the same physiological institute that had so influenced Helmholtz. He was impressed enough to resolve to make a career in academic physiology rather than medicine. He returned to Heidelberg, obtained certification for teaching in an unusually short time, and embarked on his life-long university teaching career.

Wundt's Early Psychology

Wundt's first book, a physiological treatise on muscular movement, was published in 1858. In the same year he began another book, *Contributions to the Theory of Sensory Perception*, which marked the beginnings of his interests in psychological problems. In its preface, he outlined the possibility of three new scientific disciplines, the realizations of which were to occupy the rest of his life.

First, he suggested the possibility of an *experimental psychology*, whose purpose would be to vary systematically the stimuli and conditions that produce differing mental states. The facts of consciousness ought to be amenable to experimental manipulation and observation, he wrote, just like the facts of physics, chemistry, or physiology. Second, he suggested the possibility of a psychology based on historical, comparative, and ethnographic analysis. These non-experimental methods should be especially useful in the study of the higher human functions such as thought, which are closely related to linguistic and cultural variables, and do not lend themselves easily to experimental manipulation in a laboratory. Third, Wundt proposed the development of a truly scientific metaphysics that would integrate and interrelate the findings of all the sciences, from physics to psychology. None of these ideas was thoroughly worked out in 1862, but they clearly indicated the directions in which Wundt's thought was developing.

In 1858, Wundt was also named assistant to Hermann Helmholtz, who had just become professor of physiology at Heidelberg. Apart from Wundt's gradual shift toward psychological interests, Helmholtz did not seem to influence his development directly. Relations between the two were always proper, but no close friendship or collaboration developed. Wundt apparently found Helmholtz to be rather distant and forbidding, and his attitude could hardly have been improved by the nature of his duties as assistant. In 1858, the government had just passed a new regulation requiring all medical students to take a laboratory course in physiology. Helmholtz had formal responsibility for the course, but Wundt had to run the laboratory sessions. He was not inspired by the job of showing uncooperative and unenthusiastic students how to dissect frogs, especially for a niggardly wage that just barely kept him above the poverty line.

Despite the drudgery of his official duties, Wundt continued to write and to teach a few small classes of his own. Perhaps because of Helmholtz's influence, or perhaps because of his sheer satiation with physiology, Wundt's private interests grew more purely psychological. In 1864, he was promoted to a rank roughly equivalent to an associate professorship, which improved his financial prospects enough so that he could resign as Helmholtz's assistant and concentrate on his own interests. At first, the courses he taught covered such traditional topics as experimental physiology and medical physics, but they began to contain more and more psychological material until 1867, when his course was officially named "Physiological Psychology".

By this time Wundt was beginning to be known internationally among the small group of people who were interested in the possibility of a fully scientific psychology. One such person was William James, who in 1867 was a young man trying to recover his health by travelling through Germany. He wrote a friend,

It seems to me that perhaps the time has come for psychology to begin to be a science—some measurements have already been made in the region lying between the physical changes in the nerves and the appearance of consciousness (in the shape of sense perceptions), and more may come of it. . . . Helmholtz and a man named Wundt at Heidelberg are working at it, and I hope I live through this winter to go to them in the summer.[6] *

When Helmholtz left Heidelberg in 1871 to become professor of physics in Berlin, Wundt appeared to be his natural successor. In fact, he was given many of Helmholtz's duties. But he was not promoted, and his salary was only a quarter of what Helmholtz's had been. Understandably eager to escape from Heidelberg, Wundt began work on what was to be his most influential psychological work, the *Principles of Physiological Psychology,* which in 1873 and 1874 mapped out his "new domain of science." This book elaborated upon the experimental psychology he had only suggested in the preface to his earlier work. Wundt argued that conscious states could be scientifically studied through the systematic manipulation of antecedent variables, and analyzed by carefully controlled techniques of *introspection.* Considered by some to be the most significant book in the history of psychology, this was the first call to arms for the development of a purely psychological laboratory.

In 1874, Wundt's industry and ingenuity were finally rewarded with an appointment as professor of inductive philosophy at Zurich. The following year a more attractive offer came from Leipzig. The chair of philosophy there had been vacant for ten years, partly because of political infighting among the faculty. Finally, it was decided to divide the professorship in half and hire two younger men for the price of a single famous philosopher. Wundt was appointed as a representative of "scientific philosophy" and another man was

* James did not actually meet Wundt on this trip, since the hills of Heidelberg turned out to be more than his frail back could tolerate. Their first face-to-face meeting did not occur until 1882 in Leipzig, where James was impressed with Wundt personally, but somewhat disappointed that Wundt did not find more time for him.

chosen to represent the more classical approaches to philosophy. Thus Wundt, a medically trained physiologist who had had but one formal course in philosophy himself, and who had initiated the idea of an experimental, physiologically oriented *psychology,* found himself twice appointed as professor of philosophy. Nothing could better illustrate the lack of distinct boundaries between the various disciplines which combined to bring about the development of psychology.

The Institute at Leipzig

Once established at Leipzig, Wundt set about making his proposed experimental psychology into a concrete reality. In 1879, he converted his small demonstration laboratory—actually a single room in a rather decrepit old building—into a "private institute" where students could conduct experiments. The university administration was not particularly enthusiastic about this project, fearing that prolonged use of Wundt's experimental introspection techniques by psychology students was likely to drive them insane. Nevertheless Wundt persisted, and supported the institute out of his own pocket until 1881, when it was clear to all that experimental psychology was both harmless and a popular success. Far from driving its practitioners insane, it was attracting growing numbers of students from all over the world. Wundt's lectures became the most popular in the university. Increasingly interesting research projects were devised and carried out, and then published in a new journal that Wundt started in 1881. The journal, entitled *Philosophische Studien* ("Philosophical Studies"), was, in spite of its title, the world's first to be primarily devoted to experimental psychology.

These successes made Wundt one of the most influential members of the Leipzig faculty, and in 1889 he was honored by being elected rector of the university. In 1892, his laboratory was moved into an eleven-room suite and, in 1897, into an entirely new building which he had helped design. In 1909 he was named the official orator for the university's 500-year jubilee. When Wundt retired in 1917 after more than forty-two years continuous service to the university, he himself had become something of an institution.

Anecdotes about Wundt from his Leipzig days abound. Many centered around his lecturing style, which everyone agreed was impressive. Even William James, who visited Wundt's class in 1882, found that he had "a more refined elocution than anyone I've yet met in Germany." [7] A more memorable description was written by Edward Bradford Titchener (1867–1927), later to become Wundt's most ardent disciple in America, immediately following his first attendance at a Wundt lecture:

The [teaching assistant] swung the door open, and Wundt came in. All in black, of course, from boots to necktie; a spare narrow-shouldered figure, stooping a little from the hips; he gave the impression of height, though I doubt in fact if he stands more than 5 ft. 9.

He clattered—there is no other word for it—up the side-aisle and up the steps of the platform: slam bang, slam bang, as if his soles were made of wood. There was something positively undignified to me about the stamping clatter, but nobody seemed to notice it. . . .

Wundt made a couple of mannered movements—snatched his fore-finger across his forehead, arranged his chalk,—and then faced his audience with both elbows set on [an adjustable book-rest]. A curious attitude, which favours the impression of height. He began his lecture in a high-pitched, weak, almost apologetic voice; but after a sentence or two, during which the room settled down to silence, his full lecturing voice came out, and was maintained to the end of the hour. It is an easy and abundant bass, somewhat toneless, and at times a little barking; but it carries well, and there is a certain per-suasiveness, a sort of fervour, in the delivery that holds your interest and prevents any feeling of monotony. . . . The lecture was given without reference to notes; Wundt, so far as I could tell, never looked down once at the book-rest, though he had some little shuffle of papers there between his elbows. . . .

He stopped punctually at the stroke of the clock, and clattered out, stooping a little, as he had clattered in. If it wasn't for this absurd clatter I should have nothing but admiration for the whole proceeding.* [8]

At the beginning of each academic year, Wundt would post the particulars of his research seminar in an undecipherable handwriting and ask all students to assemble at his institute at a certain time. On the appointed day the students would stand before him in a row, their arrangement determined either randomly or by the order of their arrival in the room. Wundt then read down a list he had brought, naming the specific research projects he wished to see carried out that year and the laboratory hours during which each was to be conducted. The first student in the row got the first assignment, the second the second, and so on. No one dared to question these assignments, and the students went dutifully off to conduct their research—which in most cases became their doctoral theses. Wundt consulted with each student occasionally while the research was being conducted, and then supervised the writing of the report for publication. Though he occasionally permitted students to express their own views in their reports, he often exercised his editorial blue pencil. One of his last American students reported that "Wundt exhibited the well-known German trait of guarding zealously the fundamental principles of his standpoint. About one-third of my thesis failed to support the Wundtian doctrine of assimilation, and so received elimination." [9]

Despite his customary dogmatism and formality in the classroom, Wundt could unbend with his students in other situations. He sometimes bantered with his American students about a perpetually forthcoming trip to the United States—a trip he never actually made. He was extremely helpful to students preparing for their oral doctoral examinations. Many students reported that he seemed as nervous as they, and that he

* When Titchener became professor of psychology at Cornell, he ran his own lectures in much the same way Wundt had, right down to the black academic robes which he is reputed to have said gave him the right to be dogmatic. Presumably, however, he took pains to see that his shoes did not clatter as he walked.

coached them and let them know what kinds of questions to expect from the non-psychological examiners.

Wundt's methods were extremely effective, and he and his students performed hundreds of original experiments on a great variety of psychological topics. These studies cannot be completely summarized here but, as examples, three kinds of experiments will be described: those dealing with the subject of *mental chronometry*, those using the technique of *introspection*, and those studying Wundt's theory of *apperception and perception*.

Mental Chronometry. About one-sixth of the total number of Leipzig experiments measured the times required to perform various elementary mental operations. This subject was not original to Wundt, but grew out of previous work on the measurement of *reaction times*. Early in the nineteenth century, astronomers had realized that a person's reaction to a stimulus is not instantaneous, but requires a measurable amount of time. A straightforward physiological reason for the reaction time phenomenon was provided by Helmholtz when he showed that the nervous impulse travels at a measurable rate of speed along the nerve fiber: the reaction time is the sum of 1) the time required for an impulse to pass along a sensory nerve to the spinal cord or brain, 2) the time required for processes in the brain preceding the excitation of a motor nerve, and 3) the time required for an impulse to pass along the motor nerve and initiate the muscular responses.

Though Helmholtz abandoned the study of reaction time in human subjects because of the variability of his results, his friend F. C. Donders (1818–1889) took up the subject and refined the techniques by devising the *complication experiment* and the *subtractive procedure*. Donders reasoned that the times required for the nervous impulses to traverse the sensory and motor nerves in any given reaction should remain relatively constant. Therefore differences in an individual's reaction times are attributable to differences in the times required for the central processes in the brain, with more complicated processes requiring longer times. Thus, by measuring an individual's times for increasingly complicated reactions, and subtracting the simpler reaction times from the more complicated ones, it was possible to determine the amount of time required for the increasingly complicated central processes.

Those central processes were assumed to be the physiological underpinnings of *mental* processes. Wundt's idea was that by carefully controlling the mental processes required by a subject in various kinds of reaction experiments, the subtractive procedure could be used to measure the time required for various elementary mental acts. Wundt thus carried the complication experiment to new levels of refinement, even though he did not invent the technique.

One of the discoveries made at Leipzig with the complication experiment was that a subject's reaction time was about one-tenth of a second longer if his attention were focused on an expected *stimulus,* rather than on the desired *response.* Thus, if the stimulus was a tone and the response the pressing of a button, the subject responded more quickly when he was consciously thinking about the movement to be made than when he was concentrating on the expected tone. According to Wundt, this extra tenth of a second was the time necessary for the process of *apperception* to occur. When the subject was concentrating on the stimulus, the stimulus first had to be *perceived,* that is, simply registered in consciousness, and then *apperceived,* or consciously "interpreted" in light of the response that was associated with it. With attention focused on the response, the added step of apperception or conscious interpretation of the stimulus was not necessary. The stimulus could be merely perceived and responded to mechanically. Though this condition was faster, it represented a more "thoughtless" approach to the situation, one that was more likely to lead to premature or false responses.

Still other complications were added to the experiment to measure the time of mental processes more complicated than apperception. In one condition, several different kinds of stimuli were randomly presented, only one of which was to be responded to. Reaction times here were longer than when the subject was concentrating on a single kind of expected stimulus. The difference was said by Wundt to represent the time for *cognition* to occur; that is, the stimulus had not only to be perceived and apperceived, but also recognized and differentiated from the other stimuli that were not supposed to elicit responses. Wundt and his students found the reaction times longer still if different stimuli were presented, with each calling for a different response (e.g., press a right hand button at the flash of a light, but a left hand button to the sound of a tone). The time this required in excess of the cognition reaction was assumed to be the time for a process of *association* to occur.

This research on mental chronometry illustrated one of the major features of Wundt's experimental psychology: the tendency to analyze mental phenomena in terms of their simplest possible units. By various experimental methods, Wundt attempted to break down complicated mental states somewhat as a chemist breaks down compound substances into their constituent elements. Perception, apperception, cognition, and association were all thus regarded as elementary mental acts that could be combined with one another in many different ways. The complication experiments provided a means of sorting out their effects.

Introspective Studies. Even more important than the complication experiment in Wundt's experimental analysis of consciousness, was systematic and controlled *introspection*. For Wundt, introspection was not the simple sort of self-analysis and inner pondering that is commonly suggested by the term today. Instead, it was a rigorous and highly disciplined technique for the separation of conscious experience into its most basic elements. Subjects were always advanced psychology students who had been carefully trained to introspect properly. Some students found the technique too difficult to master, and so were discouraged from pursuing careers in psychology.

The purpose of Wundtian introspection was to analyze conscious experience in terms of elementary *sensations* and *feelings*. By sensations, Wundt meant the raw sensory content of consciousness, devoid of any "meaning" or interpretation by the subject. All conscious thoughts, ideas, impressions, etc. were assumed to be combinations of sensations which could be defined on just four basic dimensions. These were *mode* (whether the sensation was visual, auditory, tactile, etc.), *quality* (for example, the colors and shapes of the visual sensations), *intensity,* and *duration.* Thus the introspective analysis of the experience of looking at a moving picture would not contain references to the objects in the picture, but the minute description of patches of light with differing colors, intensities, and durations.

Any complete introspective analysis of an experience would also have to describe the feelings that accompanied the various sensory impressions. Wundt's method of analyzing feelings changed over the years, but his final view, the so-called *three-factor theory,* held that all feelings could be introspectively analyzed and described on just three dimensions. The classic experiment was one in which Wundt himself served as subject, and listened to a metronome beating at varying rates of speed. First, he reported that he found some speeds to be more pleasant that others; thus, the first dimension of feeling was *pleasantness-unpleasantness.* Secondly, he reported that he experienced a slight amount of tension just before each anticipated beat sounded, followed by a slight relaxation just after it occurred. These feelings occurred regardless of whether the overall pattern seemed pleasant or unpleasant, so Wundt postulated *tension-relaxation* as a second independent dimension of feeling. Finally, and quite independently of his feelings on the first two dimensions, Wundt discovered that some of the faster metronome patterns gave him a mild feeling of excitement, whereas some of the slower ones had a slight calming effect. This seemed to indicate the existence of an *activity-passivity* dimension running through his feelings.

A major goal of Wundtian introspection was to cut through the learned categories and concepts that define our everyday experience of the world. Wundt believed that his trained introspectors' sensations and feelings were the pristine building blocks from which even the earliest childhood experiences are constructed, just as chemical compounds are constructed from hydrogen, oxygen, and the other chemical elements. The sensations and feelings revealed by introspection were often far removed from ordinary levels of awareness, just as the chemical elements are often masked by being locked in complex compounds with one another.

Apperception and Perception. Though Wundt stressed the importance of discovering the elements of consciousness, he most emphatically believed that conscious experience is something more than just the sum of its elements. He has been erroneously charged by some commentators of having believed that the elements of consciousness combine with one another in a strictly mechanical, additive fashion. This was actually far from the case. Wundt recognized very well that the same mental elements may combine together in many different ways, and that the same sensory input may yield different conscious experiences at different times. But Wundt also realized that there are some occasions when mental processes *do* seem to run on in habitual, predetermined, and mechanical ways.

Wundt accounted for these differences in mental functioning by positing separate processes of *apperception* and *perception* (whose durations were measured in the complication experiments). In describing the difference between the two processes, Wundt used the visual field as an analogy. The visual field contains a small spot near the center, corresponding to the part of the retina known as the fovea, where objects are in very clear focus. Visual acuity diminishes rapidly in areas surrounding this spot, and is quite poor in the periphery of the visual field. The eye is an extremely mobile organ, however, which may be moved rapidly so that the field of focus is constantly shifting from one object to another. According to Wundt, conscious experience generally is much like that. A small number of ideas are always in *attention,* while many others are experienced only peripherally, and not very distinctly. Attention shifts rapidly from one small group of ideas to another. Those sensations which receive attention are *apperceived;* those on the periphery of consciousness are merely *perceived.*

Perceived sensations and feelings organize themselves mechanically and automatically along lines that have been rigidly laid down by past experiences. The flow of perceived experience is completely determined by external stimulation and the associational history of the individual. Apperceived sensations and feelings, by contrast, can be combined in a variety of ways so as to create many different conscious experiences. The course of apperceived mental events is flexibly determined by "inner" variables such as motives, innate predilections, memories, and emotions, as well as the external stimulation impinging on the individual. Wundt regarded these motivational and non-mechanical influences on apperception as so important that he sometimes referred to his entire psychological system as *voluntarism.*

To differentiate perception from apperception, consider as a simple example a person's response to a stimulus card on which the digit 1 has been printed immediately over the digit 2. If the symbols are just *perceived,* the conscious response will be the idea most frequently associated with the symbols in the past. Perhaps that is the idea of "three," since the symbols resemble an arithmetic problem. If the symbols are *apperceived,* however, there will be many more possible responses besides the most common associate from the past. In addition to "three" the symbols may elicit such responses as "minus one," "twelve," "twenty-one," ideas about a secret code or cipher, or any number of other concepts limited only by the imagination of the subject and the circumstances of the situation. When full attention is focused on a stimulus, strongly ingrained and habitual responses may be overcome and replaced by new ones. When attention is less strongly focused, the old habits are likely to dominate. In Wundt's terminology, a *creative synthesis* takes place at the center of attention, as the result of all acts of apperception.

Psychology in the University

One of the most famous studies at Leipzig measured the size of the attention span, that is, the number of ideas which could be apperceived at once. It was found that when complex stimuli were flashed before a subject for a short period of time, the number of apperceived units varied between four and six. For example, if the stimuli were an array of random letters, somewhere between four and six of them could be clearly apprehended at once (as measured by the subject's ability to recall them after a very brief exposure). The important variable here was the *unit*, rather than the absolute size or complexity of the stimuli to be apperceived. Thus, if a random list of six-letter words rather than individual letters were flashed, the subject could simultaneously apperceive four to six words, made up of twenty-four to thirty-six individual letters. Such a subject did not actually "see" all of the letters individually, however, but only their configurations as meaningful and whole words which had been thoroughly learned in the past. For unfamiliar words, apperception was reduced to the level of individual letters. Thus readers of this book can apperceive the entire word *taller* with scarcely more than a single glance. Unless they are familiar with the Polish language, its equally long Polish equivalent *wyzszy* will have to be apperceived as an unfamiliar series of six letters.

In designing these and all of his other experimental studies, Wundt vigorously sought to avoid the sort of armchair theorizing that had characterized earlier attempts to analyze conscious mental processes. Accordingly, he always employed groups of subjects who had been carefully trained in the requirements of the experiment, and subjected the data they produced to statistical analysis. The hallmarks of all of his experiments were systematic control over the variables and repeated measurement of the effects.

Consistent with the program he had proposed in 1862, however, Wundt believed that there were limits beyond which the rigorously controlled experimental method could not reach. Experiments could be useful in discovering the basic components of consciousness, and in determining certain quantitative facts about the ranges of sensitivity and capacity of the mental processes. But Wundt did not believe that the *qualitative* nature of the higher mental processes was amenable to direct experimental manipulation in a laboratory. Thinking, memory, and cognition had to be taken as givens and studied naturalistically in the context of the finished products of human culture and history. Such analyses would have to be consistent with the results of experimental psychology, but their methods would be very different.

Völkerpsychologie

Wundt devoted much of the last twenty years of his life to the development of a non-experimental psychology of higher mental processes, which he referred to as his *Völkerpsychologie* (roughly translated, "ethnic psychology," or "group psychology"). The cornerstone of this work was an analysis of language, which illustrates Wundt's general approach to the higher mental processes.

According to Wundt's naturalistic analysis of linguistic phenomena, the most basic unit of thought is not a word or other linguistic element, but rather a "general impression" (*Gesamtvorstellung*) that is independent of words. The process of formulating speech or any other linguistic communication requires the apperception of the general impression, followed by its analysis into discrete words and linguistic structures that represent it more or less adequately.

Wundt was certain, because of a number of experiences people commonly have as they speak or contemplate speech, that the general impression was not identical with the words used to express it. Perhaps the most striking of these experiences occurs when a person is speaking, and suddenly realizes that his words are not conveying his thought accurately. "That's not what I meant to say. Let me start over again," the person may exclaim. Clearly the thought—the general impression that inspired the speech to begin with—was not identical with the words that incorrectly represented it. On other occasions, general impressions may arise and clearly fix themselves in consciousness before they can be adequately described. Sometimes a listener becomes aware of a point of disagreement between himself and a speaker, for example, and interrupts the conversation with a "What?" or "Wait a minute!" before he has had time to formulate his objection in words.

The act of *comprehending* language also provides evidence for its non-identity with thought. In Wundt's analysis, the listener's task is to apperceive speech sounds and creatively synthesize them into a general impression that is similar to the one the speaker wishes to convey. This clearly involves something other than a word-for-word memorization of the speech, because when a listener is asked to repeat a message that has just been communicated to him he often conveys the ideas perfectly, but in words which are different from those of the original message. Indeed, if a listener must focus attention too carefully on the specific words being spoken to him (as when he is relatively unfamiliar with the language), he often loses the drift of the conversation completely.

For Wundtian linguistics, then, the ultimate unit of language was not the word but the *sentence,* the structure that contains a complete thought and thus expresses a general impression. When speaking or listening, one's attention is not only focused on the specific word currently being uttered, but also on the role of each word in an overall sentence structure. Thus the speaker knows, as he speaks, that each of his words occupies a specific place in an overall "thought structure" that is currently "filled" with the specific general impression he wishes to convey. The listener automatically fills in the vacant parts of his thought structure as he hears the different words of a sentence. Wundt noted that, psychologically, the sentence is at once "a simultaneous and a sequential structure":

It is simultaneous because at each moment it is present in consciousness as a totality even though individual subordinate elements may

145

occasionally disappear from it. It is sequential because the configuration changes from moment to moment in its cognitive condition as individual constituents move into the focus of attention and out again one after the other.[10]

Wundt's psycholinguistics made good use of many of the concepts he had developed in his experimental psychology. For example, general impressions had to be apperceived, and some individual words brought to the focus of attention, while others were retained on the periphery of attention. In general, the completion of the ten-volume *Völkerpsychologie* in 1920 marked the fulfilment of the ambitious psychological program Wundt had set for himself almost sixty years earlier. He had now integrated the findings of experimental psychology into a sophisticated analysis, pursued mainly by historical and naturalistic methods, of the higher mental functions.

Wundt remained in full harness until the very end of his long life. He retired from teaching in 1917 at the age of 85. For three more years he looked after the completion of his *Völkerpsychologie,* and he spent much of 1920 working on his autobiography. He completed it on August 23 and died eight days later, leaving behind not only his voluminous published works, but also most of the 24,000 students he had taught during his long and prodigiously productive career.

Wundt's Influence on Modern Psychology

For many years American psychologists tended to follow James's lead by regarding Wundt as a rather plodding, arrogant, and dogmatic figure whose talents were mainly administrative. He was credited with founding the new science of experimental psychology, but charged with leading it in poorly chosen and scientifically unproductive directions. One historian went so far as to refer to Wundtian psychology as "an interruption in the development of a natural science of man," [11] a temporary eddy running counter to the general stream of scientific progress.

Psychology in the University

The most common criticism of Wundtian psychology focused on its use of introspection. The unreliability of introspective reports and the difficulty of verifying them was stressed by John B. Watson in 1913 when he founded the movement known as *behaviorism*.* The dominant force in American psychology for many years, behaviorism held that the only proper subject matter for psychology was the objectively observable behavior of organisms, unadorned by subjective introspective accounts of mental states. Such accounts could never be verified, Watson argued, and there existed no way to resolve the differences if two subjects gave divergent introspective reports of the same experimental situation.

Disagreement over method was not the only reason for the American antagonism to Wundt, however. Even before Watson had proposed behaviorism as a distinct alternative, there were underlying cultural differences between Germany and America which made wholehearted American acceptance of Wundt problematic. The German intellectual tradition from the time of Kant had been preoccupied with the description of the human mind *in general*. The major question that Wundt, as a representative of that tradition, tried to answer was "What are the universal characteristics of the mind that can account for the universal aspects of human experience?" Americans, with their pioneer tradition and historical emphasis on individuality, were more concerned with questions of *individual differences* among people, and the usefulness of those differences in the struggle for survival and success in a socially fluid atmosphere. These attitudes made Americans especially receptive to Darwin's ideas about individual variation, evolution by natural selection, and the "survival of the fittest" when they appeared in the nineteenth century. They also led to a certain natural resistance against Wundtian psychology.

Finally, the natural intellectual differences between Wundt and the American psychologists were exacerbated by the all-too-physical antagonisms of World War I. Wundt was an ar-

* See Chapter 8 of the present volume for details of Watson's attack.

dent German patriot, a fact that was bitterly resented by many of his former American students. Relationships with Germany being poisoned, American psychology self-consciously withdrew from all things German. This was one of the factors leading to an insularity of American psychology—a lack of interest in psychological developments in the rest of the world—that persists to a certain degree today.

In this hostile atmosphere most of Wundt's later works, including the impressive ten-volume *Völkerpsychologie,* were never translated into English. A tradition began of paying lip service to Wundt as the founder of experimental psychology, while denigrating the specifics of his psychological theories in the absence of any first-hand knowledge of what they really were.

In recent years this has begun to change, as some American and Canadian psychologists have taken the trouble to read Wundt in the original, and have discovered the relevance of his work to their own current concerns. They find that their studies of such cognitive phenomena as "information processing," "selective inattention," and "perceptual masking" are much in the tradition of Wundt's studies of apperception. They measure the times for very brief mental operations in a manner reminiscent of the Leipzig studies of mental chronometry. They are also finding that Wundt's three-factor theory of feelings—even though based on the discredited method of introspection—has been rather closely replicated by their own factor-analytic studies of emotion and attitude. A current theory of schizophrenia, which holds that it is caused by a deficiency in attention, is directly traceable to Wundt's view that schizophrenic personalities are deficient in apperceptive processes. And perhaps most striking of all, the North Americans are recognizing that Wundt's theory of language, never translated completely into English, is a striking anticipation of the currently influential "transformational grammar" expounded by such linguists as Noam Chomsky.

Thus, American psychologists must now recognize Wundt as more than just the "founder" of an ineffective experimental psychology, more than a dogmatic tyrant who suppressed everyone else's point of view, and more than an indefatigable author of weighty tomes. He was a genuine innovator whose accomplishments earned him a place in the history of psychology fully as distinguished as that of his great American rival, William James.

William James: Early Years

William James was born on January 11, 1842, in New York City. During his boyhood and adolescence, he moved with his family from New York to London, Geneva, Paris, Boulogne-sur-mer, Newport, Dresden, and Boston before finally settling down in Cambridge, Massachusetts in 1866. Such travel was made possible by the inherited wealth of his remarkable father, Henry James, Sr.

Henry Sr. had gone to divinity school for two years, but left because of dissatisfaction with stern Presbyterian doctrines. Most of his subsequent adult activities, including the years of constant travelling, were directed toward the independent education of his five children, and the promulgation of an obscure Swedenborgian religious view. This Swedenborgian philosophy was the direct result of a severe personal crisis he experienced in 1844—one that was to be closely echoed in his son William some twenty-six years later. The crisis followed years of philosophic and religious questioning, but arrived with totally unexpected suddenness and ferocity. The elder James has provided a vivid description of its onset:

One day, . . . towards the end of May, having eaten a comfortable dinner, I remained sitting at the table after the family had disappeared, idly gazing at the embers in the grate, thinking of nothing, and feeling only the exhilaration incident to a good digestion, when suddenly—in a lightning flash, as it were—"fear came upon me, and trembling, which made all my bones to shake." To all appearance it was a perfectly insane and abject terror, without ostensible cause, and only to be accounted for to my perplexed imagination, by some damned shape squatting invisible to me within the precincts of the room, and raying out from his fetid personality influences fatal to life. The thing had not lasted ten seconds before I felt myself a wreck; that is, reduced from a state of firm, vigorous, joyful manhood to one of the almost helpless infancy.[12]

Henry James Sr. remained badly shaken for more than two years following this incident, subject to chronic anxiety and a general feeling that the foundations had been pulled from beneath his existence. He consulted many eminent physicians, who could do nothing better than prescribe vacations, trips in the open air, and cheerful companions. Finally, he learned that the Swedish mystic, Emanuel Swedenborg, had many years earlier written about anxiety attacks like his own, calling them "vastations." He began reading every book he could find by or about Swedenborg. Somehow, this activity brought him the assurance he needed, and enabled him to gain control over his neurosis. He spent the rest of his life trying unsuccessfully to communicate his new philosophy to others in books and lectures.*

Whatever its popular defects, the elder James's philosophy gradually restored him to vibrant good spirits, and enabled him to attend with passionate energy to his other dominant interest—the education of his family. He believed strongly that his children should receive the best possible education, but could never quite decide what that was. After trying several private schools and home tutoring in New York, he concluded that a European education would be superior. Then began an odyssey in which his five children, among them, attended scores of different schools in Europe and America. No school ever worked out quite as well as had been hoped.

Nevertheless, the children picked up a familiarity with several different languages and cultures, and carried with them wherever they went the most important educational benefit of all: their tremendously stimulating home environment. Every-

---

* After publication of one of his typically obscure books, entitled *The Secret of Swedenborg*, a friend jocosely remarked that Henry Sr. had not only discovered the secret, but also kept it.

one was encouraged to engage in intellectual discussions, to express opinions freely, and to be prepared to defend them against lively familial opposition. In the heat of dinner table discussions, the boys would sometimes leave their seats to gesticulate on the floor, or invoke humorous curses on their father—that "his mashed potatoes might always have lumps in them," for example.[13]

The vagabond and intellectually roistering life style the elder James created for his children had mixed effects. The three youngest children—Garth Wilkinson, Robertson, and Alice—were clearly somewhat intimidated by the vigorous antics of their father and elder brothers. Despite their early promise, they grew up susceptible to neurotic illnesses and led generally unhappy adult lives. For William and his brother Henry Jr., the famous writer, the results were much more positive. Much of the vitality, sensitivity, and worldly sophistication that later characterized their writings undoubtedly had roots in their childhood experiences. But all was not smooth sailing for them, either, as both grew up subject to periodic emotional disturbance.

Henry Jr. was born just fifteen months after William, close enough to be a companion, but young enough to feel always overshadowed. Unable to match the venturesome antics of his brother, he retreated into the world of books and literature. William, as the oldest, was always "out front"—the first and prime result of his father's educational experiments. In many respects he revelled in this role. Despite a propensity towards ill health, he was naturally outgoing, adventurous, and high-spirited—all characteristics which drew favorable attention to himself (and made it all the more difficult for Henry to compete with him directly). From boyhood on, he liked to experiment with things, to ingest various substances to determine their pharmacological effects on himself, and to mix chemicals indiscriminately. He created any number of explosions and foul smells with this activity, which led his father to conclude very early that William was destined for a career in science.

But family life was not totally unclouded for William, even though his external personality and circumstances were so different from his siblings'. As the oldest and therefore most capable child, he was forced to bear the brunt of responsibility. It was usually in *his* supposed interests that the various educational pilgrimages were planned. And while purportedly promoting independence, many of the elder James's educational decisions did not have quite that effect. After deciding William was cut out to be a scientist, for example, he was not thrilled to see his seventeen-year-old son come under the sway of a Newport artist and express an interest in art as a career. He hoped to discourage this ambition by packing the family off to Europe for a year, and only after William's artistic interest persisted did he reluctantly bring them back to Rhode Island. When William demonstrated, after all, only moderate artistic talent, he guiltily admitted he had been wrong and went off to study chemistry at Harvard. This appeased his father to a degree, but engendered the worry that William would become too materialistic as a scientist and lose sight of the spiritual values that Henry Sr. found so important. It was no wonder that William was to have a difficult time making a career choice, and to require many years to find his vocation as a psychologist and professor.

James's Academic Training

When James entered Harvard in 1861 he was officially a chemistry student, but the only previous training he had had in chemistry came from his explosive home experiments. He found chemistry at Harvard to be difficult and not really absorbing, and he became more interested in physiology (in which he had had *no* prior training). This science was making great strides at the time under the influence of figures such as Müller, Helmholtz, and du Bois-Reymond. Soon James waged an internal debate over whether to pursue a career in academic science, medicine, or business. The family fortune had begun to show its first signs of being finite, and for the first time in two generations a James had to take financial considerations into account. Without too much enthusiasm, he finally chose medicine because it offered both scientific training and a reasonable income. In 1864, James enrolled in Harvard's Medical School.

A major diversion occurred in young James's life in 1865, when Louis Agassiz (1807–1873), Harvard's eminent biologist and the most outspoken American critic of Darwinism, conducted a specimen-hunting expedition to the Amazon. William went along as an unpaid assistant, with hopes of discovering untapped biological talents within himself. The trip, however, was far from a personal success. He was miserably seasick for most of the journey south, causing him to write to his parents, "No one has a right to write about the 'nature of Evil,' or to have any opinion about evil, who has not been at sea." [14] His enthusiasm was hardly increased by his first task upon arriving at Rio, the collecting and crating of jellyfish. Soon after, he was stricken with smallpox, and when he recovered he began making plans to return home. He stayed on in Brazil for a few months out of a sense of duty to the expedition, and did go on some productive collecting expeditions to the interior. But it was by now abundantly clear that the life of a field biologist was not for him, so James returned home and resumed his medical studies at Harvard.

Unfortunately, his real troubles were just beginning. Smallpox had left him with an eye weakness, and he began to experience severe back pain which made walking difficult. Handicapped in his reading, and prevented from making medical rounds or conducting laboratory research on his feet, he found little left to do in medical school. The fashionable treatment for back problems at the time was to take mineral spring baths in Europe, so William departed in April of 1867 for Germany, where he hoped to perfect his German as well as cure his back.

After a year and a half he had succeeded at the former but failed at the latter. His eyes improved, and he read omnivorously, especially in the physiologically oriented psychology then developing in Germany. It was then that he first heard of Wundt, and made his abortive attempt to visit him and Helmholtz at Heidelberg. In Berlin he attended the lectures of du Bois-Reymond, and was greatly impressed by the explanatory power of the new mechanistic physiology. By the end of 1868, it was clear that his back was not improving, however, and he returned home in a greatly dispirited condition.

James's back improved slightly after returning to Cambridge, and he went through the motions of completing his medical degree. Outwardly he was filled with enthusiasm, but inwardly he was in a state of turmoil and deep depression. In the spring of 1870, the death of a favorite female cousin brought his emotional crisis to a climax, and precipitated a sudden breakdown highly reminiscent of his father's "vastation" twenty-six years earlier. James described his experience, disguised as the case of a fictional "Frenchman," many years later in his *Varieties of Religious Experience:*

Whilst in this state of philosophic pessimism and general depression of spirit about my prospects, I went one evening into a dressing-room in the twilight to procure some article that was there; when suddenly there fell upon me without warning, just as if it came out of the darkness, a horrible fear of my own existence. Simultaneously there arose in my mind the image of an epileptic patient whom I had seen in the asylum, a black-haired youth with greenish skin, entirely idiotic, who used to sit all day on one of the benches, or rather shelves against the wall, with his knees drawn up against his chin, and the coarse gray undershirt, which was his only garment, drawn over them inclosing his entire figure. He sat there like a sort of sculptured Egyptian cat or Peruvian mummy, moving nothing but his black eyes and looking absolutely non-human. This image and my fear entered into a species of combination with each other. *That shape am I,* I felt, potentially. Nothing I possess can defend me against that fate, if the hour for it should strike for me as it struck for him. There was such a horror of him, and such a perception of my own merely momentary discrepancy from him, that it was as if something hitherto solid within my breast gave way entirely, and I became a mass of quivering fear. After this the universe was changed for me altogether. I awoke morning after morning with a horrible dread at the pit of my stomach, and with a sense of the insecurity of life that I never knew before, and that I have never felt since.[15]

In the aftermath of this experience, James was more incapacitated than he was ever to be again in his life (though he always remained subject to milder bouts of depression). Constantly aware of "that pit of insecurity beneath the surface of life," he was unable to concentrate on his work. He abandoned all intentions of practicing medicine without any prospects for another career.

One of the ideas that most oppressed James during this low period in his life was the vision of a mechanistic universe promulgated by the German physiologists. Though intellectually impressed by mechanism, he was troubled by its philosophical implications. If all things in the universe, including physiological and psychological phenomena, were mechanistically determined, then all of his own physical and mental suffering was nothing more than the inevitable and predetermined result of interacting physical particles. The difference between himself and the epileptic mental patient was likewise predetermined, and there was nothing either of them could do personally to alter his fate.

William's emotional recovery, like his father's before him, was inspired by the chance reading of a peculiarly apt philosophical document. In William's case, it was an essay on free will by the French philosopher, Charles Renouvier (1815–1903), which he happened to read on April 29, 1870. The next day, he wrote in his diary:

I think that yesterday was a crisis in my life. I finished the first part of Renouvier's second "Essais" and see no reason why his definition of free will—"the sustaining of a thought *because I choose to* when I might have other thoughts"—need be the definition of an illusion. At any rate, I will assume for the present—until next year—that it is no illusion. My first act of free will shall be to believe in free will. . . . Hitherto, when I have felt like taking a free initiative, like daring to act originally, without carefully waiting for contemplation of the external world to determine all for me, suicide seemed the most manly form to put my daring into; now, I will go a step further with my will, not only act with it, but believe as well; believe in my individual reality and creative power.[16]

James's trial adoption of a belief in free will was successful, and lasted not just to the end of the year but to the end of his life. In a curious way, his adoption of this most unmechanistic of beliefs freed him of his intellectual inhibitions and enabled him to regard the mechanistic ideas of the new physiology and psychology even more seriously. He could entertain the mechanistic ideas and carry them as far as they would go *scientifically,* without allowing their implications to paralyze him *personally.* From his personal point of view it was *useful* to think and behave as if he had free will, just as from a scientist's point of view it was useful to assume that all physiological and psychological phenomena have mechanistic causes. Both views were articles of faith incapable of absolute confirmation or denial. In the absence of any absolute criterion for resolving the free will-determinism issue, utility seemed as good as any other. And since it was useful to him as an individual to believe in personal freedom, James would go ahead and do so. Evaluation of ideas in terms of their utility became a life-long habit, and the foundation of James's later philosophy of *pragmatism.*

James's physical and emotional condition improved steadily following this crisis, though his complete recovery was a slow process. He had completed his medical studies while still living with his parents in Cambridge, and now spent his time reading and conversing with friends. Approaching thirty, he had never held a paying job, and even though he was storing up a large amount of useful information he remained very much tied to the parental purse and apron-strings.

A turning point came in 1872, when Harvard's president Charles Eliot, a Cambridge neighbor and a former professor of James's, asked him to teach half of a newly instituted physiology course. After much deliberation, he accepted. He was a natural for the job, and did so well that he was asked to take over the entire course the next year. James did not yet feel sufficiently recovered from his crisis to undertake this responsibility, especially since it would have involved preparing some radically new material for him. He begged off for a year and toured Europe, but then returned to Cambridge and accepted the position. For the rest of his life his primary identity was that of a professor at Harvard, where he became one of its almost legendary figures.

James as a Teacher

James was a born teacher, bringing his own infectious zest for his subject matter into the classroom, and treating his students as intellectual equals engaged in a common quest for knowledge. In an age when professors were noted for their authoritarianism, James frequently walked to and from his classes with his students, constantly engaged in animated conversation with them. He seemed almost shockingly informal, and one prominent visitor to his class noted that he looked more like a sportsman than a professor.

Students remembered his lectures for the sense of intense absorption in his subject that he conveyed. As one student recalled, "James would rise with a peculiar suddenness and make bold and rapid strokes for a diagram on the blackboard—I can remember his abstracted air as he wrestled with some idea, standing by his chair with one foot upon it, elbow on knee, hand to chin." Once James brought his own portable blackboard to class: "He stood it on a chair and in various other positions, but could not at once write upon it, hold it steady, and keep it in the class's vision. Entirely bent on what he was doing, his efforts ended at last in his standing it on the floor while he lay down at full length, holding it with one hand, drawing with the other, and continuing the flow of his commentary." [17]

James was genuinely interested in his students and their responses to his classes. He was probably the first professor in the United States to solicit course evaluations from his students at the end of the semester. He always permitted students to ask questions, in class and out, and won over more than one hostile undergraduate with his wit, gaiety, and courtesy.

One of the best known James anecdotes concerns Gertrude Stein, who was one of his top students when she was a Radcliffe undergraduate. After looking at the questions in James's final philosophy examination she wrote, "Dear Professor James, I am sorry but really I do not feel like an examination paper in philosophy today," and then left the classroom. James wrote back, "Dear Miss Stein, I understand perfectly how you feel. I often feel like that myself." [18] He gave her the highest mark in the class.*

An important reason for James's success as a teacher lay in his approach to subject matter. Far from regarding his subjects as dry and dusty disciplines with no relationship to everyday life, he constantly sought to extract from them what was useful for living. Indeed, his own motive for study was to understand himself and his world more clearly. Just as he had found philosophical and psychological ideas to be useful in resolving his own crisis, so he tried to convey some sense of the personal value of knowledge to his students. He was no ivory tower professor, and his practical orientation accounted as much as anything else for his developing antipathy to the Wundtian style of academicism.

The subject matter of James's courses changed with his interests. He had no formal academic training after his medical degree, but always served as his own teacher first before becoming the teacher of others. Initially appointed to teach anatomy and physiology, by 1875 he was labelling his course "The Relations between Physiology and Psychology." (It was in connection with this course that he developed his small demonstration laboratory in 1875). He dropped anatomy and physiology from his curriculum in 1878, and for several years his courses were explicitly psychological. By the time James had summarized his view of psychology in *The Principles of*

---

* Gertrude Stein's ploy has since been tried by many other students, with many other professors. Results have not been so universally positive as to make it a generally recommended practice.

Psychology in the University

Psychology in 1890, his personal interests were becoming more philosophical in nature. He began to think of himself as more of a philosopher and less of a psychologist, and his course offerings during the last years of his life were almost exclusively in philosophy.

Even though his tenure as a psychologist was temporary and relatively brief, it was extraordinarily influential. With his lectures, articles, and textbooks, he made the new science come alive for anyone who cared to read or listen to him. Wundt had succeeded in bringing psychology to the university; James brought it recognition in the world at large.

The Principles of Psychology

In 1878, just as James was beginning to teach his first pure psychology courses, he contracted with the publisher Henry Holt to write a psychology text. He thought that writing it would be a straightforward matter since he was already well acquainted with the German, French, and English literature, and he confidently promised to complete it in two years. But when 1880 arrived he had hardly begun, and now felt the entire task was like a dark cloud destined to hover above him perpetually. During the next decade, however, he wrote several magazine articles on psychological subjects, and realized that these could rather easily be shaped into the chapters of his text. The book finally began to materialize in the late 1880s, and James wrote sardonically to his publisher of "the enormous *rat* which . . . ten years gestation has brought forth." [19] At last, in January of 1890, he sent Holt the first 350 manuscript pages, with assurances that the remaining four-fifths of the book would soon follow. (He could not understand why his publisher would want to wait for the rest before sending it off to be set in type.) He was almost as good as his word, and the massive two volumes of *The Principles of Psychology* were finally published in late 1890.

No one could have been more relieved than James to have the awful burden removed from his conscience. He had grown understandably weary of the subject after twelve years, and the final installments of the manuscript were accompanied by a letter to his publisher saying, "No one could be more disgusted than I at the sight of the book. *No* subject is worth being treated of in 1000 pages! Had I ten years more, I could rewrite it in 500; but as it stands it is this or nothing—a loathsome, distended, tumefied, bloated, dropsical mass, testifying to nothing but two facts: *1st,* that there is no such thing as a *science* of psychology, and *2nd,* that W.J. is an incapable." [20]

Two aspects of James's critique were perhaps correct: the book *was* huge, and it did reveal psychology as an unsystematic and incomplete science ("like physics before Galileo's time," as he put it in a letter to a friend). But it was also a beautifully written document, which quickly became the best selling psychology text in English. Psychologists throughout the world, with the predictable exception of Wundt, greeted it with enthusiasm, and its quality is such that it can still be read with pleasure by students today.

James employed the same practices in the *Principles* that made his classroom teaching such a success, constantly stressing the utility and potential personal relevance of psychological ideas for his reader. Further liveliness was added because James was unusually frank in commenting on the works of other psychologists. He could criticize the faults he saw in a man like Wundt, while at the same time praising some of his ideas and citing him as one of the men whose writings most directly inspired the *Principles*.

It is impossible to summarize the contents of *The Principles of Psychology* briefly, except perhaps by noting that it includes chapters on such topics as brain function, habit, "the automaton-theory," the stream of thought, the self, attention, association, the perception of time, memory, sensation, imagination, perception, reasoning, voluntary movement, instinct, the emotions, will, and hypnotism, among others. A few brief examples will be cited here to give a flavor of his style.

Habit. One of James's best known chapters is "Habit," where he describes the enormously important influence of *repetition* on all organic behavior. After pointing out that repetition is a basic fact of physics as well as physiology ("The laws of Nature are nothing but the immutable habits which the different elementary sorts of matter follow in their actions and reactions upon each other."),[21] he asserts that the repetition of learned acts in all people is what holds human society together:

Habit is thus the enormous fly-wheel of society, its most precious conservative agent. It alone is what keeps us all within the bounds of ordinance, and saves the children of fortune from the envious uprisings of the poor. It alone prevents the hardest and most repulsive walks of life from being deserted by those brought up to tread therein. . . . It dooms us all to fight out the battle of life upon the lines of our nurture or our early choice,and to make the best of a pursuit that disagrees, because there is no other for which we are fitted, and it is too late to begin again. It keeps different social strata from mixing. Already at the age of twenty-five you see the professional mannerism settling down on the young commercial traveller, on the young doctor, on the young minister, on the young counsellor-at-law. You see the little lines of cleavage running through the character, the tricks of thought, the prejudices, the ways of the 'shop,' in a word, from which the man can by-and-by no more escape than his coat-sleeve can suddenly fall into a new set of folds. On the whole, it is best he should not escape. It is well for the world that in most of us, by the age of thirty, the character has set like plaster, and will never soften again.[22]

After pointing out the inevitability and power of established habits, James characteristically tries to draw some sort of a lesson. Obviously, it is of the utmost importance to a person what kind of habits he develops. Yet the laws determining habit-formation are impartial, capable of fostering positive as well as negative actions:

Every smallest stroke of virtue or of vice leaves its never so little scar. The drunken Rip Van Winkle, in Jefferson's play, excuses himself for every fresh dereliction by saying, "I won't count this time!" Well! he may not count it, and a kind Heaven may not count it; but it is being counted none the less. Down among his nerve-cells and fibres the molecules are counting it, registering and storing it up to be used against him when the next temptation comes.[23]

The practical problem is to see to it that positive habits become established instead of negative ones. James believed that his college-aged audience still had some flexibility left for the development of intellectual and professional habits, and offered some advice. When trying to develop a new positive habit, the student should "never suffer an exception to occur till the new habit is securely rooted in your life. . . . Seize the first possible opportunity to act on every resolution you make. . . . Keep the faculty of effort alive in you by a little gratuitous exercise every day." [24] If students do this, they need have no anxiety about the upshot of their education: "If [the student] keep faithfully busy each hour of the working-day, he may safely leave the final result to itself. He can with perfect certainty count on waking up some fine morning, to find himself one of the competent ones of his generation." [25] The production of "competent ones," of course, was the major goal of James's psychology in general.

The Stream of Consciousness. Another famous chapter from the *Principles*, "The Stream of Thought," presents James's most influential critique of Wundtian experimental psychology. Here James argues that the proper metaphor for thought is a *stream*, not a collection of discrete elements or ideas. He cites the Greek philosopher Heraclitis, who asserted that one never descends twice into exactly the same stream, and points out that, analogously, no person ever has exactly the same sensation, thought, or other experience twice. Every experience is inevitably molded by all the experiences that have gone before it, and since no two experiences ever have exactly the same background they can never be precisely alike.

Thought is streamlike because it is consciously experienced as continuous. Even when gaps in consciousness occur, as in sleep, the continuity is maintained subjectively. James likens the last conscious experience before sleep, and the first one after it, to "broken edges of sentient life" which, upon awakening, "meet and merge over the gap, much as the feelings of space of the opposite margins of the 'blind spot' meet and merge over that objective interruption to the sensitiveness of the eye." [26] Because conscious thought is experienced as a flowing and continuous stream, it can never be "frozen" and studied analytically without doing damage to its essential nature. This is the essence of James's critique of the introspective analysis of thought into static elements, such as Wundt's sensations and feelings: "The attempt at introspective analysis . . . is in fact like seizing a spinning top to catch its motion, or trying to turn up the gas quickly enough to see how the darkness looks." * [27]

Emotion. One of James's few original theoretical contributions to psychology in his textbook was his view of *emotion* as nothing more than the perception of internal bodily changes that have occurred in response to some stimulus.** Accordingly, it is a *consequence* rather than a cause of bodily changes —the reverse of the common sense view of emotion:

Common sense says, we lose our fortune, are sorry and weep; we meet a bear, are frightened and run; we are insulted by a rival, are angry and strike. The hypothesis here to be defended says that this order of sequence is incorrect, that the one mental state is not immediately induced by the other, that the bodily manifestations must first be interposed between, and that the more rational statement is that we feel sorry because we cry, angry because we strike, afraid because we tremble, and not that we cry, strike or tremble because we are sorry, angry, or fearful, as the case may be.[28]

As usual, James tried to draw a practical lesson from his theory of emotion, and suggested some behavioral devices to be employed in times of emotional distress:

* This is not quite the devastating critique of Wundt's psychology that it might seem because Wundt, it will be remembered, agreed that thought is something much more than the sum of its elements. He argued that knowledge of what the elements are is useful, however, when considered *in conjunction with* knowledge of the processes of apperception and creative synthesis. James candidly admitted that he never really understood Wundt's theory of apperception, so this may have contributed to his negative view.

** A theory virtually identical to James's was independently published at about the same time by the Danish scientist, Carl Lange (1834–1900). To honor both men, it has come to be known as the *James-Lange theory of emotion.*

Whistling to keep up courage is no mere figure of speech. On the other hand, sit all day in a moping posture, sigh, and reply to everything with a dismal voice, and your melancholy lingers. There is no more valuable precept in moral education than this, as all who have experience know: if we wish to conquer undesirable emotional tendencies in ourselves we must assiduously, and in the first instance cold-bloodedly, go through the *outward movements* of those contrary dispositions which we prefer to cultivate. The reward of persistency will infallibly come, in the fading out of the sullenness or depression, and the advent of real cheerfulness and kindliness in their stead.[29]

A striking feature of this theory is its consistency with James's own personal experience. He had resolved his own personal crisis as a young man by deciding purposefully to believe in free will, that is, to behave, regardless, as if free will existed. After a time the behavior following from a belief in freedom became habitual (in accordance with James's observations about the nature of habits), and the crisis was largely resolved. The theory of emotion crystallized in James's mind shortly after the death of both his parents in 1882, and it is likely that a similar purposeful combatting of grief played an important role in its genesis. For all of its stiff-upper-lip oversimplicity, James's theory has its merits and is still employed by psychologists today to account for at least some aspects of emotional experience.

Will. Another of the clear ways in which James's personal experience shines through *The Principles of Psychology* is in its regular emphasis on *will* as a factor in human behavior. In addition to stressing how the will may be employed to influence such phenomena as habits and emotions, James devoted an entire chapter to the subject by itself. There he described *effort,* or the sensation of effort, as the primary subjective indication that an act of will has occurred: "The most essential achievement of the will . . . when it is most 'voluntary,' is to ATTEND to a difficult object and hold it fast before the mind. . . . Effort of attention is thus the essential phenomenon of will." [30]

James openly addressed the difficult question of whether psychology should admit of there being free will. The question, as he saw it, reduced to one of whether the feeling of effortful attention was strictly a mechanistically determined function of the object of thought, or whether the subjective consciousness supplied certain indeterminate and unpredictable influences of its own, independent of the object. Scientific psychology assumed the former to be true, while personal, subjective experience suggested the latter.

In a passage hauntingly evocative of his own past, James argued that if there were indeed freedom of the will, it would still be possible to conceptualize a completely determined universe:

If . . . the will *be* undetermined, it would seem only fitting that the belief in its indetermination should be voluntarily chosen from amongst other possible beliefs. Freedom's first deed should be to affirm itself. We ought never to hope for any other method of getting at the truth if indeterminism be a fact. Doubt of this particular truth will therefore probably be open to us to the end of time, and the utmost that a believer in free will can *ever* do will be to show that the deterministic arguments are not coercive.[31]

Furthermore, from a scientific point of view it was desirable and *necessary* to postulate complete determination: "Before . . . indeterminism, science simply *stops*." The benefits and advances of the scientific point of view were clear, and certainly *most* psychological phenomena were explainable deterministically even if free will was sometimes brought into play. As James expressed it, "The operation of free effort, if it existed, could only be to hold some one ideal object, or part of an object, a little longer or a little more intensely before the mind. . . . And although such quickening of one idea might be *morally and historically momentous*, yet, if considered *dynamically* it would be an operation amongst those physiological infinitesimals which calculation must forever neglect." [32]

The essence of James's position, then, was that psychology was unable to solve the free will-determinism controversy; but that was a matter of small consequence *for psychology* which could progress only by assuming determinism. This did not mean that belief in free will must be abandoned in *other* contexts, however, because "Science . . . must constantly be reminded that her purposes are not the only purposes, and that the order of uniform causation which she has use for, and is therefore right in postulating, may be enveloped in a wider order, on which she has no claims at all." [33] In his role as a psychologist, James would accept the tenets of determinism, and allow them to go as far as they could. But in his role as a feeling, willing, and socially responsive human being, he would continue to act on his belief in free will. Psychology, for James, did not and could not contain all the answers.

Such was the essence of James's psychology. It was not a finished system, nor did it offer absolutely certain conclusions. It was much more in the nature of an intellectual journey, offering tantalizing glimpses into potentially fascinating but only partially explored regions. Though James served as an accomplished and helpful guide, he did not promise more than he could produce.

James's Influence on Psychology

Partly because of his sense of the limitations of psychology, James's interests after 1890 turned increasingly to philosophical questions. Even as his textbook was making him famous as a psychologist, he began, half-jokingly, to complain about his identification with such a limited science. Psychology, he told a Harvard colleague, was "a nasty little subject," and added, "all one cares to know lies outside." When he learned he was to receive an honorary degree from Harvard in 1903, he professed a dread that President Eliot would publicly proclaim him "Psychologist, psychical researcher, willer-to-believe, religious experiencer." The "psychologist" on this fantasied list seemed scarcely more respectable than the other titles.[34]

Apart from the classic *Varieties of Religious Experience* (1902), which explored the relationships between religious experience and "abnormal" psychology, James's psychological writings after 1890 were abridgements and popularizations of what he had already said in *Principles*. He continued to keep abreast of psychological developments, and in 1894 was the first American to call favorable attention to the recent work of the relatively obscure Viennese physician, Sigmund Freud.* But he did no more original thinking in psychology itself, confining his creative efforts to philosophy. In that field he promulgated the doctrines of *pragmatism* and *radical empiricism,* which extended his notion that ideas should be evaluated for their utility rather than for some illusory absolute truth. This point of view had been implicit in his approach to psychology, of course, but he now applied to it many other areas as well, including ethics. This work was influential enough that at his death in 1910 James was hailed as "the most famous American philosopher since Emerson." 36

Despite his relatively brief tenure as a psychologist, James's impact on the discipline itself was enormous. Rather than expounding a theory, he provided a *point of view* that captured the imagination of psychologists, especially in America. He directly inspired the movement there known as *functionalism,* which flourished during the early years of the twentieth century and which emphasized the purpose and utility of behavior, rather than merely its description. From this point of view, *individual differences* in psychological characteristics were very important, because they determined how well or poorly different people could adapt to their environments. The functionalist movement itself lasted for only a few years before giving way to behaviorism. But its most basic tenet—a concern for the

* In 1909, just a few months before his death, James travelled to Clark University "to see what Freud was like" in person when Freud made his only visit to America. He was impressed, but had some reservations. He wrote a friend, "I hope that Freud and his pupils will push their ideas to their utmost limits, so that we may learn what they are. They can't fail to throw light on human nature; but I confess that he made on me personally the impression of a man obsessed with fixed ideas." 35

practical implications of psychological knowledge, and its usefulness for the individual person—have remained hallmarks of American psychology to the present.

Perhaps most important of all, James transformed psychology from a somewhat recondite and abstract science that some students avoided because of the difficulty of introspective methodology, into a discipline that spoke directly to personal interests and concerns. James's characterization of psychology as a "nasty little subject" that excludes all one would want to know is nowhere more clearly belied than in his own textbooks on psychology.

Suggested Readings

Unfortunately, no full length biographies of Wilhelm Wundt are yet available in English. Brief biographical sketches may be found in E. B. Titchener's "Wilhelm Wundt," *American Journal of Psychology* (*32*: 161–178, 1921); Chapter 16 of Edwin G. Boring's *A History of Experimental Psychology* (New York: Appleton-Century-Crofts, 1957); and Wolfgang G. Bringmann et al., "Wilhelm Wundt 1932–1920: A Brief Biographical Sketch," *Journal of the History of the Behavioral Sciences* (*11*: 287–297, 1975). Fascinating anecdotes about Wundt by his former students are included in "In Memory of Wilhelm Wundt, by his American Students," *The Psychological Review* (*28*: 153–188, 1921). A "traditional" American account of Wundt's psychological system is presented in Chapter 16 of Boring, cited above. More recent and appreciative accounts have been published by Arthur Blumenthal in his *Language and Psychology: Historical Aspects of Psycholinguistics* (New York: Wiley, 1970), and his paper "A Reappraisal of Wilhelm Wundt," *American Psychologist* (*30*: 1081–1088, 1975). Interesting sketches of both Wundt and James are included in George Miller and Robert Buckhout's *Psychology: The Science of Mental Life* (New York: Harper & Row, 1973).

An excellent James biography is *William James: A Biography,* by Gay Wilson Allen (New York: Viking, 1967). Biographical material interspersed with delightful examples of James's own writing is included in Henry James, ed., *The Letters of William James,* 2 vols. (Boston: Atlantic Monthly Press, 1920). Also see Ralph Barton Perry's *The Thought and Character of William James* (Boston: Little, Brown, 1935); and F. O. Matthiessen's *The James Family* (New York: Knopf, 1961). Both volumes remain in print of James's *The Principles of Psychology* (New York: Dover, 1959); and his *A Textbook of Psychology: Briefer Course* is available in several paperbound editions.

5

Early Hypnotists and the Psychology of Social Influence

In the fall of 1775, the Prince-Elector of Bavaria appointed a commission to investigate the most celebrated exorcist of the day, a country priest named Johann Joseph Gassner (1727–1779). Gassner's method of exorcism was simple but often produced spectacular results when applied to people who were apparently physically ill. Gassner always began by ensuring that the patient was a believer in the divinity of Jesus Christ, undergoing a trial exorcism willingly. Then Gassner invoked the name of Christ and ordered any demons present in the patient's body to produce the symptoms of the illness forthwith, in extreme intensity. If nothing happened, Gassner concluded that the illness had purely physical causes, and sent the patient to a physician. In many cases the suggested intense symptoms *did* appear, however, and the patients suffered convulsions, paralyses, ravings, or pains. Having produced the evidence that demons did indeed afflict the patient, Gassner proceeded to "tame" them by commanding them to cause a new series of symptoms in different parts of the body. Upon his suggestion, pains and paralyses moved all over the body accompanied by abnormal emotions ranging from grief and dread to silliness or anger.

Finally, after establishing control over the demons in this fashion, Gassner would order them to leave the body altogether, leaving the patient cured.

Gassner's activity caused considerable controversy in the Church. Exorcism was an accepted practice, but it seemed to many officials that Gassner carried it too far and applied it too indiscriminately. Not surprisingly, the medical profession joined in his condemnation. Gassner also had supporters, however, and several pamphlets and tracts were written presenting both sides of the issue. The controversy culminated in the appointment of the investigative commission.

The commission's deliberations reached a turning point with the testimony of a previously little-known physician from Vienna named Franz Anton Mesmer (1734–1815), who had been called because of rumors that he had developed a new form of treatment with results similar to Gassner's. Mesmer's treatment was based on a theory of *magnetism* rather than demonology, however, and was much more in tune with the emerging scientific consciousness of the late eighteenth century. The commission was interested in learning if science could duplicate the effects that Gassner attributed to faith.

Mesmer gave a number of demonstrations in which he caused symptoms in selected patients to appear and disappear upon command, attributing the effects to a magnetic fluid concentrated within his body. He convinced the commission that Gassner's cures, while real enough, had had natural rather than demonological causes. The commission declared exorcism an improper treatment for ordinary physical symptoms, and forbade Gassner from practicing it. He was banished to a country parish, where he died in obscurity a few years later.

Mesmer's fame was just beginning, though his role as the representative of "science" and "enlightenment" was both ironic and temporary. This paradoxical figure had truly made some accurate observations about the phenomenon now called *hypnotism*, which he tried to explain in a scientific way. He was so cavalier in his methods, however, and so grandiose in his claims, that he himself soon ran afoul of the scientific and medical community. Within ten years of his testimony on Gassner, *he* was the subject of a royal commission's inquiry, and he fared no better than Gassner had. As a result of that inquiry, the entire subject of hypnotism was branded as unscientific and unrespectable, and to the present day it has not quite lived down that early reputation.

In addition to these negative after-effects, however, Mesmer also left a more positive legacy. His faltering attempts were the starting point for a small but hardy group of investigators who resisted the establishment and began the truly scientific study of hypnosis. The study of hypnosis, in turn, was to provide psychologists with valuable ideas about the general ways in which one person may manipulate or influence the behavior or attitudes of another. Thus, without realizing it, Mesmer and the early hypnotists laid the groundwork for the study of *social influence processes,* one of the most important areas of modern social psychology.

Mesmer and Animal Magnetism

Little is known about the life of Mesmer until 1766, when he acquired his doctor of medicine degree in Vienna at the age of 32. He listed several other academic degrees on the title page of his dissertation, but searches of Europe's university archives have failed to confirm that he actually earned any of them. Even more damaging to his posthumous reputation, most of his dissertation was plagiarized from a work by a colleague of Isaac Newton's. These indiscretions were undetected in 1766, however, and Mesmer obtained his medical degree with no trouble.

The dissertation, entitled "On the Influence of the Planets," maintained that the heavenly bodies influence the well-being of human beings—a thesis that seems uncomfortably astrological today, but that was not so implausible in the immediate wake of Newton's laws of universal gravitation. One of the few unplagiarized parts of Mesmer's dissertation was the postulation of a force called *animal gravitation* which supposedly acted directly from the planets on the human body.

After his graduation, Mesmer married a wealthy Viennese aristocrat much older than himself and settled down to a life of ease. He practiced medicine only sporadically, but was impelled by a lively curiosity to keep informed about scientific and cultural developments. When Benjamin Franklin invented a curious musical instrument called the glass harmonica, Mesmer acquired one and became an accomplished performer. The instrument was played by rubbing damp fingers on a revolving glass drum, resulting in a sound similar to that produced by rubbing a wet finger around the rim of a wine glass. In a more orthodox musical vein, the Mesmers were friendly with Leopold Mozart, whose young son Wolfgang was then receiving much publicity as a prodigy. When the twelve-year-old Mozart wrote his first opera, *Bastien und Bastienne*, it was first performed in the spacious Mesmer home. Another, ultimately more consequential diversion for Mesmer occurred in the early 1770s when he made the acquaintance of Maximillian Hell, a Jesuit priest who made magnets as a hobby. The two men's conversations about the peculiar powers of magnetism were soon to have startling results.

Mesmer's routine was dramatically altered in 1773, when a twenty-seven-year-old woman suffering from a bewildering array of symptoms appeared in his consulting room. She had already been to many other doctors who had been totally unsuccessful in curing her. Mesmer began by treating her with conventional methods, and with no more success than his predecessors had had. Then, recalling his conversations with Father Hell, he had the unusual idea of applying magnets to her body. When he did, the patient went into what Mesmer described as a "crisis," with trembling, twitching, convulsions, and intense pains in the locations of each of her symptoms. After a while, she spontaneously returned to normal and remarked that her symptoms seemed much improved. Repetitions of the magnetic applications produced more crises and the disappearance of all symptoms. Mesmer tried the treatment on other patients, always telling them in advance what the expected crisis state would be like. Results were encouraging, and he was on his way to a new career.

As Mesmer attempted to account for these surprising events, he first theorized that every person's body was permeated with a magnetic force-field that sometimes became misaligned in particular places. These sites of misalignment became the locations of the symptoms. Application of magnets realigned the magnetic field and restored health. Then Mesmer discovered that he did not have to use magnets at all to induce the crisis state: all he had to do was pass his hands near the body of a patient who expected to go into crisis. Instead of drawing the most plausible conclusion from this finding—that the therapeutic effects really had nothing to do with magnetism—Mesmer decided that he possessed a large quantity of potentially therapeutic magnetic force within his own body. He argued that this magnetic force must pervade the entire organic world, but in uneven distribution. Some individuals, such as himself, contained unusually high concentrations of it and were natural healers because they could transmit small portions of their magnetism to others who were deficient in it and thus prone to illness.

Mesmer's theory was developed to this stage when he was called upon by the Gassner commission. He testified that Gassner's successes had not been due to exorcism, but to the fact that Gassner was, unknowingly, a highly magnetized person. In fact, Mesmer modestly admitted that Gassner was naturally more highly magnetized than he was himself. This reasoning was the genesis of the persistent misconception that the secret of hypnotic phenomena lies in some mysterious power residing in the *hypnotist,* rather than in the suggestibility of the *subject.*

As word of Mesmer's magnetic therapy spread, he became involved in controversy. Father Hell claimed priority for the discovery, insisting that he had suggested the magnetic treatment to Mesmer. Mesmer responded ungenerously, and soon

5. Mesmer treating patients in crisis.
The Bettmann Archive, Inc.

Vienna was full of newspaper stories and pamphlets supporting one side or the other. Mesmer argued that he had known
of the healing power of magnetism long before he ever met
Father Hell, as was proven by his frequent use of medicines
with iron in them! His most effective argument was that he
had anticipated the new therapy in his doctoral dissertation.
There, he claimed, he had already given a name to "that
property of the animal body by virtue of which it is susceptible
to universal attraction, *gravitas animalis* [animal gravity] or
magnetismus animalis [animal magnetism]." [1] This was a lie,
of course, since Mesmer had only postulated animal *gravitation* there, not *magnetism*. Nevertheless, the claim helped him
to win the priority dispute, and also established the term
animal magnetism as the name for his newly discovered
phenomena.

In 1777 Mesmer became embroiled in another controversy. He had undertaken the magnetic treatment of a seventeen-year-old girl who had been blind since the age of three. Details of the case are unclear, but Mesmer reported that the girl temporarily regained her sight while in his presence. She could never see in his absence, however, or when there was an objective witness present. The girl's own testimony was ambiguous, and Vienna's orthodox physicians accused Mesmer of being a charlatan. Though it is possible the girl's blindness was psychologically caused, and that Mesmer actually helped her, he found it convenient to leave town. Leaving his wife behind, Mesmer fled to Paris where he was soon to achieve even greater notoriety.

French society was in a state of turmoil and instability in those prerevolutionary days and was especially prone to crazes. The pseudo-scientific theory of animal magnetism, loudly and publicly proclaimed by the flamboyant Mesmer, quickly attracted a wide and enthusiastic following. Soon he found he had more patients than he could handle individually, even when he charged enormous fees. Mesmer's solution was to mass-produce cures by means of his famous *baquet,* or tub.

The therapeutic sessions were held around a *baquet* filled with magnetized iron filings. Metal rods were inserted into the *baquet*, with their ends protruding to form handles. The patients came into the treatment room in groups and sat around the *baquet* grasping the handles. The lighting was dim, and Mesmer, in an adjoining room, played soft music on his glass harmonica. When the stage was properly set, he emerged, dressed in a flowing lilac-colored robe, and began pointing his finger or an iron rod at the various patients. Some of them invariably began to experience tinglings and peculiar bodily sensations which quickly passed into a crisis state. Soon other patients followed suit. Those with the most severe crises were carried by Mesmer and his assistant to an adjoining, and clearly marked, *chambre de crises* ("crisis room") where they received individual attention. By the end of the session, a few patients had experienced severe crises, a few none at all, and most were somewhere in between. Many of the patients reported alleviation of their symptoms.

By treating his patients in groups, Mesmer increased not only his profits, but also the strength of the responses in many individuals. This was due to the *contagion effect,* a phenomenon well known to modern stage hypnotists. As soon as one person responds to a suggestion, others are likely to lose their inhibitions and follow suit. As more and more people respond, a pressure to go along naturally builds up even in the most resistant subjects. Thus, many people who would not respond to hypnotic suggestions if they were alone with the hypnotist, respond readily when in a compliant group.

Though Mesmer's *baquet* was a popular and commercial success, he was not really happy because the medical profession continued to scoff at the magnetic theories he propounded to explain his results. Thus, he pressured all of his aristocratic connections, and finally in 1784 induced the King to appoint a special, blue-ribbon commission to investigate his claims. Among the eminent members of this commission were the chemist Lavoisier, the physician Guillotin (proponent of the "humane" execution device that now bears his name), and the American ambassador Benjamin Franklin. They quickly reached a decision: "The commissioners . . . have unanimously concluded, on the question of the existence and the utility of [animal] magnetism, that there is no proof of its existence, that this fluid without existence is consequently without utility." [2] The *effects* of magnetic treatment, which unlike the theory itself did have a degree of reality, were dismissed as the result of "imagination". In that day and age, "imagination" was tantamount to "simulation," so the commission in effect cast out Mesmer's genuine contribution along with his worthless theory. The commission's report effectively branded the entire subject of animal magnetism as bogus science, and discouraged legitimate scientists and practitioners from taking it seriously for years to come. The development of hypnotism after Mesmer was left in the hands of scientifically untrained amateurs.

Of these there was no dearth, however. While animal magnetism was a fad, Mesmer took advantage of its popularity among wealthy aristocrats by creating an expensive school, called the Society of Harmony, where students could be taught the fundamentals of his practice and the details of his theory. Most of its members provided little more than missionary zeal, but a few made genuine scientific contributions to the study of magnetism. It was thanks to them that the objective study of hypnotic phenomena remained alive in the years following Mesmer's official disgrace. The most important of these men was Amand-Marie Jacques de Chastenet, the Marquis de Puységur (1751–1825).

Puységur and Artificial Somnambulism

The starting point for Puységur's contribution was his dislike of the rather violent, convulsive nature of the "crisis state" in magnetic treatments. It was obviously painful for many patients, and sometimes the magnetizer needed considerable physical strength to deal with the patients' violent agitation. Puységur's dislike of the violent crises must have unconsciously influenced the way he administered directions. One day, as he was magnetizing one of his young male servants, the patient spontaneously entered a peaceful, sleeplike state instead of the crisis. Unlike a person really sleeping, however, he continued to respond to Puységur's voice, answering questions and even performing complex motoric activities upon command. At Puységur's suggestion, the servant talked about his work, pretended to shoot for a prize, and made rapid movements in his chair as if he were gaily dancing to imagined music. When he awoke, he had no recollection of these events, though he immediately remembered them upon being re-magnetized.

Puységur quickly discovered that he could reproduce this peaceful trance state in patients simply by suggesting it overtly in the course of magnetic induction; the entire violent crisis could be by-passed. At first he named the new state the "perfect crisis," but later, inasmuch as it seemed to resemble sleepwalking and sleeptalking more than a crisis, it was renamed *artificial somnambulism*. The therapeutic results with artificial somnambulism were just as good as they had been with crisis states, and since the procedure was so much less strenuous, other magnetizers quickly adopted Puységur's techniques.

In investigating the properties of artificial somnambulism, Puységur and his colleagues discovered almost all of the properties of the hypnotic state that are known today. They conclusively demonstrated that the state is characterized by drastically increased *suggestibility*. All they had to do was state that certain things were happening, and somnambulistic subjects would begin to behave as if they really were. Paralyses and pains could be artificially produced in various parts of the body, and made to move about at the will of the magnetizer. Parts of the subject's body could be rendered insensitive, so pinpricks, burns, or other painful stimulation could be tolerated without the slightest sign of discomfort.

Puységur also demonstrated the phenomenon now called *post-hypnotic suggestion*, whereby a somnambulistic subject is told to perform a certain act after the trance has ended. When the subject performs it he has often forgotten that the suggestion was ever made, just as he may have forgotten the other events from the trance. These memory deficiencies, now called *post-hypnotic amnesia*, are among the most intriguing and mysterious of all hypnotic effects. Obviously, the forgotten memories have not been completely "lost" because in the post-hypnotic suggestion they retain enough efficacy to produce the suggested response. Furthermore, the post-hypnotic amnesia can be easily overcome if the subject is re-hypnotized, or simply told by the hypnotist that his memory will return.

Because of the extreme suggestibility of somnambulistic subjects, their specific responses to magnetic or hypnotic situations varied tremendously. This accounted for the difference between Mesmer's "crisis states" and Puységur's "perfect crises." Mesmer's patients went into crisis because they were expected to, because there were all sorts of implicit and explicit suggestions that they should. All of the trappings of the *baquet*, for example, from the presence of strong assistants to the clearly observable *chambre de crises*, led patients to believe they were supposed to respond violently. Most of them had also undoubtedly heard about other patients' crises, which were models for their own subsequent behavior. Then, in the group setting around the *baquet*, the early responders provided vivid examples of crisis for the rest of the group to follow. Puységur somehow altered these expectancies when he induced the first perfect crisis, and hypnotists ever since have followed his example.

While most of Puységur's observations on artificial somnambulism have stood the test of time, he made two unfortunate errors that remain part of the popular mythology about hypnotism. First, he believed that many abilities could be increased in the trance to a degree unattainable in the waking state, and that even such paranormal phenomena as clairvoyance could be produced. It is now known that this is false. Sometimes performances of tasks can be *optimized* by hypnotic suggestion, but this is the result of increased concentration or self-confidence rather than of an actual alteration in ability.* Clairvoyance, of course, has yet to be conclusively demonstrated in *any* situation.

Another of Puységur's mistaken beliefs was that people could not be magnetized against their will, or induced to perform acts while in trance that were contrary to their moral

---

* Highly skilled performers of tasks tend to function *normally* in a state that partly resembles hypnosis. Typically, their attention is concentrated on a relatively high-order goal, and they are largely unconscious of the more molecular aspects of their performance, which follow automatically. For example, accomplished pianists lose themselves in their conceptions of the music they play, while their finger movements occur without conscious deliberation. In these cases the specific fingering skills have been previously developed by conscious practice, of course, and they are not spontaneously produced by the states of concentrated attention.

scruples. The problem here is with the imprecise definitions available of "will" and "moral scruples," for while many instances supporting Puységur can be cited, so can some contradictory examples. For example, modern stage hypnotists can deal easily with many defiant subjects—people who proclaim loudly that they can never be hypnotized, and challenge the hypnotists to try. Such subjects are invited to sit in a chair, and are given the firm command *not* to fall asleep. Often they fall immediately into a state of hypnosis, and may be manipulated freely by the hypnotist. Have they been hypnotized against their will? On the question of violating moral scruples, there are cases on record of crimes being committed by persons under hypnosis. Though the persons committing such acts may have had deep underlying aggressive tendencies, there was no evidence that they would have committed the crimes without the hypnotist to tell them to. In one celebrated Danish case, a hypnotized subject committed a murder, was apprehended, and received a two-year sentence. The hypnotist received life imprisonment.[3]

On reflection, of course, there is no reason to expect behavioral safeguards in hypnosis that do not apply to other situations where one person has a degree of authority over another. There are many such situations where people are induced to do things counter to their normal wishes or morals. Soldiers are regularly induced to face dangers they would rather avoid, and to commit acts of aggression that they would condemn in civilian life. Successful teachers and coaches regularly induce people to reach beyond themselves, motivating them to levels of performance they would not otherwise attain. Great political leaders are sometimes great precisely because they can convince large numbers of citizens to follow paths of conduct that, all things being equal, they would rather avoid. In general, then, many other social influence situations offer the same possibilities for abuse as hypnotism.

In spite of his errors, Puységur rendered invaluable service to the cause of hypnotism. He discovered a range of intriguing and reproducible phenomena that could be produced outside the flamboyant and distracting settings that had been devised by Mesmer. Although the whole subject of magnetism was in official disgrace, Puységur's work ensured that a small band of amateurs would keep the topic alive. It was then only a matter of time until a vanguard of legitimately trained scientists saw the amateurs' magnetic demonstrations and recognized that there was something valid there to be studied. When this resurgence began some forty years later, it was localized mainly in Great Britain, and inspired by the observation of traveling stage magnetizers, known as "mesmerists," who repeated many of Puységur's findings for the entertainment of paying crowds.

The Founding of "Hypnotism"

One demonstration that stage mesmerists included in their repertoire was the induction of artificial anaesthesia. A subject would be told that a part of his body was becoming numb, and then would show no sign of pain as the magnetizer applied painful stimuli to the anaesthetized area. By the mid-1830s a few daring surgeons began to consider magnetism as a possible surgical anaesthetic. No effective anaesthetic had yet been discovered, and operations were then excruciatingly painful experiences.

One of the first of these surgeons was John Elliotson (1791–1868), an unorthodox physician accustomed to bucking the conservatism of the medical community. As a young physician he had been one of the first people in England to recognize the value of the newly invented stethoscope. When he had shown it to his colleagues, it had been subjected to immediate ridicule and called a mere "piece of wood," "just the thing for Elliotson to rave about." One of his superiors admonished him, "You will learn nothing by it, and, if you do, you cannot treat the disease any better." [4] These responses were only a rehearsal for what happened when Elliotson embraced magnetism. In 1837 he observed a traveling mesmerist, was convinced of the genuineness of what he saw, and made plans to investigate the anaesthetic properties of magnetism. Immediately, the governing board of his hospital passed a resolution "to prevent the practice of mesmerism or animal magnetism in future within the Hospital." [5] Elliotson promptly resigned his position, and began studying magnetism independently. He never had an opportunity to test its anaesthetic properties, but he did recognize its potential as a therapy for neuroses, particularly hysteria. In 1843, he founded a journal named the *Zoist,* whose subject matter was "cerebral physiology and mesmerism, and their applications for human welfare." [6] For all his pioneering zeal, however, Elliotson remained an outsider to the established scientific world, and his journal and views were never really taken seriously.

Meanwhile, other physicians were actually beginning to experiment with the anaesthetic properties of magnetism. In 1842, the surgeon W. S. Ward performed a successful leg amputation with magnetism as the anaesthetic, but his report was widely ridiculed. Marshall Hall, England's leading neurophysiologist, went so far as to argue that the patient had been an impostor. Another authority contended that even if Ward's account were true, which he doubted, its findings were useless "because pain is a wise provision of nature, and patients ought to suffer pain while their surgeons are operating; they are all the better for it and recover better." [7] A third critic felt the whole situation would be best dealt with simply by expunging all record of Ward's report from the Medical Society's minutes, as if to signify that the experiment had never taken place at all.

James Esdaile (1808–1859), a Scottish physician practicing in India, was the first person to use magnetism as an anaesthetic on a large scale, and to keep track of his results. He taught his native assistants to put patients into somnambulistic trances, and performed more than 1300 operations on magnetized patients in the late 1840s. Many of his operations were for the removal of scrotal tumors, a procedure from which only half of the patients normally recovered. Of those who had been successfully magnetized, however, the mortality was only five per cent. Impressive as Esdaile's findings were, they were dismissed in England on the racist grounds that they were obtained from highly suspect "native" patients who had been magnetized by equally suspect "native" assistants. The patients actually liked to be operated on, it was said, and they had merely tried to help Esdaile.

Magnetism thus was among the first successful and systematically applied anaesthetics to be used in western medicine. In spite of the skepticism with which it was regarded, it was clearly gaining ground and would probably have been eventually accepted as a standard medical practice if it were not for another series of events. In 1844, the American dentist Horace Wells demonstrated the anaesthetic effects of nitrous oxide for the extraction of teeth. Within three years ether and chloroform had been similarly employed and the day of chemical anaesthetics was at hand. These chemical methods were much more understandable than magnetism to mechanistically trained physicians, and had the further genuine advantage of being more reliable and universally applicable. Thus, after a brief flurry of excitement, the idea of magnetism as a surgical anaesthetic faded into the background.

A somewhat more successful attempt to bring magnetic phenomena into the mainstream of British science was made by another Scottish physician, James Braid (1795–1860). When Braid first encountered a traveling stage mesmerist, he was highly skeptical. The mesmerist had brought his own subject along with him, whom Braid naturally suspected of simulating all of the effects. He was therefore surprised when the mesmerist permitted him and a colleague, a respected ophthalmologist, to examine the somnambulistic subject. He was even more surprised to find that the subject's pupils remained dilated when his eyelids were forced open and that his insensitivity to pain seemed genuine. Braid became convinced it would be worthwhile to investigate these magnetic effects scientifically and systematically. When he did so, he made no fundamentally new discoveries, although he did make three extremely important contributions.

First, he scientifically demonstrated the reality of the principal somnambulistic effects and published his results in respectable medical journals. These studies were performed only a short time after Elliotson's, and the results were not very different, but they were much more acceptable to the medical establishment coming from Braid who was himself an establishment figure.

Second, Braid's experiments convinced him that the major effects were mainly the result of the *susceptibility of the subject* rather than the power of the magnetizer. Mesmer had taught that the effects were caused by magnetic powers within the body of the magnetizer, and even after the magnetic theory was discredited it was natural to attribute the effects to something like the "will" of the magnetizer. Braid came to believe that the really crucial events take place in the subject rather than the magnetizer, however, and though this shift in emphasis was subtle, it was influential in shaping the next stage of experimentation.

Third, Braid provided magnetic phenomena with a new and more scientific sounding name. Noting the sleeplike features of the somnambulistic trance, and believing that the state must be caused by physiological changes in the nervous system, Braid coined the new term "neuro-hypnology" (from the Greek *neuro* for "nervous" and *hypnos* for "sleep"). Shortly thereafter, common use shortened the new term to "hypnology," and then to the word used today, "hypnosis." Though the simple act of renaming a phenomenon may seem insignificant, it complemented Braid's other achievements in making magnetic phenomena seem more scientifically respectable.

Even with its new name and scientific legitimacy, however, hypnotism was not fully accepted as more than a curiosity or diversion. It was to be several more years before its general interest, and relevance to other important phenomena, would be demonstrated by a series of events in France.

The Nancy School

The founder of the so-called "Nancy School" of hypnotism was Auguste Ambroise Liébeault (1823–1904), a country doctor who practiced in a village just outside the French city of Nancy. After establishing a highly successful orthodox practice, Liébeault determined to follow up on a longstanding interest in magnetism by using it as a therapy for his patients. So great was the disrepute of the subject in France, however, that he could find no patients willing to submit to it. Finally, he agreed to treat patients hypnotically for free, or by orthodox methods for his usual fee. This won him a few volunteers, and his success with them was so great that his practice was soon endangered by a preponderance of nonpaying clients.

Liébeault's hypnotic method was simple, straightforward, and invariable for all patients. He told each patient to stare deeply into his eyes, and then gave repeated suggestions that the patient was getting sleepy. As soon as the patient fell into a light sleeplike trance, Liébeault told him that his symptoms would soon disappear. In many cases they did, a clear testimonial to the extent to which ordinary physical complaints can be caused, or removed, by psychological factors.

By the mid-1860s Liébeault's hypnotic practice was larger than he could handle, and he retired for two years to write a book entitled *On Sleep and its Analogous States, Considered Especially from the Point of View of the Action of the Mind on the Body*. The book taught that hypnotic sleep is identical with normal sleep, except that the concentration of attention on the hypnotist's voice enables the subject to remain in conscious *rapport* with the hypnotist. The work was a literary and commercial disaster, reportedly selling only one copy in the ten years following publication.

After writing his book, Liébeault returned to his clinic and began treating all patients hypnotically, this time with no fixed system of fees, but accepting whatever his patients offered to pay. He became a beloved figure among the country-folk, who called him "Good Father Liébeault." But despite his local popularity, he would undoubtedly have passed into obscurity if he had not attracted the attention of a small group of younger men who gradually formed a "school" about him. Principal among these was Hippolyte Bernheim (1840–1919), who became the Nancy school's most eloquent spokesman.

Bernheim was an Alsacian from Strasbourg, where he had begun his medical career by doing research on typhoid fever and heart disease. When Germany annexed Alsace in 1871, Bernheim's French sympathies led him to move to Nancy, where he was appointed professor of internal medicine. He eventually heard rumors about Good Father Liébeault, and curiosity prompted him to pay the hypnotic clinic a visit in 1882. Instead of finding something farcical, as he had expected, he was deeply impressed and shortly returned to study there. Soon he was devoting all of his time to hypnosis, closely studying hundreds of patients in an attempt to discover the conditions under which it could be most effective.

Bernheim was particularly struck by the observation that some patients were more responsive to hypnotic suggestion than others. In his own cases he had more success with patients from the lower than from the upper classes. He speculated that the lower class patients may have been more conditioned to strict obedience than the wealthier or better educated, and that this may have predisposed them to greater hypnotic susceptibility. Bernheim's theory was thus one of the first major attempts to follow up on Braid's assertion that the important hypnotic variables lay in the subject rather than the hypnotist.

Bernheim came to believe that human beings vary on a general trait of *suggestibility*, which he defined as "the aptitude to transform an idea into an act." [8] Individuals such as his lower class patients were assumed to have high general suggestibility, whereas more independent types were low on the trait. Bernheim believed that highly suggestible individuals responded strongly not only to hypnotic suggestion, but to other kinds of commands and suggestions as well. Eventually, this belief led Bernheim to rely on straightforward persuasion techniques instead of hypnotism per se. If he could only get his patients to *believe* that they would be cured, in many cases they really would.

It was on the point of defining the "hypnotizable personality" that Bernheim and the Nancy school became embroiled in heated controversy. During the 1880s, the subject of hypnotism was taken up by one of the most flamboyant and influential figures in all European medicine. Jean Martin Charcot (1825–1893), director of Paris's Salpêtrière Hospital and known as the "Napoleon of the Neuroses," had noted similarities between hypnosis and the neurotic illness called *hysteria*. He concluded that hypnotizability was merely one of the symptoms of hysteria. Bernheim and the Nancy school took strong issue with this, maintaining that hypnotizability, whatever else it might be, was a completely *normal* phenomenon unrelated to any kind of psychopathology. This Nancy-Salpêtrière disagreement lasted for many years, in spite of a clear preponderance of evidence in favor of the Nancy school. In order to understand why it lasted so long, it is necessary to know something about Charcot's unusual life style and personality.

Charcot: Hypnosis and Hysteria

As a relatively impoverished medical student, Charcot had been required to put in some time at the vast and crumbling Salpêtrière Hospital, used to house thousands of indigent and ill old women. Charcot immediately recognized that the hospital was a treasure-trove of neurological cases, offering unbounded research possibilities for a neurologist. He vowed to return there as a senior physician, and remain.

Immediately after receiving his degree he became private

physician and travelling companion to a wealthy banker. This gave him access to a rich and aristocratic circle of acquaintances who later became the basis of a flourishing private practice. Assured of financial security, Charcot realized his earlier ambition and returned to the Salpêtrière as senior physician in 1862.

He quickly converted the hospital into a productive research center, devoting the first ten years of his tenure to the study of epilepsy, multiple sclerosis, and poliomyelitis. He voluntarily gave regular clinical lectures which attracted large and enthusiastic audiences of professional and lay people alike. A master showman, he often imitated the symptoms of the diseases he discussed. He also publicly interviewed patients, engaging them in dramatic dialogue. Sometimes he employed special devices to show off their symptoms. When discussing tremors, for example, he brought out women patients wearing hats with very long feathers. The different kinds of vibrations in the feathers indicated different kinds of tremors.

The French government officially recognized Charcot's genuine scientific and administrative achievements in 1881 by creating a new post especially for him, professor of neuropathology at the Salpêtrière. With his increased reputation, he became physician and confidant to the elite of European society. Not surprisingly, a man as powerful and flamboyant as Charcot aroused widely divergent responses in those who worked with him. While he attracted many devoted disciples, others secretly chafed under his discipline. One colleague, who knew Charcot well enough to be familiar with his medical history, sent him anonymous letters predicting imminent death from his heart condition.

All had to admit, however, that Charcot was a brilliant clinician. His technique was unusual, in that he had little use for theory, but instead tried to immerse himself in the clinical data provided by large numbers of patients suffering from the illness under study. He described himself as a "visual," a person who *sees* things rather than thinks them and who imposes order on his observations only after long periods of careful watching. Sigmund Freud observed Charcot's technique carefully when he studied under him, and described it as follows: "He used to look again and again at the things he did not understand, to deepen his impression of them day by day, till suddenly an understanding of them dawned on him. In his mind's eye the apparent chaos presented by the continual repetition of the same symptoms then gave way to order: the new nosological pictures emerged, characterized by the constant combination of certain groups of symptoms." [9] One of Freud's anecdotes illustrates Charcot's attitude toward theory as opposed to observation. Freud once protested against one of Charcot's clinical interpretations on the grounds that it ran counter to the Young-Helmholtz theory of color vision. Charcot responded, in words that Freud savored for the rest of his life, *"La théorie, c'est bon, mais ça n'empêche pas d'exister"* (roughly, "Theory is fine, but it does not prevent things from existing.").[10]

From his observations, Charcot attempted to discover an underlying *type* that represented the full and complete form of each illness he studied. The *type* was usually observed in pure form in only a small minority of cases, where the underlying pathological process was complete and uncomplicated by other factors. Cases that did not meet all the characteristics of the *type* were called *formes frustes,* literally "blurred forms." The prototype for this diagnostic method had been the classification of epilepsy into *grand mal* and *petit mal* forms, corresponding to the *type* and a *forme fruste,* respectively. The *type,* or *grand mal* form, was characterized by three distinct phrases: first, an *aura,* or psychic sensation that regularly precedes a seizure; second, a *tonic phase,* in which all the large muscles of the body go rigid, the person falls and loses consciousness; and third, a *clonic phase,* in which the body convulses spasmodically. This was the "purest" form of epilepsy, contrasted to the incomplete *petit mal* seizure where the patient might simply experience "spells" or brief fainting sensations.

Charcot applied this diagnostic method to a wide variety of neurological conditions during his first years at the Salpêtrière, thereby clarifying the diagnoses of poliomyelitis and multiple sclerosis. Then in the 1870s his attention shifted to another group of illnesses, which, unlike poliomyelitis, multiple sclerosis, or epilepsy could not be traced to observable pathology of the nervous system. Charcot knew that damaged neural tissue could not be regenerated, and that complete recovery from extensive physical damage to the nerves was unlikely if not impossible. Nevertheless, there were some patients at the Salpêtrière with symptoms that mimicked the results of neurological damage in some respects, but that occasionally disappeared, changed state dramatically, or showed other uncharacteristic features. For example, some of these patients experienced paralyses whose characteristics did not conform to the anatomy of the nervous system. In genuine organic paralyses, the boundary between paralyzed and nonparalyzed body areas is never distinct. Some of these patients, however, reported paralyses that were limited to sharply circumscribed parts of their bodies, such as the part of a hand and arm normally covered by a glove.

Cases like these had been known since ancient times, when the Greeks coined the word *hysteria* to describe anomalous physical complaints in women. The name derived from the Greeks' conception of the origin of the illness: they believed that the uterus (Greek *hystera*) sometimes "wandered" from its appropriate place in the abdomen to other bodily locations, where it caused the symptoms to appear. One Greek therapy for hysteria was to try to drive the uterus back to its proper place by applying a foul-smelling substance to the afflicted area and a sweet-smelling one to the abdomen.

The prevailing medical tendency among Charcot's colleagues was to dismiss hysteria as malingering; symptoms without a clear-cut physiological or anatomical base were simply not comprehensible to most nineteenth century physicians. Charcot became convinced that there was more to hysteria than simulation of illness, however, because the symptoms of many of his patients seemed to cause genuine subjective distress.

Once again displaying his independence from medical orthodoxy, Charcot decided to study hysterics seriously. He applied his usual diagnostic techniques to large numbers of patients, and soon concluded that a few of them were perfect examples of a major *type* which he called *la grande hystérie* ("major hysteria"). Charcot believed these patients always manifested their symptoms in a perfectly predictable four-stage cycle. First there was an "epileptoid stage," in which the patients had symptoms similar to the onset of a grand mal epileptic seizure. Second there was a "large movement stage," where the patient performed seemingly automatic and sometimes violent acts. This was followed by a "hallucinatory stage," in which various imaginary sensations and physical states took on great subjective reality for the patients. Finally,

6. Charcot demonstrating *grand hypnotisme. The National Library of Medicine, Bethesda, Maryland*

the patients lapsed into a "delirious stage" before returning temporarily to relative normality. Most cases of hysteria did not display this spectacular and perfectly predictable sequence of symptoms, of course, and they were accordingly diagnosed as *petite hystérie* ("minor hysteria"), *formes frustes* of the major *type*.

Though theorizing was never his strong suit, Charcot nevertheless suggested that the underlying cause of hysteria was hereditary neurological degeneracy. Because of this degeneracy—which he assumed was progressive and irreversible—patients supposedly gradually lost the ability to integrate and interconnect their higher neurological processes. Memories and emotional states which should have been joined with one another through neurological connections in the brain became *dissociated*. Symptoms arose when single dissociated aspects of past memories were aroused. Hysterical patients were thus viewed as reliving the dissociated aspects of their past experience, without being able to place them within the full context of the memory. Emotion-laden and traumatic experiences were especially liable to dissociation, so patients often re-experienced strong emotions without being able to remember the concrete situations in which they first occurred.

Charcot's approach to hysteria was largely misguided, particularly his attempt to specify a major *type*. The few patients who manifested the four stages in perfect regularity did so for a host of reasons quite separate from the essential nature of their illness. Most of them were attractive young women whom Charcot liked to use for demonstrations at his clinical lectures. They became minor celebrities, and enjoyed special prestige at the hospital. The most famous of these was a young woman named Blanche Wittmann, whose spectacular performance of the four stages and haughty attitude toward other patients won her the nickname "Queen of the Hysterics." Consistent with his theory of the irreversible nature of hysteria, Charcot made no attempt to cure her, but continued to use her for demonstrations until her status slipped in favor of some new hysterical patients. She drifted from the Salpêtrière and a few years later wound up in another Paris hospital, where she manifested a completely different pattern of hysterical symptoms.* The *grande hystérie* that she had so successfully demonstrated had been little more than a figment of Charcot's imagination; hysteria was much too diverse a condition to be neatly packaged into major and minor *types*.

As Charcot became increasingly committed to his fanciful view of hysteria, he compounded his problems by adding *hypnotizability* to his list of major hysterical symptoms. His attention had been initially attracted to hypnosis by the observation that hypnotic phenomena and hysterical symptoms had much in common. Both conditions produced physical and mental anomalies that made little sense anatomically, and that seemed beyond the conscious volition of the subject or patient. Hypnosis produced paralyses, anaesthesia, or amnesia, and caused subjects to perform consciously inexplicable acts (post-hypnotic suggestions), just as hysteria did. Furthermore, Charcot discovered that his prize cases of *grande hystérie* could be induced to demonstrate their four stages of symptoms even more perfectly if they were hypnotized. Once hypnotized, the patients could also be led by direct suggestion to exchange or temporarily give up their symptoms. In spite of this finding, however, Charcot gave little thought to using hypnosis as a therapy for hysteria, since he believed hysteria to be ultimately incurable.

Instead, Charcot embarked on a peculiar research program into the nature of hypnosis itself. His assistants regularly hypnotized hysterical patients and presented them to Charcot for neurological examination. Charcot himself seldom if ever did any actual hypnotizing, and normal subjects were never em-

---

* There was a poignant ending to the story of Blanche Wittmann. After intensive psychotherapy at the new hospital she was cured of her symptoms. A few years later she returned to the Salpêtrière—not as a patient but as an assistant at the photography laboratory. With the invention of X-rays, whose hazards were not yet understood, she became one of the first victims of radiologist's cancer. After several years of multiple amputations and intense suffering she died. Despite the stresses of her final years she never reverted to her hysterical symptoms.

ployed. Despite these extraordinary limitations on his data gathering, Charcot convinced himself that hypnosis was a neurological condition *caused* by the hysterical degeneracy of the nervous system. Anyone who could be hypnotized was therefore said to be at least latently hysterical—even though Charcot or his followers did not try to hypnotize anyone who was manifestly normal!

Charcot went on to postulate a major *type* of hypnotism—*grand hypnotisme*—according to his usual diagnostic procedures. *Grand hypnotisme* was said to have three sequential stages, each with its own distinctive neurological properties. In the first stage, *catalepsy,* the subject became muscularly relaxed, motionless, and generally insensitive to external stimulation. *Lethargy* was the second stage, where the bodily muscles were generally flaccid, but could be temporarily activated into strong contractures and movements. In the third stage, *somnambulism,* complex automatic movements could be carried out upon suggestion. This stage was generally equivalent to the artificial somnambulism of the early magnetizers, but Charcot believed it was always produced by the neurological events of the preceding two stages. Not surprisingly, the individuals who best demonstrated the three stages of *grand hypnotisme* were those like Blanche Wittmann who also demonstrated *grande hystérie.*

In 1882, Charcot presented his formulation of *grand hypnotisme* to the French Academy of Sciences. In spite of the fact that the Academy had three times previously dismissed reports on magnetism or hypnotism, Charcot's neurologically-oriented theory appealed to the conservative biases of his audience and was enthusiastically received. Charcot thus succeeded in undoing the legacy of Mesmer by having hypnotism formally accepted by an official French scientific body. Ironically, it was precisely because of the mistaken and artificial neurological trappings of his theory that Charcot was successful in this effort.

One small group of investigators, however, remained justifiably skeptical of Charcot's theory. Led by Bernheim and a

Belgian physician named Joseph Delboeuf, the Nancy school began publishing rebuttals to Charcot. In contrast to Charcot, they had hypnotized literally thousands of subjects, and knew perfectly well that non-hysterical individuals were just as hypnotizable as hysterics. They also knew that the catalepsy and lethargy stages were not necessary predecessors to somnambulism. Delboeuf finally visited the Salpêtrière to observe personally the way experiments were performed there, and realized at once the extent to which the phenomena of *grand hypnotisme* were elicited by the blatant, if unwitting, suggestions emitted by the Salpêtrière experimenters.

At first impartial observers of the controversy favored Charcot, with his enormous personal prestige. But ultimately the greater merits of the Nancy position became clear to all, and toward the end of his life Charcot himself had the good grace to admit that he had been wrong. In disappointment, he began to question all his work on hysteria as well as hypnotism, and expressed the belief that his theories would not endure. He was correct. In 1893 the prediction of his anonymous tormentor came true, and he succumbed to a heart attack. Though the obituaries were laudatory, his reputation began to suffer almost immediately. People with widely differing theories took over the Salpêtrière, and six years after Charcot's death all that remained of *grande hystérie* was a small collection of his former patients who would re-enact full-fledged attacks if paid a small fee.

Yet, for all his scientific deficiencies, Charcot cannot be considered a failure. Quite apart from his early neurological achievements, he succeeded brilliantly in raising both hysteria and hypnosis out of obscurity and disrepute. Simply because of his own personal influence in the 1880s, other investigators were obliged to take notice. He attracted a wide variety of gifted students—prominently including Alfred Binet, William James, Pierre Janet, and Sigmund Freud—and while all of them went on to diverge considerably from Charcot's views, they remembered him with respect as a man who had illumi-

nated important problems for them. Indeed, it was as a problem *finder* rather than problem *solver* that Charcot made his
greatest contribution.

Largely as a result of Charcot's influence, the topics of hysteria, hypnosis, suggestion, and psychopathology in general
became fashionable among French intellectuals in the late
19th century. As with all fashionable ideas, they inevitably
were applied to contexts and situations different from those
in which they had been developed. Thus, it became obvious
to a number of investigators that hypnosis was intriguingly
similar to a number of other situations in which one individual exerts, or attempts to exert, influence over the behavior
of others. Principles of suggestion, hypnosis, or psychopathology suddenly seemed relevant to the explanation of many
aspects of social behavior in general.

Another prominent European social phenomenon of the
time was *crowd behavior*. A century of political and social turmoil had provided many examples of the bizarre behavior of
people in crowds suggested by the terms "craze" or "mob
hysteria." With the Nancy-Salpêtrière controversy so prominent at the same time, several observers naturally noted similarities between hypnotized subjects and people in crowds.
The most influential of these was an energetic and controversial Frenchman named Gustave Le Bon (1841–1931). His writings did much to set the patterns and the problems for the
newly emerging disciplines of social psychology and sociology.

Le Bon and the Psychology of Crowds

Born into an old and wealthy family, Gustave Le Bon had the
income and the leisure to permit the study of an extraordinarily broad range of personal interests. He became one of
France's most prolific and diverse authors. Following his graduation from medical school, he travelled in little-known parts
of central Europe, Asia, and North Africa. He was impressed
by the wide variations in what we would now call "national

character" among the groups he encountered, and described them in a half-dozen ethnographic books. On his return to France, he devised an instrument for measuring the cranial capacity of individuals, and proceeded to draw group and racial comparisons. While lost on a travelling expedition to Nepal he conceived, and subsequently developed, a photographic method for making accurate relief maps. He used the new method of "stop-action photography" to analyze the movements of horses, wrote a book on the training of horses, and developed new methods for the chemical analysis of tobacco. Around the turn of the century he published research on black light, and became embroiled in a brief (and unsuccessful) dispute with Nobel Prize winner A. H. Becquerel over priority for the discovery of radioactivity.

Only when he was past fifty did Le Bon begin to write about social psychological subjects, producing two highly popular and influential works on group behavior. Neither *The Psychology of Peoples* (1894) nor *The Crowd* (1895) treated its subject in anything like scholarly depth, but what the books lacked in scholarship was made up for by a vigorous prose style and sometimes outrageous manner of propounding opinions. Le Bon stated his hypotheses so boldly that they aroused instant responses in his readers—sometimes indignation, sometimes enthusiastic approval. At the same time, he raised issues that have continued to engage social psychologists for more than eighty years.

One of Le Bon's major ideas, first expressed in *The Psychology of Peoples* and repeated in *The Crowd,* was that the most fundamental social responses of any individual are the result of *unconscious* ideation and motivation. Citing the hypnotists' demonstrations of post-hypnotic amnesia and post-hypnotic suggestion, Le Bon pointed out that unconscious motivational factors are not restricted to hypnotic situations. Indeed, his experiences with the training of horses had convinced him that the most effective motivating ideas of *any* behavior were *always* unconscious. Thus a horse was never satisfactorily trained until the specific "ideas" of the proper responses had become completely automatic and unconscious. The horse's experience was parallel to that of a human being who focuses a great deal of conscious attention on his behavior as he is learning a task, but who performs it unconsciously and automatically after he has learned it well. According to Le Bon, the best learned and most effective motivating ideas always operate at an unconscious level, in man and horse alike.

Le Bon believed that the most important differences between national and cultural groups were those between their unconscious ideas. Certain tendencies in each cultural group were so basic and so pervasive as to be automatically assimilated by every member. They became so ingrained as to become unconscious, and beyond the reach of normal rational deliberation. Because of these unconscious national characteristics, Le Bon was deeply pessimistic about the prospects of real international harmony. Though members of different groups might be able to understand each other's *conscious* ideas and motives, the most important ones were unconscious and inaccessible to all parties. Thus international strife and warfare seemed inevitable.

In *The Crowd* Le Bon went on to discuss situations where the already limited amount of conscious control was abandoned even more completely so people behaved irrationally, like automatons. The prototype for these situations was the *crowd*, where people give up their individuality as well as rationality, and assume a kind of collective mind which impels them to perform all sorts of activities they would never dream of while alone.

According to Le Bon, one specific change that takes place in a crowd is that unconscious racial ideas become more dominant than usual: "It is . . . general qualities of character, governed by forces of which we are unconscious, and possessed by the majority of the normal individuals of a race in much the same degree—it is precisely these qualities . . . that in crowds become common property. . . . The heterogeneous is swamped by the homogeneous, and the unconscious qualities gain the upper hand." [11]

Many of the characteristics of crowds are reprehensible by

civilized standards. A crowd is "always intellectually inferior to the isolated individual," more impulsive, irritable, mobile, at the mercy of exterior exciting causes, credulous, intolerant, ingenuous, and conservative in its values.[12] But because crowd responses are more extreme than individual ones, crowds can also sometimes produce heroic or noble acts which individuals would be too timid to perform alone. Le Bon notes that history, especially in warfare, is made by the unconscious heroism of crowds: "Were peoples only to be credited with the great actions performed in cold blood, the annals of the world would register but few of them." [13]

Le Bon's analysis of why crowds behave as they do depended on three principles. First, he said the members of a crowd sense the power of their numbers and the anonymity of their individual selves. Their sense of power enables them to yield to instincts that would seem too dangerous to express in an isolated state. Their anonymity enables them to disregard the sense of personal responsibility that controls their responses as individuals.

Le Bon's second principle explaining the formation of crowds was the phenomenon of *contagion*—the fact that when people see others behaving in a certain way, they become more inclined to do so themselves. Apart from citing the obvious importance of contagion in the formation of crowds, Le Bon could not say much about its essential nature, or the reasons why it occurs. Recalling that the hypnotists had made deliberate use of contagion since the days of Mesmer's *baquet,* however, he classified it as a "hypnotic" phenomenon.

The introduction of hypnotic factors into his discussion led Le Bon to the third and most important determinant of crowd behavior: the enhanced *suggestibility* of an individual in a crowd. Once again he was unable to explain exactly *how* suggestibility was enhanced, but he referred to the physiological theories that had been propounded by people like Charcot to account for hypnosis:

The most careful observations seem to prove that an individual immerged for some length of time in a crowd in action soon finds himself—either in consequence of some magnetic influence given out by the crowd, or from some other cause of which we are ignorant—in a special state, which much resembles the state of fascination in which the hypnotized individual finds himself in the hands of the hypnotiser. The activity of the brain being paralyzed in the case of the hypnotised subject, the latter becomes the slave of all the unconscious activities in his spinal cord, which the hypnotiser directs at will. . . .

Such also is approximately the state of the individual forming part of a psychological crowd. He is no longer conscious of his acts. In his case, as in the case of the hypnotised subject, at the same time that certain faculties are destroyed, others may be brought to a high degree of exaltation. Under the influence of a suggestion, he will undertake the accomplishment of certain acts with irresistible impetuosity. This impetuosity is the more irresistible in the case of crowds than in that of the hypnotic subject, from the fact that, the suggestion being the same for all the individuals of the crowd, it gains in strength by reciprocity.[14]

After describing the general characteristics of the participants in crowds, Le Bon addressed himself to the problem of how crowd suggestibility can be acted upon and taken advantage of, the problem of *leadership*. The most effective leaders, he noted, tend to be unreflective themselves, and prone to strong and often irrational ideas:

The leader has most often started as one of the led. He has himself been hypnotised by an idea, whose apostle he has since become. It has taken possession of him to such a degree that everything outside it vanishes, and that every contrary opinion appears to him an error or a superstition. . . .

The leaders we speak of are more often men of action than thinkers. They are not gifted with keen foresight, nor could they be, as this quality usually conduces to doubt and inactivity. They are especially recruited from the ranks of those morbidly nervous, excitable, half-deranged persons who are bordering on madness. However absurd may be the idea they uphold or the goal they pursue, their convictions are so strong that all reasoning is lost upon them. . . . The intensity of their faith gives great power of suggestion to their words. The multitude is always ready to listen to the strong-willed man, who knows how to impose himself upon it. Men gathered in a crowd lose all force of will, and turn instinctively to the person who possesses the quality they lack.[15]

Le Bon went on to describe three particular techniques that are useful to a leader in conveying his faith and opinion to a crowd. First is simple *affirmation,* free of complicated reasoning or proof. The effective leader must always concisely accentuate the positive about his idea, denying any opportunity for doubt or careful consideration. Slogans and credos, which are easy to remember and direct in their appeal to belief and action, and which may be shouted repeatedly and in unison, are thus effective tools for crowd leaders.

A second technique of the effective leader is *repetition* of his message. The simple affirmations and slogans are repeated over and over again, until they finally join the ranks of the supremely powerful unconscious ideas:

At the end of a certain time we have forgotten who is the author of the repeated assertion and we finish by believing it. To this circumstance is due the astonishing power of advertising. When we have read a hundred, a thousand, times that X's chocolate is the best, we imagine we have heard it said in many quarters, and we end by acquiring the certitude that such is the fact.[16]

Third, effective leaders ensure that at least a few people are planted in their crowds beforehand who are positively disposed toward their messages. Because of the contagion effect, they can count on the fact that a "current of opinion" will be formed to spread the positive response much more widely. Needless to say, political leaders today still try to take advantage of this phenomenon by ensuring that they are greeted in public by enthusiastic crowds, preselected by "advance men." The preselected crowd's enthusiasm, they hope, will be transferred by contagion to their larger audience.

Note that Le Bon's crowd leadership techniques had a great deal in common with the techniques commonly employed by hypnotists. Hypnotists did not stop to explain to their subjects *why* symptoms should disappear, or memory should be lost, or any of the other hypnotic effects should occur.

They simply affirmed repeatedly and authoritatively that it would be so, and in due course their subjects accepted their suggestions.

In applying ideas about hypnosis and psychopathology to his analysis of group behavior, Le Bon instituted a tradition that was to persist for many years, and not only in France. From 1921 until 1964 the leading social psychological journal in the United States was entitled *The Journal of Abnormal and Social Psychology*. Because of the strong historical reliance of studies of groups upon previous studies of abnormal states like hypnosis and hysteria, the conjunction of "abnormal" with "social" did not seem at all unusual.

Today, journal titles no longer suggest the direct linkage between social and abnormal psychology, and many of Le Bon's assertions are known to be oversimplified or incorrect. Nevertheless, consider some of the research topics that are still of great interest to social psychologists, denoted by such names as "suggestibility," "persuasibility," "attitude change," "obedience," "leadership," "conformity," or "social facilitation." All of these current subjects pertain to how one person can influence the thought, feeling, or behavior of another, or how the behavior of an individual is altered when he finds himself in a group. Hundreds of experiments are performed and published annually in attempts to specify and quantify the variables involved in these processes. Though the terminologies and the specific details generated by these experiments are new, the *general* questions they try to answer were dimly discernible in Mesmer's time, and explicitly clear by the era of Bernheim, Charcot, and Le Bon.

Suggested Readings

Various aspects of the history of hypnotism are well presented in each of the following: Chapters 7 and 26 of Edwin G. Boring's *A History of Experimental Psychology*, 2nd ed. (New York: Appleton-Century-Crofts, 1957); Chapter 2 of Henri F. Ellenberger's *The Discovery of the Unconscious* (New York:

Basic Books, 1970); Frank Pattie's "A Brief History of Hypnotism" in Jesse E. Gordon, ed., *Handbook of Clinical and Experimental Hypnosis* (New York: Macmillan, 1967); and Chapter 9 of Gregory Zilbporg's *A History of Medical Psychology* (New York: Norton, 1967).

Sigmund Freud's impressions of Charcot are fully described in an obituary he wrote in 1893. Entitled "Charcot," it has been reprinted in Volume III of *The Standard Edition of the Complete Psychological Works of Sigmund Freud* (London: Hogarth, 1962). Freud also describes Charcot's role in the development of psychoanalysis in *An Autobiographical Study* (New York: Norton, 1963).

A general history of social psychology, which places much of the material from the present chapter in broader perspective, is Gordon W. Allport's "The Historical Background of Modern Social Psychology," in Gardner Lindzey and Elliott Aronson, eds., *The Handbook of Social Psychology,* 2nd ed., Vol. 1 (New York: Addison Wesley, 1968). Gustave Le Bon's *The Crowd* is available in paperback (New York: Viking Press, 1960).

6

Man in Conflict:
The Psychoanalytic Psychology
of Sigmund Freud

"But Doctor, I'm not asleep, you know; I can't be hypnotized." Those half apologetic, half taunting words rang in the ears of Sigmund Freud one afternoon in 1892.[1] They had just been uttered by one of his patients, whom he knew he could cure of her symptoms if only he could induce her to enter a state of deep hypnosis. Accordingly, the thirty-six-year-old physician had been repeating, over and over again, "You are feeling drowsy; your eyelids are getting heavier and heavier; soon you will be fast asleep."

The patient suffered from *hysteria,* a condition which baffled and irritated most nineteenth-century physicians, since its major symptoms were peculiar physical complaints which had no discernible physical basis. Some patients complained of paralysis, but thorough neurological examinations revealed no organic damage. Equally baseless were other hysterics' reports of blindness, deafness, anaesthesia (numbness), lameness, and numerous other sensory and physical symptoms. Many physicians were understandably tempted to dismiss hysterical patients as malingerers and fakers, since the bases of their complaints seemed so obviously imaginary.

Freud knew the situation was more complicated than that,

however. He had studied with the French neurologist Jean Charcot, who taught him that hysteria was to be taken seriously. As one of the few Viennese doctors who would deign to accept hysterical patients, Freud had learned that the symptoms had a subjective reality for the patients, even if objective physical causes were not evident to their physicians. Most patients were sincere in their complaints, and if they were malingering they themselves were unaware of the fact.

When Freud began his practice, there were few established therapies for hysteria. The most fashionable treatments bore the impressive sounding names *hydrotherapy* and *electrotherapy*. The former consisted of various kinds of baths, the latter of passing mild electric currents through the afflicted body areas. Freud quickly realized that the beneficial effects of these treatments were produced largely by *suggestion,* so he next sought something to make use of suggestion even more directly. He knew that members of the so-called "Nancy School" in France had been using hypnosis as a therapy for hysteria, and he visited their clinic to learn their techniques. These were very straightforward: patients were hypnotized and then given direct suggestions that their symptoms would disappear. Sometimes they did, and although relief was usually partial or temporary, hypnosis was clearly an improvement over hydrotherapy and electrotherapy.

Freud began using direct hypnosis on his own patients, with some success. Still not satisfied, however, he sought a more complete and permanent cure. In the course of his search he remembered a remarkable case that had been described to him several years previously by his older friend, Josef Breuer (1842–1925). Breuer was a prominent Viennese physician who seldom treated hysterics, but during the years 1880–1882 he had worked intensively with a single hysterical patient. After much experimentation he developed a technique that seemed to cure her completely.

The patient suffered from a whole array of hysterical symptoms, and Breuer discovered that he could remove them, one by one, if he hypnotized her and asked her while under

hypnosis to try to recall the first time she had ever experienced
a physical sensation similar to that produced by the symptom.
Invariably she gradually remembered a "forgotten" memory of
an emotion-laden experience. For example, one symptom was
contraction of the muscles around her eyes, forcing them into
a perpetual squint. When the patient was asked under hypnosis
to recall the first time the squint occurred, she remembered
an emotionally painful experience that had occurred while she
was keeping a vigil beside the bed of her desperately ill father.
She had been very worried about him, with tears in her eyes.
Suddenly her father roused himself into momentary consciousness and asked for the time. The patient, not wishing to betray

7. Sigmund Freud (1856–1939). *The National Library of Medicine, Bethesda, Maryland*

her concern, choked back her sobs and tried to look at her watch. Because of the tears it was necessary to squint.

As she newly recalled this painful scene, she re-experienced its entire emotional impact. Further, in the therapy she allowed herself the previously denied luxury of expressing the emotion openly. Following this emotional catharsis, the symptom disappeared. Breuer discovered that he could treat each of the other symptoms in the same manner, which he came to call the *cathartic method,* and gradually the patient was restored to health. Ironically, however, Breuer never treated another hysterical patient.

It was Freud who carried on with the cathartic method several years later, after recalling Breuer's description of it. When he tried it on his own patients he had generally good results, and concluded that a cure for hysteria was close at hand. It was clear, as he and Breuer phrased it, that "hysterics suffer mainly from reminiscences" [2]—not ordinary reminiscences, to be sure, but reminiscences of emotionally charged experiences that have been somehow forgotten and placed beyond the reach of normal consciousness. With hypnosis these memories could be recovered and the emotions associated with them fully expressed. It seemed that the emotional energy had been bottled up or "strangulated" as long as the memory was out of consciousness. Denied the normal path to conscious expression, the *emotional* energy had been converted into *physical* energy, and expressed itself as a physical symptom. When permitted access to consciousness, it expressed itself in the normal way and then dissipated.

The remarkable discovery that Freud and Breuer had made was that physical symptoms could be created by mental states. Accordingly, they gave the name *pathogenic* (disease-producing) *ideas* to those unconscious but emotion-laden memories underlying hysterical symptoms. And those mystifying symptoms, which had defied rational analysis for so long, were now shown to have a comprehensible cause and a straightforward cure. All the physician had to do was hypnotize his patient, and then. . . .

But there was the problem: while hypnosis offered a key to the cure of hysteria, not all hysterical patients could be hypnotized. Many patients did not respond to Freud's hypnotic induction by falling into a state in which their memories were exceptionally fluent. Instead, they remained puzzled, anxious, or even defiant: "But Doctor, I'm not asleep, you know; I can't be hypnotized."

Freud's eventual solution to this problem led directly to his most fundamental discoveries, and to the most revolutionary psychological system of the twentieth century. The solution did not emerge suddenly, however, nor was it simply the product of Freud's isolated genius. Developing over a period of several years, it owed a great deal to Freud's extremely rich intellectual and personal background.

Freud's Education and Early Career

Sigmund Freud was born on May 6, 1856 in the Moravian town of Freiberg. The family moved to Vienna in 1860, where Freud remained until 1938 when the rise of Nazism caused him to move to England shortly before his death. Freud's family constellation was unusual, in that his father was twenty years older than his mother, and had had two sons by a previous wife. One of these boys had a son of his own just before Sigmund was born. Sigmund was the first of eight children to be borne by his mother within a period of ten years. Thus he grew up as the oldest child within a large immediate household, but he also had half-brothers the age of his mother, and a nephew who was older than himself. It is likely that this rather unusual situation made Freud particularly sensitive to the vagaries of family relationships when he later formulated his theories.

As the oldest child in his immediate family, Sigmund became the unchallenged leader of his full siblings. He also did outstandingly well at school, prompting his family to give him the luxury of a room of his own where he could study undisturbed at night. And even though his father was a financially struggling wool merchant, Sigmund was always encouraged to buy books. Even as a youth he had high intellectual aspirations, reading history and philosophy omnivorously. He and a friend passed their spare time for several months teaching themselves Spanish, so they could read *Don Quixote* in the original and form a secret society whose communications could be in a language little known in Vienna.

Until his last year in secondary school, Freud's interests and abilities seemed to be drawing him toward a career in law or politics. During that year, however, he encountered an essay by Goethe on Nature, which suddenly awakened him to the attractions of science. Almost on the spur of the moment, he decided to indulge this new interest by enrolling in the medical school of the University of Vienna.

At the university, Freud encountered many outstanding teachers. For the first year or two the most influential of these was Franz Brentano (1838–1917), a philosopher who had just written a textbook on psychology. Brentano taught that motivational influences were extremely important in deter-mining the flow of thought, and that there were profound differences between the "objective" reality of physical objects and the "subjective" reality of private thought—both themes that would later emerge in more powerful form in psycho-analysis. Brentano also seriously considered the question of whether unconscious ideas exist, and though he concluded that they did not, many of his specific points were included in Freud's later, positive case. Brentano was a charismatic teacher; Freud briefly came under his spell and determined to take a degree in philosophy after completing his medical training. Soon he was dissuaded by the teaching of an even more influen-tial figure, however.

Ernst Brücke (1819–1892), director of Vienna's Physiological Institute and Freud's teacher of physiology, was later described by Freud as the person "who carried more weight with me than anyone else in my whole life." Brücke, together with his close friends Hermann Helmholtz, Émile du Bois-Reymond, and Carl Ludwig, had been a founder of the mechanist movement in physiology.* The mechanist point of view dominated Brücke's Institute, as workers tried first to determine the fine anatomical structure of the nervous system, and then to deduce how such structures interacted mechanically to produce physiological and even psychological phenomena. In the years following the successes of men like Helmholtz, it seemed only a matter of time until the "new physiology" would uncover all of the secrets of life. Freud was captivated by Brücke and the new physiology, and delayed his direct progress towards a medical degree so he could conduct research at the Institute. In 1880, he would happily have settled into a research career in physiology.

Such was never a real possibility for Freud, however. Jobs were scarce and low-paying to begin with, and pure science was still very largely the prerogative of the rich. Further, Freud was a Jew in an anti-semitic society that proscribed Jews from most official positions. His personal dilemma became acute in 1882, when he fell in love with Martha Bernays. Suddenly recognizing the need to earn enough money to marry and support a family, Freud reluctantly decided to leave the Institute and undertake the training to qualify him for a career in medical practice.

In choosing his specialty, Freud naturally inclined toward neurology and neuropathology, the fields most closely related to his neurophysiological work at the Institute. He studied under Theodor Meynert (1833–1893), the foremost brain anatomist in the world, and soon became an expert at diagnosing the effects of different kinds of brain damage. He did so well, that in 1885 he was awarded a fellowship to study for six months under the celebrated Jean Charcot in Paris. While there, Freud assimilated not only Charcot's teachings on organic neurological diseases, but also many of his views on hysteria and hypnosis.

---

* Several men whose works have already been described in earlier chapters played important roles in Freud's training. Among them were Brücke and Helmholtz (Chapter 3); Wernicke (Chapter 2); and Charcot and Bernheim (Chapter 5).

When Freud returned to Vienna and tried to convince his medical superiors of these views—particularly the notion that men as well as women could suffer from hysteria—he was not enthusiastically received. In fact, Freud felt that he was firmly, if unofficially, placed among the "opposition" by the Viennese medical establishment. He realized that he would have to make his way professionally largely through his own independent efforts, without much help from the power structure.

At first, Freud tried to specialize in cases of organic brain damage. He bolstered his reputation by writing extended works on cerebral palsy in children, and a small book on aphasia that critically discussed certain aspects of Wernicke's localization theory. Though these works were well received, there were simply not enough paying cases of organic neurological disease to support a young and unestablished physician, however great his promise. There were, however, patients with hysteria who could not get sympathetic treatment from other doctors, and Freud began seeing them to augment his income. Soon he was at the point described at the opening of this chapter, seeking a universally applicable substitute for hypnotism.

The Free Association Technique

Freud took the first step toward solving his problem by recalling an almost casual observation he had made on his visit to the Nancy clinic. A subject had been hypnotized, made to experience a number of the common hypnotic effects, and then wakened from the trance. Upon awakening, the subject had no recollection of what had occurred in the trance—a simple case of post-hypnotic amnesia. Freud had been surprised, however, when the hypnotist placed his hand on the subject's forehead and said, "Now you can remember." Immediately, the subject recalled the entire hypnotic experience in minute detail.

In reflecting on this experience, Freud reasoned that if

such a simple technique could work to help a subject overcome post-hypnotic amnesia, it might also work to help his
hysterical patients recall their forgotten pathogenic ideas. To
test his idea, he experimented with a *pressure technique* and
had patients lie on a couch with their eyes closed, but in a
completely normal waking state. Freud would then ask them
to try to recall the first time they had experienced physical
sensations like those of their symptoms. They then would begin
to articulate trains of recollections that inevitably stopped
somewhere short of the goal. At these points Freud pressed his
hand on the patient's forehead and confidently asserted that
important new memories would come to mind. On a number
of occasions new memories *did* emerge, and the chain of
reminiscences could be continued. Often, after repeated applications of this new technique, truly pathogenic ideas were recalled, with subsequent emotional catharsis and symptom
relief.

As time went by, Freud became increasingly subtle in his
use of the pressure technique. From the first it had been clear
that patients did not always respond to the pressure with
obviously relevant memories; instead, they sometimes reported
only vague and apparently irrelevant images or ideas. Initially
Freud dismissed these reports as unimportant, and felt he must
start the procedure all over again. Gradually, however, he
learned that even these vague responses were significant, and
ought to be listened to and used.

One crucial experience occurred when a patient responded
to the pressure on her forehead by reporting flickers and
flashes of light with a starlike quality. Freud was disappointed,
and assumed that she was simply experiencing phosphenes,
those flashes of light that often occur when pressure is placed
on a closed eye. He was almost ready to give up, when the patient said that the images had begun to assume geometrical
shapes—crosses, circles, triangles, etc.—that resembled Sanskrit
figures. Now intrigued, Freud asked her to recount any ideas
that came to mind in association to the figures. She said the
cross-like figures represented "pain," and a circular, sun-like

figure symbolized "perfection." This led to an emotional description of her own feelings of pain and lack of personal perfection. She said that she had been made to feel especially inadequate recently by reading an article, translated from the Sanskrit, in a spiritualist magazine. The experience of recounting this was cathartic and therapeutic for her. Thus her response to the pressure technique turned out to have been highly significant after all, and from several similar experiences Freud learned to pay attention to *everything* his patients said, even if it seemed unimportant at first.

Trial and error gradually convinced Freud that he did not really have to apply physical pressure to the forehead at all. He had only to encourage his patients to begin by thinking about their symptoms, letting their thoughts run completely free, and reporting to Freud everything that came to mind. The only essential rule was that nothing must be held back, even if it seemed stupid, irrelevant, embarrassing, or obnoxious. Everything was of potential importance.

Freud called this new technique *free association,* and discovered that it could be just as effective as hypnosis in recovering pathogenic ideas. Since it did not require hypnosis, to which some people were resistant, it could be used on anyone. Freud abandoned hypnosis altogether and began to rely exclusively on free association in his treatment of patients. The change was to have far-reaching implications, since the added subtlety of free association enabled him to see features of hysteria that had been masked by hypnosis. Among these were the phenomena of *overdetermination* and *repression,* and the importance of *sexuality* as a causative factor.

Overdetermination. From his patients' free associations, Freud quickly learned that the relationships between symptoms and their underlying pathogenic ideas were usually not simple. Instead of there being a single pathogenic idea for each individual symptom, there more commonly was a whole series of emotion-laden scenes associated with a single symptom. One of his patients, for example, suffered from hysterical twitching of her hands. Analysis revealed three strong pathogenic ideas associated with this symptom: memories of being badly frightened while playing the piano, of receiving a disciplinary strapping on the hands as a schoolgirl, and of being forced to massage the back of a detested uncle. As each of these previously forgotten memories was recalled, the symptom diminished somewhat in intensity. Freud's term for this phenomenon was "overdetermination," since the symptom was not determined by a single pathogenic idea, but *over*determined by several of them. Freud noted that the overdetermined symptom conveniently symbolized the three pathogenic ideas, which all had to do with the hands. He discovered that most symptoms were simultaneously overdetermined by, and symbolic of, several different pathogenic ideas.

Repression. Even more important than the discovery of overdetermination was Freud's gradual realization that unconscious pathogenic ideas had not been simply "forgotten" in the sense that unimportant details of experience are forgotten. He found that the pathogenic ideas had been actively and willfully—though perhaps not consciously—*repressed* by his patients. Pathogenic ideas were not so much a matter of patients' *not being able* to remember as of their *not wanting* to.

The evidence leading Freud to this conclusion was varied in nature, but unmistakable in its implication: patients often manifested *resistance* to the free association process and the uncovering of pathogenic ideas. The most obvious examples of resistance occurred just at points when the therapy seemed to be going most smoothly. The patient would be free associating, and Freud would feel sure that important pathogenic material was about to be recalled. Suddenly the patient would stop and say that his mind had suddenly gone blank or engage in some other behavior that served effectively to end the train of associations. He might say, with visible signs of anxiety and embarrassment, that what he had just thought of was too ridiculous to mention, or too personal to be shared. Another common example of resistance was a sudden shifting of the subject to Freud himself, perhaps a questioning of his medical credentials or the usefulness of his strange therapeutic technique. In short, patients used many different devices to avoid the uncovering of their pathogenic ideas. This avoidance or *repression* was thus shown to be a *motivated* state, since behavior protecting the repression tended to occur automatically when the free associations got too close to the pathogenic ideas. Freud also noted that much of the resistance seemed to be unconscious as well as automatic; patients often did not realize they were avoiding the issue.

Freud's discovery of unconscious resistance taught him an extremely important lesson because it indicated that his patients' true attitudes toward their illnesses were far from simple. On the one hand, they experienced real discomfort and distress from their symptoms, and genuinely wanted to be rid of them. The very act of seeking therapy was a sign of that. On the other hand, however, their resistances tended to undermine the progress of therapy. It was as if one conscious part of each patient wanted very much to be cured, while another unconscious part resisted therapy out of fear that the pain involved in a successful cure would be too great to bear. This was one of the first situations where Freud saw the importance of *conflict* in determining human behavior, where different aspects of an individual clamored for mutually exclusive goals. By the time he had fully developed his theories, Freud saw conflict as characterizing much more than just hysterical conversion symptoms.

The presence of conflict complicated Freud's therapeutic task greatly. He now had to try to ally himself with the positive, health-seeking attitudes of his patients against their unconscious resistances. In practice, this meant he had to warn his patients constantly to be on the lookout for resistances and to try to combat them. The patients were told explicitly that they would sometimes not want to continue their associations, but that those were precisely the times when it was most important and useful to do so. Usually the resistance could gradually be combatted and significant pathogenic ideas revealed if Freud worked hard and patiently to win the confidence of his patient.

Sexuality. As Freud gathered more experience in combatting resistance, he began to gain a clearer understanding of why it existed, and what it was really directed against. He found that patient after patient began eventually, after much resistance had already been overcome, reluctantly to produce associations of a *sexual* nature. Particularly frequent were recollections of sexual experiences dating from childhood, often of sexual mistreatment at the hands of parents or other close relatives. The patient with the hand twitch, for example, eventually revealed that the uncle whose back she had been forced to rub had attacked her sexually afterwards. Freud gradually concluded that all of his patients had pathogenic ideas of a sexual nature, which were the deepest and most important causes of the hysterical symptoms. As long as those sexual ideas remained repressed, the patient always remained at least potentially hysterical. Any therapy short of bringing the ideas to consciousness was destined to be imperfect at best.

At first Freud incorporated these ideas—prematurely, it would turn out—into the *seduction theory* of hysteria, which asserted that all hysterics had undergone sexual mistreatment as children. The memory of the event was supposedly so painful and embarrassing as to become repressed. Then, in later life, events which would normally have called the memory to consciousness were incapable of doing so because of the repression, and the patient experienced a symptom instead of the memory. Thus the patient with the hand twitch experienced an intensification of her symptom whenever she came into contact with her uncle. Instead of remembering the childhood seduction she experienced a symbolic physical pain. According to the seduction theory, the symptom was a *defense* against consciously recognizing a sexual pathogenic idea. Symptoms appeared in consciousness as the lesser of two evils, as unpleasant but less anxiety arousing substitutes for the repressed ideas themselves. The defensive function made symptoms valuable to the patient, and explained the presence of resistance in therapy. Hysteria thus came to be regarded by Freud as a *neurosis of defense.*

When Freud published his seduction theory of hysteria, its implausibility caused it to be regarded derisively in medical circles. His colleagues ostracized him and stopped sending him patients. What was worse, Freud himself gradually began to have doubts about certain aspects of the theory. In spite of the regularity with which his patients reported childhood sexual traumas, and the sincerity with which they believed in the reality of those events, often their stories did not quite ring true. Sometimes Freud was personally acquainted with the alleged seducing relatives, and he felt certain that they would never have actually done such things. Besides, the theory, if correct, indicated a much higher rate of perversion among parents in the general population than one might reasonably expect. In general, then, Freud came to suspect that the "memories" of sexual mistreatment produced by his patients were not true memories at all.

But what were they, if not memories? This question was to haunt Freud for several months. He could not believe that his entire theory of hysteria was useless. His therapy still was the most effective one available, and it still made sense to regard symptoms as defenses against pathogenic ideas of *some* type, even if they were not actual memories. Furthermore, sexuality must have been important in some way, or else why would so many patients report those scenes of childhood seduction in their free associations? The seduction theory was obviously wrong in some of its details, yet right in others. When Freud finally sorted out which aspects of the theory were valid, it was largely the result of a new series of investigations he had undertaken in the middle 1890s—investigations into the meaning and nature of dreams.

The Interpretation of Dreams

It is not known precisely how Freud first became interested in investigating dreams. Some of his teachers had speculated about the similarities between dreams and mental illness, and

his patients occasionally described their dreams in the course
of their free associations. It is known that Freud himself
frequently recalled his own dreams. In any event, some combination of circumstances finally led Freud to subject dreams
to free association. When he did, he discovered that they could
be analyzed and interpreted just as hysterical symptoms could,
and that they could be shown to have comprehensible
meaning.

Manifest and Latent Content. Freud found that dreams, once
subjected to free association, had two distinctively different
levels of content. On the one hand, there was the conscious
dream itself, as experienced and recalled by the dreamer. This
was a primarily visual hallucinatory experience, often frag-
mented and disjointed in its chronology and containing fan-
tastic or bizarre images. Freud referred to this as the *manifest
content*. The manifest content, of course, was the most immediate and obvious aspect of dream experience.

Though the manifest content was generally unintelligible,
Freud found that if it were subjected to free association a
series of ideas inevitably emerged that did make sense in terms
of the life experience of the dreamer. The manifest content
was like an hysterical symptom, inexplicable and mysterious
by itself, yet linked by a chain of associations to ideas of the
utmost personal significance. Since the ideas revealed by the
free associations made sense of the manifest content, Freud
concluded that they should be considered to constitute a second
level of dream content, which he labelled the *latent content*.

As Freud reflected on the relationships between the manifest and latent content of dreams, he was astonished to discover
how similar they were to the relationships between hysterical
symptoms and their pathogenic ideas. Resistance hindered the
uncovering of latent content, just as it hindered recognition
of pathogenic ideas. In dream after dream, even those of non-
hysterical individuals, free association led to tabooed and
anxiety-arousing ideas which encountered resistance. Just as in
treating hysterical patients, steps had to be taken to overcome
the resistance.

An example of this tendency to resist was illustrated by Freud's analysis of one of his own dreams. The manifest content contained a sequence in which a patient of Freud's was administered an injection of the substance propyl (a completely ridiculous medical procedure) by a colleague. Following the injection, Freud hallucinated vividly the letters and numbers constituting the chemical formula for the substance *trimethylamin*. On free associating to this nonsensical manifest content, Freud came up with the thought that at least it was not *he* who had administered the ridiculous injection. His colleague was therefore to blame for any unfavorable outcome of the case. This led further to the disagreeable recollection that his best friend had in real life performed an irresponsible surgical operation on the patient from the dream. The patient, legally under Freud's care, had almost died as a result. Thus the latent content contained reproaches against his best friend that Freud was reluctant to acknowledge consciously. Freud's associations to the hallucinated formula for *trimethylamin* culminated in yet another taboo topic when he reflected that trimethylamin may have been an organic chemical involved in sexual responses, and that his patient's illness was of a sexual nature. Sexuality thus appeared in dreams just as in hysteria.

Freud's analysis of this dream fragment, and many others like it, led him to hypothesize a distinctive mental process by which dreams must come into being. He labelled this process the *dream work,* and argued that it consisted of the three distinct components of *displacement, condensation,* and *concrete representation.*

The Dream Work. Free associations revealed that the manifest content of a dream, like an hysterical symptom, could be thought of as *symbolizing* in a relatively "safe" way ideas that were in themselves disturbing or anxiety arousing. The technical term which Freud used to denote this symbolic process was *displacement,* to suggest that the energy that would normally have been used to activate the unconscious, tabooed idea was "displaced" to a related but emotionally more neutral idea that came into consciousness instead. Displacement served a defensive purpose, and was a key dynamic principle underlying symptom and dream formation alike.

Still another similarity between dreams and hysteria lay in the fact that manifest dream images, like symptoms, were frequently overdetermined by several latent dream thoughts. Thus Freud's associations to the *trimethylamin* of his dream involved not only sexual chemistry, but also the recollection that he had had a conversation on that topic with the same best friend who had been implicated in the associations to the propyl injection. "Trimethylamin" was overdetermined in the sense of being closely associated with two separate latent trains of thought—one related to his conflicted feelings about his friend, the other to sexual ideas. In the case of dream analysis, Freud used the word *condensation* to describe such overdetermination. The idea suggested by the term is that several different latent dream ideas may "condense" onto a single manifest image.

A third characteristic of the relationship between manifest and latent content was also reminiscent of hysterical symptom formation. In both cases something that was initially an *idea*— a pathogenic idea or a latent thought—was expressed in an extremely concrete way. In hysteria the idea was converted into a physical ailment, in a dream it was translated into a concrete sensory image. In either case, a thought that was initially at the level of an abstraction came to be given concrete representation.

Primary and Secondary Processes. Freud's analyses clearly suggested that both symptoms and manifest dreams were the end results of emotionally charged ideas which had undergone three basic kinds of transformation processes: displacement, overdetermination-condensation, and concrete representation. An interesting point about these processes was that they all ran directly counter to the intellectual qualities normally associated with logical and mature mental functioning. In order to deal effectively and logically with the environment, it is necessary to think in explicit rather than allusive concepts, to employ concepts with precisely limited rather than surplus meanings, and to progress from concrete particulars to abstract generalizations in forming ideas. Thus, Freud discovered that there are two diametrically opposed modes of mental activity, one associated with dream and symptom formation, the other with rational thought. Since the latter is not present in childhood, but only acquired after several years of intellectual experience and training, Freud referred to it as the *secondary process*. The former seemed a more primitive, irrational mode of thought, which Freud thought was probably characteristic of the mental activity of an infant, and he referred to it as the *primary process*. Dreams and hysterical symptoms came to be seen as instances where mature, secondary process thinking is abandoned in favor of the primary process— where *regression* to earlier, more primitive modes of thinking takes place.

Freud noted one more contrast between the primary and secondary processes: the secondary process was directly accessible to consciousness, whereas the primary process was unconscious. The rational deliberation of a secondary process train of thought was subject to voluntary control, and always at least potentially available to awareness. Primary process thought, however, was not subject to voluntary or conscious control; dreams and symptoms both carried the subjective sensation of coming "out of the blue." *

Freud's conceptualization of the primary and secondary processes made him stand out markedly from the academic psychologists of his time. Those psychologists tended to limit their investigations to phenomena such as perception,

* Note that these primary process characteristics are not confined to "abnormal" phenomena such as dreams or symptoms, but also seem involved in artistic creativity. Artists and poets deal with *symbols* as their stock-in-trade, making their points by allusion in a manner similar to displacement. Artistic symbols are often interpretable on several different levels of meaning, like condensations in dreams. They also often give concrete representation to abstract ideas, and appear to the artists to originate unconsciously in flashes of insight coming from sources outside themselves.

memory, judgement, and learning, all of which were *conscious*, and aspects of Freud's secondary process. In fact, psychology was defined by the leading academicians of the time as "the science of conscious experience." Since Freud's theory of mental functioning extended beyond these conscious, secondary process activities to include the unconscious primary process, he referred to it as *metapsychology* rather than psychology.

Freud's metapsychological investigations were greatly facilitated by his discovery that dreams were explicable as primary process mechanisms, quite analogous to hysterical symptoms. Dreams were much more common than symptoms, and more easily available for analysis—especially since Freud himself was a prolific dreamer. So valuable was the study of dreams that Freud called it "the royal road to the unconscious." Among the discoveries it provided was the clue to the solution of the seduction theory dilemma.

The Wish Fulfillment Hypothesis. In the summer of 1895 the startling hypothesis occurred to Freud that *all dreams represent the fulfillments of wishes*. Precisely how he happened to think of this idea is unclear. It is far from a self-evident truth, of course, since many dreams on the surface seem to be anything but wish fulfillments. Nevertheless, by 1900, when his masterful *The Interpretation of Dreams* was published, Freud reported that he had thoroughly analyzed large numbers of dreams, and had never encountered one whose latent content could not be shown to contain a wish fulfillment.

Some of the dreams Freud described in *The Interpretation of Dreams* had been presented to him as challenges by people who were skeptical about his theory. For example, a woman who prided herself on being a superb hostess dreamed that she had been prevented from giving a dinner party because of lack of food in the house. In the manifest dream she had felt extremely disappointed, and upon waking she did not see how the dream could ever be interpreted as a wish fulfillment. Free association revealed a number of interesting facts, however. The woman was recently married, and very jealous of her husband's attention to other women. She was particularly worried about a woman who frequented her husband's place of business. She had been reassured, however, when her husband remarked that this woman was not really attractive to him because she was too thin for his taste. On the day before the dream, Freud's patient had met her potential rival, who remarked in a complimentary way that she hoped to be invited soon for dinner, since the dreamer always prepared such good meals that she stuffed herself. The dream's latent content now was clearly revealed as the wish that the other woman would remain in a slender, unthreatening condition.

In another apparently disconfirming dream, a patient dreamed of the death of a young nephew of whom she was very fond. This, of course, seemed the very opposite of a wish fulfillment. Her associations to the dream included recollections of the funeral of her nephew's older brother, of whom she had also been very fond and who had actually died some time earlier. She vividly remembered all of the other people who had attended the funeral, among whom was a former paramour who had rejected her, but to whom she was still attracted. The funeral was the last time she had seen him. Thus, the funeral in the dream became interpretable as a hypothetical situation in which she might see him again. The wish indirectly expressed by the very unpleasant manifest content was clear.

Having discovered that the most important latent ideas underlying dreams were wishes, Freud was brought to the following conclusion: dreams and hysterical symptoms were strikingly similar to one another in their essential structural qualities. Both symbolized anxiety-arousing unconscious ideas by allusion, both represented several unconscious ideas simultaneously by means of single images or symptoms, both gave concrete representation to ideas, and both were created unconsciously and involuntarily. The only major difference lay in their presumed causes: dreams were presumed to be caused by latent *wishes,* symptoms by traumatic sexual *memories.*

But it was precisely on this point that the seduction theory was manifestly wrong! The childhood sexual traumas "remembered" so regularly by Freud's patients had never occurred in reality. Here then was a potential solution to Freud's problem: since dreams and symptoms were so similar on other points, why not regard them as similar in their origins as well? The seduction scenes recalled by hysterical patients could then be seen not as actual memories, but as reflections of *wishes* of a sexual nature. The wishes ran counter to all of the civilized and consciously adopted values of the patients, and so had to be repressed. But they were real nonetheless, and they demanded at least partial and symbolic expression through the primary process mechanisms of hysteria.

With this new formulation of the cause of hysteria, Freud was forced to reconceptualize the nature of "reality." From the very beginning of his investigations of primary process phenomena he had been confronted with paradoxical relationships between appearance and reality. Hysterical symptoms had no objective cause, yet they were subjectively very real for their victims. Dreams obviously lacked external reality, yet they were just as vivid and compelling as real waking experiences. Now Freud recognized that the pathogenic ideas of his patients, which *seemed* like real memories and were taken even by the patients themselves to be real memories, were disguised wishes rather than accurate reconstructions of real events.

From these considerations Freud recognized that the human psyche responds to far more than just external reality. Under certain conditions, it responds to wishes as if they were objectively real, and produces mental events such as dreams or symptoms that have all the earmarks of objective "reality." Even in everyday waking life, wishes influence what is experienced as real. Consider two people walking down the same city street on a cold winter's day. One person is very hungry, the other very cold. These two people, while encountering the identical "objective" environment, experience it in very different ways. The hungry person will focus attention on those aspects of the environment which promise food—a restaurant or delicatessen, perhaps. The cold person will pay more attention to potential shelter, perhaps a subway station or a vacant taxi. Thus the subjective experience of the environment is determined by needs and wishes as well as the objective properties of the environment.

Freud concluded that all mental experience is made up of some combination of wishes and external reality. In different situations, the relative proportions of the two components may differ. Sometimes, as when one is being chased by an angry bear, the reality component is greatly superior and all of one's energy is devoted to dealing with it. In other situations, however, the wishful component may predominate to such a degree that the wish is mistaken for objective reality, and a primary process phenomenon may take place. In Freud's terms, wish and external reality combine for every individual, at every moment in time, to constitute a *psychic reality* which is the true motivator of behavior. To understand the behavior of another person, one must take into account that person's psychic reality. Once again Freud had noticed the importance of conflict in human behavior: just as the course of therapy was determined by the clash between the resistance and the conscious desire to get well, so was the psychic reality of an individual found to be determined by the conflict between wishful and reality-oriented factors.

Freud's Self-Analysis

After resolving the difficulties with his theory of hysteria, Freud had to do some difficult thinking about the nature of human motivation. He had uncovered evidence that his patients—most of whom were outwardly proper and morally virtuous—secretly and unconsciously harbored sexual fantasies and wishes that could hardly be acceptable in society at large. Furthermore, these wishes seemed to date back so far as to indicate a *childhood* interest in sexuality. Previously, Freud had shared the common nineteenth-century belief that the sexual instinct was normally dormant in human beings until puberty. Thus his initial hypothesis must have been that hysterics were individuals who suffered from an abnormally precocious sexuality, who experienced strong sexual impulses in childhood and as a result were more predisposed than their peers to hysteria in adulthood. The real causative agent in hysteria then could be seen as a physiologically-based deviation of the sexual system.

He quickly realized that such an hypothesis was untenable, however appealing it might have seemed. His immediate reason for rejecting it was an intensely personal and painful one. From 1896 to 1898 Freud submitted *himself* to a thorough analysis, free associating to his own fantasies, dreams, and overt behavior. As a result of this self-analysis, Freud was forced to conclude that he too, just like his hysterical patients, was subject to consciously unacceptable sexual wishes dating from childhood.

The self-analysis began shortly after the death of Freud's father in the autumn of 1896. Though the death of his old and ill father was not unexpected, Freud discovered that he was much more shaken by the event than he had expected to be. He wrote to a friend that he felt "as if I had been torn up by the roots," [3] and later he was to remark that the death of a father is "the most important event, the most poignant loss, in a man's life." [4] For many months after his father's death Freud was plagued by anxiety, depression, and an inability to work. The severity of his symptoms finally led him to regard himself as a patient, and he undertook his self-analysis by free associating to his symptoms and dreams. The associations were very disturbing.

The interpretation of a childhood dream was a major part of Freud's self-analysis. The memory of the dream had always remained vivid, and sometimes parts of it returned to haunt his adult dreams. He described the childhood dream as follows: "I saw my beloved mother, with a peculiarly peaceful, sleeping expression on her features, being carried into the room by two (or three) people with birds' beaks and laid upon the bed." [5] This turned out to be a highly condensed manifest dream image, since free association yielded a welter of significant latent thoughts. First, it became clear that the dream was about death. The beaked figures were reminiscent of some pictures of Egyptian funerary gods that Freud had seen in the family Bible. Further analysis revealed that the peculiar expression on his mother's face was not really characteristic of *her,* but was identical to one he had seen on his *grandfather's* face shortly before his death. The reclining figure, then, was a type of condensation referred to as a *composite figure,* where a single dream character takes on the features of two or more real individuals and symbolizes them all at the same time. The figure represented both his mother and his dying grandfather. From the image combining his mother and dying grandfather, it was but a short associative step to the thought of a dying *father,* and Freud was forced to acknowledge that one of the important latent wishes expressed in the dream had been for the death of his father. He realized with a shock that he must have harbored unconscious hostile wishes toward his consciously loved father as far back as early childhood.

The unpleasant dream interpretations did not stop here. Further associations showed that the dream had clear *sexual* allusions as well. Freud recalled that the German slang verb for sexual intercourse (*vögeln*) was derived from the word for bird (*Vogel*). Furthermore, he had first learned the slang term from a slightly older friend named *Phillip,* and the family Bible implicated in the images of the beaked figures was an edition of the Old Testament known as *Philippson's Bible.* The worst was still to come: having determined that a sexual wish must be expressed by the dream, Freud was forced to the conclusion that the object of his childhood sexual wish must have been his mother. Though as a young boy he had only imperfectly understood the nature of adult sexuality, he had been clearly aware that it involved great sensual delight. He also had seen his mother as the most desirable source of sensual pleasure that he could understand. Thus, in all honesty, Freud had to classify the latent dream ideas about his mother as sexual in nature.

The Oedipus Complex. Freud's childhood dream image was thus revealed as complicated condensation representing two repugnant but nevertheless deeply felt wishes: the wish for for the father to be dead, and for the mother to be available as a sexual object. The concepts of death and sexuality did not have quite the same meaning for a young boy that they have for an adult, since, for a child, the primary meaning of death was simply the *absence* of someone, and sexuality entailed any kind of sensual, physical gratification. Nevertheless, Freud was compelled to admit that the feelings expressed in his dream had been the obvious precursors of the adult concepts of death and sexuality.

Other aspects of Freud's self-analysis confirmed his discovery that these feelings had been present in childhood, and further suggested that many aspects of them persisted into adulthood. Part of his peculiar reaction to his father's death was explained because the death was the fulfillment of a longstanding childhood wish. Such a wish was understandably regarded as intolerable by the conscious side of his personality. A severe conflict therefore developed and resulted in his symptoms.

Although uncovering these childhood wishes was agonizingly painful for Freud, he finally saw that he was not particularly unusual or deviant for having had them. To the contrary, he discovered that *anyone* who subjected himself or herself honestly to analysis would discover traces of similar wishes. His hysterical patients' "seduction memories" were now seen as examples of incestuous wishful fantasies. Furthermore, analysis of the dreams and behaviors of "normal" people, as well as the consideration of a number of common myths and legends, convinced Freud that the desire to sexually possess the opposite-sexed parent and to be rid of the same-sexed parent (the chief rival for the affections of the opposite-sexed parent) was a virtually universal consequence of childhood experience. Since the great Greek play *Oedipus Rex* portrayed a situation where these childhood wishes were fulfilled, (the hero,

Oedipus, unwittingly killed his father and married his mother), Freud named this universal constellation of wishes the *Oedipus complex*.

Further investigation showed Freud that the Oedipal wishes and fantasies were far from the only objectionable residues of childhood. Often, associations emerged concerning activities of the mouth or the anus which, from an adult point of view, could only be regarded as disgusting or perverted. Freud concluded that these too represented wishes dating from childhood—wishes that were regarded with horror by the conscious, adult side of the personality, but that continued to press unconsciously for expression via the primary process mechanisms. As a result of these discoveries Freud was led to a new and revolutionary view both of childhood and of sexuality, a view that was in direct opposition to the prevailing ethos.

Theory of Childhood Sexuality

The predominant late-nineteenth-century view held that childhood was a time of purity and innocence, with corruption coming only later through the iniquities of adult society and the physical coarsening of biological maturation. The sexual instinct was assumed to be totally absent in children, making its first appearance at puberty. Furthermore, the instinct was assumed to be very specific in nature when it did appear, impelling the individual to a single goal: the propagation of the species through "normal" heterosexual intercourse.

Freud's evidence from free association suggested that these views were incorrect on all counts. The existence of the fantasies of the Oedipus complex suggested that much of the mental life of a young child was very primitive and savage in nature, containing aggressive and anti-social impulses as well as sexual ones. Furthermore, childhood sexuality seemed not only to exist, but also to be a much broader kind of sexuality than the "normal" adult kind, including types of gratification that were regarded as highly deviant from an adult perspective.

Freud accounted for his surprising findings with a completely new conceptualization of the sexual instinct, hypothesizing that it exists in substantial strength from birth onwards. Far from being a highly specific drive toward a very restricted form of heterosexual gratification, however, it was a *generalized* striving, potentially capable of gratification in a multitude of different ways. The essence of sexuality was a general desire for physical, sensuous pleasure of *any* kind, with genital stimulation being only one variety.

Freud described the newborn infant as being *polymorphously perverse;* that is, capable of taking sexual (that is, sensuous) pleasure from the gentle stimulation of literally any part of the body. In the course of early development certain types of stimulation occur more easily and frequently than others, thus singling out certain parts of the body, and certain types of stimulation, as the most important vehicles for gratification. Particularly important for the infant and young child are the oral and anal zones, both of which receive regular, gentle stimulation through the acts of sucking and defecation. A little later, as the child develops more control over his own body, the pleasure derived from stimulating the genitals becomes salient.

In addition to these physical developmental variables, *social* considerations also have a bearing on the sexual instinct. Many kinds of sexual gratification are viewed as highly inappropriate by the child's parents, who restrict him accordingly through such practices as toilet training, or by punishment for the act of masturbation. The child gradually learns that only a relatively small number of gratifications are permitted. As a result of all these pressures and influences, the originally undifferentiated sexual instinct becomes more and more channelled, more and more prescribed in its manifestations. By adulthood, it usually reaches the highly specific form of genital heterosexuality.

Here then was the explanation for the Oedipal fantasies and perverted manifestations of childhood sexuality as revealed in free association. They were traces of "naive" sexuality, of the sexual instinct from the time before it had been molded into the final adult form. Children naturally experience and manifest taboo sexual impulses because they have not yet learned that they are inappropriate. When they do, they become "civilized" and consciously abandon their childish means of sexual gratification. The traditional picture was thus precisely wrong. Children are not innocents who become corrupted sexually by the evils of the world; rather, they are born with undisciplined and "perverted" tendencies that they learn to curb only as they mature and become civilized.

As Freud conceptualized the typical course of sexual development, he concluded that the unruly childish sexual impulses reach a peak at about the age of five. At that point the opposite-sexed parent has been clearly identified as the most desirable person for satisfying the impulses, and the same-sexed parent as the most formidable rival for that gratification. This gives rise to a desire to possess the one parent, and to be rid of the other; thus the Oedipus complex is born. The complex brings much internal conflict for the child, however, because the same-sexed parent is seen not only as a rival, but also as a much more powerful individual. Just as the child has negative wishes toward the parent, so he fears the parent may have negative inclinations toward him. Since the parent is so much stronger, there is no doubt in the child's mind about who would win any battle between them. Therefore the Oedipal wishes themselves come to be perceived by the child as dangerous because they threaten to cast him into a battle he has no hope of winning. His wishes have come into conflict with the harsh demands of external reality.

The only resolution of this conflict available to the child is to *repress* the Oedipal wishes, to force them into a state of unconsciousness so that they will never come to mind to arouse anxiety. All vestiges of childhood sexuality, associated as they are with the Oedipal impulses, disappear from consciousness. The child now enters what Freud called the *latency period,* which lasts until the physical maturation of puberty re-awakens the sexual drive. During the latency period, the child is largely freed from the preoccupations and anxieties generated by the sexual instinct, and is optimally predisposed to undertake the relatively "neutral" learning tasks imposed, generally at school, by society.

But the wishes and impulses characteristic of childhood sexuality have not been destroyed, merely repressed. They persist into adulthood, remaining just beneath the surface of consciousness and seeking whatever indirect and disguised forms of expression they can find. Dreams provide a "normal" outlet, and so manifest themselves in nearly everyone. Hysterical symptoms represent a more unusual and more maladaptive solution to the same problem, though the mechanisms in both cases are similar. Repressed childhood sexuality provides the unconscious latent content or pathogenic ideas, which in turn receive partial and symbolic gratification through the mechanisms of the primary process.

Freud thus came to see dreams and symptoms alike as reflections of conflicts that are inevitable in human experience —conflicts between childishness and maturity, between instinct and society, between wish and reality. As he developed his theory further, such conflicts and their attempted resolution came to seem to him the most crucial feature of human psychology.

Psychoanalytic Psychotherapy

Even as Freud extended his investigations into such phenomena as dreams and the psychological development of the child, he continued to make his living as a practicing psychotherapist. Like his theoretical work, his therapy underwent considerable change and development over the years.

At first, with the discovery of free association, the therapeutic task had seemed relatively simple and straightforward to Freud. All he had to do, it seemed, was encourage his patients' free associations until their repressed pathogenic ideas were brought to consciousness. Then the symptoms that had previously symbolized those ideas would be unnecessary and would disappear. Freud quickly discovered, however, that his patients' *resistances* were formidable barriers to the quick and easy accomplishment of this goal. As he gained increasing knowledge of the multifarious ways in which unconscious motives could hinder treatment, he realized that complete "cures" were almost impossible to accomplish, and that even modest improvement was often to be won only with considerable difficulty.

One particularly instructive case was "Dora," an eighteen-year-old woman brought to Freud by her father in late 1900, following her suicide threat. She suffered from some mild hysterical symptoms, and because of her lively intelligence seemed an ideal candidate for Freud's therapy. She took quickly to free association, and seemed to understand Freud's interpretations of her associations in terms of infantile sexuality. Her symptoms began to improve after only a few sessions, and Freud wrote confidently to a friend that "the case has opened smoothly to my collection of picklocks." [6] His optimism was premature, however, as Dora was soon to terminate the therapy before it could be successfully completed. With hindsight, Freud was able to analyze the case and understand why she had done so, and why the general therapeutic task was so much more complicated than he had previously thought.

The Case of Dora. Dora's problems stemmed from her relationships with her parents and their closest friends, a neighboring couple referred to by Freud as "Herr and Frau K." Her father was a personable man who suffered from poor health and often required extensive nursing. Her mother was a drab woman, more interested in housekeeping than in nursing, who showed little warmth toward either Dora or her father. The nursing tasks came to be taken on more and more by Frau K., and as Dora entered adolescence she realized that her neighbor had become her father's mistress as well as his nurse. Herr K., a handsome but passive man who made no fuss about his wife's liaison with his friend, contented himself with amorous adventures with his servants. He also occasionally turned his attentions to Dora as she became an attractive young woman. He bought her gifts, including an expensive jewel-case, and once attempted to kiss her. The kiss disgusted Dora, who was repelled by the strong smell of tobacco smoke on his breath.

This sordid situation reached a climax in the summer before Dora's treatment with Freud, when her family and Herr and Frau K. shared a vacation house. Herr K. proposed directly to Dora on a walk around a lake, complaining emotionally, "I get nothing out of my wife." Dora retreated indignantly, but said nothing to her parents. Every night for two weeks afterwards she had a vivid and unpleasant dream. Then she announced that she would stay in the vacation house no longer, but would accompany her father on a business trip. When she did, and told him about Herr K., her dream ceased, but she began to suffer from hysterical symptoms. They worsened, until finally her father brought her to Freud for help.

After Dora had been in analysis a short time, her dream began to recur. Freud naturally asked her to free associate to it, and her fluent and easily comprehensible responses were among the reasons he felt so optimistic about the case. The dream's manifest content was brief: "A house was on fire. My father was standing beside my bed and woke me up. I dressed myself quickly. Mother wanted to stop and save her jewel-case; but father said: I refuse to let myself and my two children be burnt for the sake of your jewel-case. We hurried downstairs, and as soon as I was outside I woke up." [7]

Dora's free associations revealed a latent content full of complicated and conflicting emotions. Herr K. was strongly involved through associations to the jewel-case and to the fire, which suggested the tobacco smoke Dora had smelled on his breath. She also recalled that she had always dressed herself quickly while at the vacation house—as in the dream—because her bed was in an exposed hall and she had feared that Herr K. would see her in a state of partial undress. The fire also represented the sexual stirrings that Dora naturally was beginning to feel as a young woman. In general, then, the dream expressed a certain amount of attraction to Herr K., as well as the conflicting feelings of fear and repugnance that he elicited.

Consistent with Freud's theory, there were also clear allusions to *childhood* sexuality. The fire led to associations to water, which, in combination with the other sexual allusions, recalled childhood memories of bedwetting and masturbation. When Dora remarked that her father had used to wake her at night and take her to the bathroom to prevent her incontinence, Freud felt sure he understood the real meaning of the dream, and the wish it expressed.

According to his interpretation, the dream replaced Dora's current and conflict-laden attraction for Herr K. with her earlier, Oedipal attraction for her father. As Freud expressed it, "She summoned up an infantile attraction for her father so that it might protect her against her present affection for a stranger." [8] The *wish* expressed by the dream was to run away with her father, to be protected by his reassuring company from the disturbing impulses of her maturing sexuality. In fact, she shortly fulfilled this wish in reality when she went with him on his business trip. Significantly, the dream then ceased to occur.

Freud had reason to feel satisfied with this clarification of Dora's emotional life. But, he later realized, he failed to carry the dream's analysis as far as he should have. For while the interpretation explained why the dream had occurred while Dora was at the vacation house, it did not explain its reappearance in the middle of her analysis with Freud. The answer to this question became clear toward the end of the third month of treatment, when Dora suddenly announced that she would return no more. Though her therapy had made great progress, it was far from completed. Freud was initially stunned by her abrupt departure.

He shortly realized that Dora had warned him of her intentions, though he had failed to interpret her message. The dream had not recurred in the middle of treatment to express Dora's complicated feelings toward *Herr K.,* who was no longer a major figure in her real life, but toward *Freud* instead. On reflection, Freud could see that he had been implicated in Dora's free associations just as strongly as Herr K. He was himself a heavy smoker, and one of the expressions he frequently used to encourage his patients' associations was "There can be no smoke without fire." While his intentions were not dishonorable like Herr K.'s, he had talked openly with Dora about sexual subjects that must inevitably have aroused disturbing impulses in her. Thus the dream was useful once again for Dora to express her fear of emotional or sexual entanglement with another older stranger, and her wish to flee to the relative safety of her father. Just as she actually fulfilled that wish the first time, so she did again by withdrawing from therapy.

Transference. From this experience with Dora, and from similar if less dramatic interactions with other patients, Freud learned an extremely important lesson about the relationship between himself and his patients. Inevitably, he found, his patients would manifest what he called *transference* feelings; that is, they would transfer onto *him* motives and attributes that were characteristic of important people from their past lives, people who were implicated in the feelings that originally gave rise to their neuroses. Regardless of what Freud was objectively like, his patients' fantasies created a psychic reality where he could become like mother, father, or some other emotion-laden figure such as Herr K.

Freud realized that the transference phenomena greatly complicated his therapeutic task. As with Dora, they could all too easily become part of the resistance. They dictated that Freud and his patients would have to pay just as much attention to the present relationships between themselves as to the uncovering of the patients' past pathogenic experiences.

With this discovery, individual symptoms came to seem much less important to Freud. He realized that they were simply one, relatively superficial, manifestation of *underlying emotional conflicts* that express themselves in a great variety of ways, including dreams, the transference, or a variety of different symptoms. The disappearance of an individual symptom was relatively insignificant, because the symptom was not an independent entity. The conflict that had given rise to it could always re-express itself in dreams or transference feelings, or give rise to a completely new symptom. The whole situation was so fluid that any hope of permanent relief required the analysis of the entire complex of underlying unconscious ideas.

Freud now believed that really effective therapy could seldom be accomplished in a short time, since the analysis of complete underlying complexes was likely to require months or years. He also now believed that the best criterion for deciding when an analysis was complete lay in the transference situation rather than in the state of the symptoms. Both the symptoms and the transference reflected the same underlying conflicts, but the transference was much closer to hand for constant scrutiny by the therapist. When Freud could clearly discern that a patient was beginning to respond to him more as he really was, and less as if he were a shadowy figure from the past, he could feel confident that the long analytic task was finally nearing an end.

In the end, then, Freud did not provide the quick and specific cure for hysterical symptoms that he had originally sought. Instead, he had discovered a rather difficult process that could offer patients a large degree of self-knowledge, one consequence of which was the disappearance or diminution of their need for their symptoms.

Model of the Mind: The Id, Ego, and Superego

Throughout his career, Freud always sought to place his clinical discoveries within a wider theoretical context. He continually asked himself about the nature of the structures and functions that must exist within the human organism—presumably in the brain—to produce psychological phenomena. In short, he sought to construct a theoretical model of the mind itself. In the course of his long career, he wrote several works with this end in view.

His earliest attempts, in the 1890s, were as much neurophysiological as psychological in nature. Consistent with his mechanistic training at Brücke's Institute, Freud attempted to describe neurological structures and mechanisms that could account for dreams and hysterical symptoms, as well as normal waking thought processes. The result was a long draft manuscript in 1895 that Freud never edited for publication, but that his editors published posthumously under the title *Project for a Scientific Psychology*.

Though the writing of the *Project* was an extraordinarily useful experience for Freud, and led to many novel and valuable ideas, the neurological framework imposed many unnecessary constraints on his theorizing. The nervous system was not understood well enough to allow him to specify in sufficient detail which neurological mechanisms were responsible for which psychological responses. Thus, Freud adopted a new strategy. Rather than allowing himself to be distracted by neurological technicalities, he decided to express his theory in completely psychological terms. He tried to keep his concepts *consistent with* all available neurological knowledge, and he retained most of the key ideas of the *Project,* only now cast in non-neurological terminology. He remained confident that future neurological research would discover the precise mechanisms underlying his hypothesized psychological processes. For the present, however, he decided he could make much better progress by remaining on strictly psychological grounds.

Freud's last and most definitive psychological model of the mind was published in 1923, in *The Ego and the Id,* where he introduced his now-famous division of the mind into *id, ego,* and *superego.* Consistent with his clinical work, the mind according to this conception was pre-eminently an organ responsible for the resolution of conflict.

According to Freud's conception, the human mind is constantly beset by three different kinds of demands that usually conflict with one another, and require some sort of compromise solution. First, there were the demands arising from within the body itself—the biologically-based needs for nourishment, warmth, physical or sexual gratification, etc. Freud referred to these biological demands—which can never be avoided or run away from—as the *instincts*. The second major class of demands come not from within the body, but from the world of external *reality*. The environment constantly imposes stimulation on the human organism that requires some sort of adaptive response—dangers to be fled from, instinct-gratifying objects to be sought, etc. Obviously, there occur countless occasions when instinctual demands and the constraints of reality come into conflict, where instinctual gratification must be delayed, modified, or abandoned altogether because of the realities of the world. Conflicts between instinctual wishes and reality, of course, were a major preoccupation of Freud's when he developed his early theories of dreams, hysteria, and the primary and secondary processes.

By the time he wrote *The Ego and the Id*, Freud realized that *moral demands* constituted a third category of the mind's burdens, because he had observed numerous occasions when moral considerations came into conflict with both instinctual wishes and objective reality. Often individuals refrained from performing instinctually gratifying acts for reasons of conscience, for example, even when there was no overtly inhibiting force in the objective environment. At other times, moral demands caused an individual to ignore or violate the demands of external reality, as when a person risked his or her life to help another. Moral demands thus can, and often do, motivate a person in ways quite independent of the demands of reality and the instincts. Any complete model of the human psyche must make room for them.

In the new model of the mind, Freud conceptualized a psychic agency to account for each of these three parties to human conflict. He suggested, first, that there is a part of the psychic apparatus which can be called the *id*, that responds directly to the instincts. The id stores all of the wishes and impulses that arise in direct consequence of the organic needs of the body.

Second, there is a *perceptual system*, which conveys sensations from the external world into the psyche. Through this perceptual system, located at the boundary between the mind and external world, the demands made on the organism by external reality come to be recognized.

Third, Freud postulated a moral agency within the psyche, which he called the *superego*. Whereas both the id and the perceptual apparatus give the psyche access to energies from outside itself, the superego is contained wholly within the psychic system. The arrangement of these three agencies is suggested by Figure 6–1.

As is also indicated in Figure 6–1, the *ego* is located squarely in the middle of the psychic apparatus. This central location suggests that it is here where the demands of instinct, reality, and conscience converge and conflict. It is in the ego where mental work must be done to resolve the conflicts as much as possible, and to decide on appropriate courses of action. Inevitably, the ego's first task in reconciling contradictory demands is to inhibit the overly hasty satisfaction of

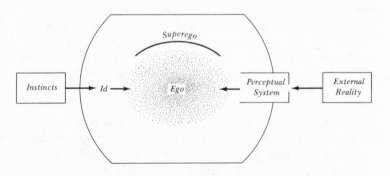

Figure 6–1 *Freud's Model of the Mind*

241

any one of them. Then, after achieving a temporary delay in the action, the ego must produce some kind of *compromise* action that will be at least minimally acceptable to all sides.

Toward the end of his career, Freud analyzed in increasing detail the kinds of compromises produced by the ego. It became clear to him that everything a person does is the result of some sort of compromise among the many conflicting demands upon his psyche. Sometimes the compromises favored one conflicting demand over the others, and they varied in their adaptiveness for the individual. But all human behavior seemed some sort of compromise response to conflict of some type.

One class of compromises were the primary process phenomena such as dreams and hysterical symptoms which had attracted Freud's attention as a young man. These occurred when the ego was relatively weak, and were rather extreme forms of compromise in which the constraints of external reality were largely ignored. The wishful pressures of the id were not completely victorious even here, however, since the pathogenic ideas and latent thoughts received disguised rather than overt expression as a result of superego pressure. The wishes in their pure form were unacceptable from a moral standpoint, and hence distorted before being expressed. Thus dreams and symptoms are compromises effected by a relatively weak ego that permits reality to lose out, and id impulses to receive symbolic expression after being modified to suit the superego demands.

Defense Mechanisms. Another important group of compromises detected by Freud directly influence the normal waking behavior of everyone, and are referred to as the *defense mechanisms*. Defense mechanisms come in many varieties, and different individuals tend to use different combinations of them. The one certain fact, however, is that everyone uses them constantly to deal with ever-present and inevitable conflicts. Among the common defense mechanisms are displacement, projection, intellectualization, denial, and rationalization.

The prototype for the defense mechanism of *displacement*

is the displacement observed in dreams and hysteria. When displacement is used as a defense mechanism, an impulse is acted out in real life toward a substitute person who resembles the original target in some way, but is "safer." Many men marry women who resemble their mothers, for example, and many women marry men who resemble their fathers. In these cases, according to Freud, the spouses are selected in part because of this resemblance. Such choices allow displaced gratification of Oedipal impulses by providing a love object who is similar to one's opposite-sexed parent, but who does not arouse the same anxiety in the role of sex object. Displacement also occurs when people "take out" their anger on inappropriate but "safe" targets, such as family members or pets, after initially being made angry by more dangerous people such as bosses or policemen. Aggression, rather than sexuality, is displaced in this case.

Projection is a common defense mechanism through which unacceptable impulses of one's own are attributed to someone else. Individuals may experience hostile feelings toward others, but be unable, because of superego demands, to admit that they are angry. They may solve this dilemma by unconsciously projecting their own anger onto the other person, arriving at the conscious perception that the other person is hostile toward them. Projection is especially common in wartime, when multitudinous evil impulses are commonly attributed to the enemy, but steadfastly denied on one's own side.

In *intellectualization,* an impulse-ridden area is approached in a purely intellectual way. Thus sexual impulses may result in a great *intellectual* interest in the subject of sexuality, without any overt sexual activity being performed. Many adolescents attempt to deal with their budding sexual feelings in this way, often achieving some useful knowledge in the process.

Some defense mechanisms permit the overt gratification of an impulse, but then alter the *memory* of that gratification so that anxiety is not experienced. A rather primitive defense mechanism of this type, common in children, is *denial.* In

243

denial, a person behaves as if something had never happened. Two fighting children, upon detecting the approach of an adult, may suddenly begin behaving in a completely cooperative and sociable way. Even after the departure of the adult they may continue to deny successfully the aggressive impulses they had been openly expressing only moments before. A rather more sophisticated version of denial, frequently practiced by adults, is *rationalization*. Here the person may act because of one motive, but explain the behavior on the basis of another. To be successful as defense mechanisms the rationalizations must be believed by the rationalizers themselves.

Sublimation is a psychic compromise similar to the defense mechanisms, occurring when the energy from an instinct is channelled by superego and reality demands in such a way as to produce something that is socially valuable. An artist, for example, may redirect originally sexual or aggressive instinctual energies into the creation of a work of art. The work may bear a symbolic relationship to the initiating impulses, just as the manifest content of a dream is related to its latent content. In the case of a work of art, however, the ego and the secondary process "work over" the final product so that it is much more polished and effective than a dream. Sublimation is not restricted to artistic creativity, but is assumed by psychoanalytic theory to underlie almost any creative activity.

Closely related to sublimation, and among the best compromises one can make, is *love,* where an individual experiences genuine concern about the well-being of another person. In many respects this provides an ideal compromise, since sexual and affectional needs can often be gratified within the context of a loving relationship, but tempered by ethical and reality-oriented considerations. Instinct, reality, and the superego can all receive gratification here.

While compromises resulting from sublimation and love are among the best, they are also the most difficult. Sublimation is difficult because it often requires an unusually high degree of skill (such as artistic ability) to be successfully accomplished, and because the instinctual gratification it affords is rather mild and far removed from the instinct's initial goal. Love presents problems because it subjects a person to the possibility of severe disappointment or pain in the event of the loss of the loved one. Few experiences are more catastrophic, and persons who have once lost at love may be reluctant to try it again as the answer to the human dilemma.

Toward the end of his life, Freud became increasingly preoccupied with the philosophical implications of these aspects of his theory. He analyzed the long-range prospects for human happiness from sublimation and love in *Civilization and Its Discontents,* published in 1930. He foresaw a potential long-range difficulty arising from the paradoxical position of the individual in society. Only in a civilized society are the "higher" gratifications of sublimation and love possible. Only socially-agreed values can provide the forms necessary for the products of sublimation, while social institutions governing family and other group ties are required for meaningful love relations. But while society provides the structure in which these satisfactions are possible, it also imposes restraints on the gratification of impulses. Freud saw growing evidence, from such catastrophes as World War I and the incipient rise of National Socialism in Germany, that "civilized" societies were increasing their restraints on the instincts of love, while decreasing them on the instincts of death and destruction. Thus, acts of carnage and murder could be committed in war, and praised as acts of patriotism and morality. At the end of *Civilization and Its Discontents,* Freud expressed the hope that this trend would soon reverse itself, and that societies would begin to offer more opportunities for compromises in the service of love. He was not overly optimistic, however, and he closed with a question: "And now it is to be expected that the other of the two 'Heavenly Powers,' eternal Eros, will make an effort to assert himself in the struggle with his equally immortal adversary [Thanatos, the instinct of death and aggression]. But who can see with what success and with what result?" [9]

In sum, Freud's message was that there are no perfect answers to the problems of human existence. A person is constantly beset by conflicts which yield to no completely adequate or permanent resolutions. The rather pessimistic, though perhaps realistic conclusion implied by Freud's model of the mind, is that the best a person can hope for is to make compromises out of the conflicting demands of life. If one is fortunate enough to have developed a strong and resourceful ego, and to live in a society that provides decent opportunities for sublimation and love, the compromises may be reasonably good ones.

The Freudian Legacy

Few people have ever been as influential—or as controversial —as Sigmund Freud. By the time of his death in 1939, Freud had inspired a large band of followers and created an official psychoanalytic movement devoted to carrying on his ideas. The movement continues today as the International Psycho-Analytic Association, with members still conducting therapy much as Freud did, and carrying on psychoanalytic research.

Another significant group of therapists began under Freud's sway, but then broke with his group for one reason or another and went on to create their own "neo-Freudian" schools. Some, including Alfred Adler (1870–1937), Carl Gustav Jung (1875–1961), and Karen Horney (1885–1952), believed that Freud overemphasized the role of sexuality in his theory, and they developed new systems emphasizing social or cultural factors. Others, such as Otto Rank (1884–1939), reacted against the long time required to complete psychoanalytic therapy, and devised techniques intended to shorten the process. Each of these individuals developed a well articulated theory of personality that attracted—and continues to attract—large numbers of followers.

Among the most influential current psychotherapists, several were originally trained in Freudian techniques but later reacted explicitly against them. Carl Rogers, for example, developed *client-centered therapy* in an attempt to combat what he saw as an unwarranted air of omniscience in the role of the classical Freudian psychoanalyst. Joseph Wolpe came to disagree with the Freudian emphasis on underlying causes of neurosis at the expense of individual symptoms. He developed one of the most popular forms of *behavior therapy* in an attempt to provide quick and specific relief for the particular symptoms that brought his patients into therapy.

As these very sketchy descriptions suggest, the psychotherapeutic scene today is extremely diverse. Therapists do not agree among themselves about the best approaches to be employed, and only a minority use exactly the same techniques that Freud did. Nevertheless, one generalization is possible: almost all therapists today employ techniques that were used by Freud himself, that were developed by his followers as outgrowths of his theories, or that were developed by dissidents in explicit reaction against psychoanalytic practices. Freud is the one dominating figure, either for whom or against whom virtually all therapists feel compelled to take a stand.

In addition to having an enormous influence on psychotherapy, Freud's theories have directly or indirectly inspired countless studies by psychologists on the development of personality. Many of the methods of personality research have been directly derived from psychoanalytic practices. *Projective tests* such as the Rorschach or Thematic Apperception Test, for example, assume that subjects' responses to "neutral" stimuli such as ink blots or ambiguous pictures may reveal, in much the same way that free associations can, conflicts and personal characteristics of which they themselves are unaware.

Psychoanalytic hypotheses have been employed by personality researchers in the explanation of many different personality types. The *authoritarian personality*—a person who is predisposed to prejudiced attitudes toward minority groups —is one such type that has been extensively studied. Research has suggested that child-rearing practices lead authoritarian individuals to make heavy use of the defense mechanism of projection. They project their own hostility onto minority groups, so that consciously they see the groups as hostile to *them*. Then those who project can behave in a hostile manner toward the minorities, while rationalizing their aggression as a matter of self-defense.

Emphasis on child-rearing variables in the development of personality is yet another extremely important general legacy from Freud. By showing the importance of early childhood experiences for the development of adult character, Freud helped open the door to a whole new area of investigation. Our culture's present concern with child-rearing techniques is a direct, though often distorted, outgrowth of Freud's pioneering investigations.

Other current research areas influenced by Freudian ideas include sleep, dreams, hypnosis, sexuality, sex differences, aggression, and creativity. In fact, there is probably no area of research in personality or abnormal psychology that is untouched by the Freudian influence.

Of course Freud's influence has not been limited to psychology and its related disciplines. His demonstration of the importance and pervasiveness of unconscious mental factors was so effective that this once revolutionary idea is almost taken for granted today. The best art and literature of our time portrays human beings as creatures in conflict with themselves, subject to forces beyond their personal conscious control, and unaware of their own identities. While many specific aspects of Freudian theory remain untested or questionable, there can be no doubt that this view of humanity has struck a responsive chord. Sigmund Freud was among the small handful of individuals whose work vitally affected not just a single field of specialization, but also an entire intellectual climate.

Suggested Readings

Anyone who was interested by the ideas presented in this chapter deserves the pleasure of reading Freud in the original. His complete psychological works have been superbly edited, translated into English, and fully documented in a

Standard Edition under the editorship of James Strachey. The following paperback volumes are all from the *Standard Edition*.

Freud presented overviews of his theories, written for non-specialists, in *Introductory Lectures on Psychoanalysis* (New York: Liveright, 1977) and *An Outline of Psychoanalysis* (New York: Norton, 1970). A reading of Freud's major works in the order in which they were written is to be recommended for those wishing a more detailed presentation. One good sequence begins with *Studies on Hysteria* (New York: Avon Books, 1966), then proceeds to *The Interpretation of Dreams* (New York: Avon Books, 1965), *Three Essays on the Theory of Sexuality* (New York: Avon Books, 1965), *The Ego and the Id* (New York: Norton, 1962), and *Civilization and Its Discontents* (New York: Norton, 1962).

Of the several general introductions to Freud available in paperback, the author may perhaps be excused for especially recommending his own *Psychoanalytic Psychology: The Development of Freud's Thought* (New York: Norton, 1973).

The Measurement of Mind:

Francis Galton and the Psychology
of Individual Differences

London's International Health Exhibition of 1884 featured a curious exhibit that attracted many spectators. Labelled an "Anthropometric Laboratory," it was contained in a long, narrow enclosure. One of the walls was made of trellis work, so the waiting spectators could get a partial view of a bench inside, with several strange-looking contrivances laid out upon it. As they watched, a volunteer subject would enter the laboratory and manipulate the device at one end of the bench while consulting with the attendant. After a minute or two, the attendant wrote something on two small cards, and the subject moved on to the second contrivance. The procedure was repeated at each stop on the bench, after which the attendant filed one of the cards away and gave the other to the person to keep. Subjects invariably left studying their cards with keen interest. By the end of the Health Exhibition, 9,337 spectators had been sufficiently intrigued by what they saw to pay a fee of three pence and become subjects themselves.

For their time and money, these people received both the gratification of contributing to science and some information about themselves. Each of the devices tested or measured them in some way, while the cards recorded their personal scores on the tests as well as the average scores obtained by subjects who had gone before. New scores were constantly added to the data file and used in the computation of later statistics.

The individual tests measured "Keenness of Sight and of Hearing; Colour Sense; Judgement of Eye; Breathing Power; Reaction Time; Strength of Pull and of Squeeze; Force of Blow; Span of Arms; Height, both standing and sitting; and Weight." [1] The device measuring force of blow was only sometimes operational. It had a padded target on the end of a strong stick. When the subject punched the target, a mechanical spring device recorded the strength of the blow. This apparatus worked beautifully so long as the target was struck head on, but some subjects struck it from the side, breaking the stick and often spraining their wrists. Such incidents caused the proprietor of the exhibit to mutter about the frustrations of testing the general public. "It is by no means easy to select suitable instruments for such a purpose," he later wrote. "They must be strong, easily legible, and very simple, the stupidity and wrong-headedness of many men and women being so great as to be scarcely credible." [2]

Most of the other testing instruments met these criteria nicely. The test of keenness of hearing, for example, employed a whistle with an adjustable screw plug at the end which could be turned to alter the whistle's pitch. The attendant systematically raised the pitch until the subject could no longer hear it, and simply noted the number of turns of the screw that had been necessary. The test of reaction time employed a pendulum which, when released, caused a sound to occur. The subject was told to respond to the sound by immediately pressing a button with his finger. The finger response caused an elastic string that was swinging parallel to the pendulum to be stopped in front of a graduated scale. This provided a measure of how far the pendulum had swung before the response, and hence of the subject's reaction time.

Most surprising about these tests from a present day perspective is that many were thought of by their inventor as *mental* tests, measuring aspects of *intelligence*. Today it is taken for granted that intelligence involves "higher" mental processes, such as thinking, reasoning, and logic. It is hard to see how physical variables like sensory acuity, reaction time, or the strength of one's blow could possibly measure intelligence. Yet there was a plausible, if ultimately incorrect logic in seeing these as mental tests, based upon the predominant psychological views of the 1880s. Intelligence was supposed to involve the active manipulation of ideas, and ideas were supposedly built up out of elementary *sensations*.* Thus, the most intelligent people should be the ones with the most efficient and accurate senses. As the proprietor of the Anthropometric Laboratory put it, "the only information that reaches us concerning outward events appears to pass through the avenue of our senses; and the more perceptible our senses are of difference, the larger the field upon which our judgment and intelligence can act." [3]

His view seemed supported by certain "facts" that he had been led to believe. For example, he thought the severely mentally retarded were deficient sensorily as well as intellectually. "The discriminative faculty of idiots is curiously low," he wrote. "They hardly distinguish between heat and cold, and their sense of pain is so obtuse that some of the more idiotic seem hardly to know what it is." [4] Furthermore he, like most Victorian males, was certain that women were intellectually inferior to men. It therefore seemed more than coincidental that jobs requiring extreme sensory acuity—piano tuning, wine or tea tasting, or wool sorting, for example—were invariably held by men. He noted that "Ladies rarely distinguish the merits of wine at the dinner-table, and though custom allows them to preside at the breakfast-table, men think of them on the whole to be far from successful makers of tea and coffee." [5] These naïve examples correlating "in-

---

* Wundt's notion, described in Chapter 4, that the contents of consciousness could be introspectively analyzed into separate component sensations was perhaps the most influential variant of this assumption.

telligence" and "sensory acuity" provided presumptive evidence for the validity of sensorily-based intelligence—at least for the upper class males of Victorian England.

The proprietor of the Anthropometric Laboratory was Francis Galton (1822–1911). At the age of twenty-two he had inherited a substantial fortune which enabled him to devote his entire adult life to the pursuit of his personal interests. Like many other upper class Victorians, he often demonstrated a smugness and insensitivity to the position of people less fortunate than himself. In other respects, however, Galton was extraordinarily atypical. He was an energetic, humorous, and above all *curious* man who became a self-financed explorer, geographer, instrument-designer, meteorologist, and biological

8. Sir Francis Galton (1822–1911). *The National Library of Medicine, Bethesda, Maryland*

theorist before turning his attention to the measurement of psychological attributes.

As his psychological ideas developed, many of them, such as his view of intelligence, were simplistic or incorrect. But this ought not mask the fact that Francis Galton was one of the great founders of modern psychology. For while often wrong in their specifics, his theories provided basic foundations on which others could build. Among his important contributions was the very *idea* that tests could be employed to measure psychological differences between people. He also offered provocative theories about the origins of those psychological differences, and suggested how social policy might be changed so as to foster positive psychological characteristics in the general population. He thus elevated the scientific study of *individual differences* to the level of a major psychological specialty with important social implications. Most of the general issues that he raised in the last century still preoccupy psychologists today.

Galton's Early Life and Career

Francis Galton was born near Birmingham, England, on February 16, 1822, the seventh and last child in an old and distinguished family. His father was a prosperous banker, descended from one of the founders of the Quaker religion. His mother was a Darwin, half-sister of Charles Darwin's father. Francis never became really close to his eminent half-cousin, who was thirteen years older than himself, but they maintained cordial relations with one another as adults, and Darwin's evolutionary theories had a dramatic impact on Galton's viewpoint and career.

Until the age of eight, Galton received his education at home under the tutelage of an older sister. It is a pity she never recorded her teaching methods, because he developed as a prodigy. At the age of two-and-a-half he could read and write; by five he could read any English book, some Latin, and could solve most basic arithmetic problems. A year later he was thoroughly familiar with the *Iliad* and the *Odyssey*, and could quote from them appropriately in conversation. By the age of seven he was reading Shakespeare and Pope for pleasure.

Despite this remarkable beginning, Galton's later academic career was not outstanding. At the age of eight, he was sent away to the first of a series of boarding schools. Even the best English schools of the time stressed rote learning of the classics, and completely discouraged any independent efforts to learn anything scientific or mathematical. For so intensely curious a youth as Galton the schools were an unmitigated disaster. The diaries he kept at the time contain hardly a single reference to a scholarly idea, but are replete with references to canings, floggings, mandatory sermons, punitive homework assignments, fights with local boys, and general hell-raising. Many years later, Galton summed up his boyhood education as follows: "The literary provender provided at . . . school disagreed wholly with my mental digestion. The time spent there was a period of stagnation for myself, which for many years I bitterly deplored, for I was very willing and eager to learn, and could have learnt much if a suitable teacher had been at hand to direct and encourage me." [6]

To his great satisfaction, Galton was taken out of boarding school when he was sixteen. His father had begun to fear—unrealistically, as it was to turn out—that the family fortune might be insufficient to guarantee Francis a life of leisure, so he sought a more practical education for his son. Following the tradition of many of his Darwin relatives, medical training was decided upon.

Galton's introduction to the medical profession was both rough and abrupt. A physician friend was summoned one evening to perform an autopsy on a neighboring housemaid who had just died of peritonitis. The young physician-to-be was invited to go along and observe. Seventy years later the awful memory still remained vivid in his mind: "I can easily reproduce in imagination all the ghastly horror of the scene and could describe it in detail, but it would be unfitted for these pages. . . . I returned home chilled, awed and sobered, and seemed for the time to have left boyhood behind me." [7]

A few months later he began his medical training in earnest, at the Birmingham General Hospital. Training there was offered simply, practically, and on the spot, so from the beginning Galton had to assist in the setting of fractures and in the treatment of other serious and painful injuries. Anaesthetics did not exist in those days, and the worst part of the job was having to listen to the screams of the patients. With time, and the application of great self-discipline, he adapted to this situation: "It seemed after a while as though the cries were somehow disconnected with the operation, upon which the whole attention became fixed." [8] His hard won ability to objectify his patients' medical problems would later predispose Galton to take a detached and analytic view of psychological characteristics as well. For the present, it enabled him to undertake his medical duties with detachment and a degree of zest, as reflected in a letter he sent home describing his first attempt at tooth extraction:

A boy came in looking very deplorable, walked up to me and opened his mouth. . . . I did not manage the first proceedings well, for first I put in the key (that is the tooth instrument) the wrong way, then I could not catch hold of the right tooth with it. At last I got hold. I then took my breath to enable me to give a harder wrench; one–two–three, and away I went. A confused sort of murmur something like that of a bee in a foxglove proceeded from the boy's mouth, he kicked at me awfully. I wrenched the harder. When, hang the thing,—crash went the tooth. . . . Well, there was another tooth which he wanted out and against which I took proceedings. I at last fixed the instrument splendidly and tugged away like a sailor at a handspike, when the boy, roaring this time like a lion with his head in a bag, broke away from me and the sawbone that was holding his head, bolted straight out, cursing all the Hospital doctors right manfully. So much for my first tooth-drawing.[9]

Another of Galton's duties was the preparation of medicines, and this offered him ample opportunities to indulge his curiosity. He quickly discovered that a decoction of quassia wood was the bitterest tasting substance that could be imagined. Then, proceeding more systematically, he began taking small doses of all the medicines listed in the pharmacopoeia, beginning with the letter A. It was, he later remarked, "an interesting experience, but had obvious drawbacks. . . . I got nearly to the end of the letter C, when I was stopped by the effects of Croton Oil. I had foolishly believed that two drops of it could have no noticeable effects as a purgative and emetic; but indeed they had." [10] Despite such experiences, Galton's tendency to perform experiments on himself remained strong throughout the rest of his life.

After a year of practical experience in Birmingham, Galton enrolled in the medical school of King's College in London for a more theoretical approach. Then he decided to interrupt his medical education temporarily, and take an arts degree at Cambridge University. He was a candidate for an honors degree in mathematics, but in his third year fell victim to Cambridge's extremely intense academic competition and pressure. He suffered an emotional breakdown, during which "a mill seemed to be working inside my head. I could not banish obsessing ideas; at times I could hardly read a book, and found it painful even to look at a printed page. . . . It was as though I had tried to make a steam-engine perform more work than it was constructed for, by tampering with its safety valve and thereby straining its mechanism." [11]

During his Cambridge career, Galton was constantly preoccupied with his standing relative to his fellow students. His letters home betrayed an obsessive concern with examinations, including the way they were constructed and marked at Cambridge so as to yield a precise ranking of all students. Undoubtedly, his disappointment at not being able to place at the very top of the list was an important factor in his breakdown. Recovery came only slowly, after Galton abandoned any thought of competing for honors, and settled for an "ordinary" or "poll" degree. His preoccupations with examinations and the ranking of intellectual ability would persist in milder form throughout his life, however, and would contribute to his later development of mental tests.

During his recovery, one of Galton's diversions was some informal experimentation with hypnosis, or magnetism, as it was still called. After learning how to magnetize his friends, he began to investigate some commonly held beliefs about the state:

I had been assured that success was the effect of strength of will on the part of the magnetiser, so at first I exerted all the will-power I possessed, which was fatiguing. I then, by way of experiment, intermitted a little, looking all the time in the same way as before, and found myself equally successful. So I intermitted more and more, and at last succeeded in letting my mind ramble freely while I maintained the same owl-like demeanor. This acted just as well. The safe conclusion was that the effect is purely subjective on the part of the patient, and that will-power on the part of the operator has nothing to do with it.[12]

Unfortunately, Galton decided that magnetism was "an unwholesome procedure" shortly after making this discovery, and abandoned further research in the subject. This was probably a loss to the field, since his discovery occurred even before James Braid had clearly established that the secret of hypnotism lies in the predilections of the subject rather than the powers of the hypnotist.*

After taking his non-honors degree at Cambridge in 1843, Galton returned to London to complete his requirements for the medical degree. Before he had finished his father died, however, in the autumn of 1844. Emotionally upset, Galton had little inclination to continue his studies. As he wrote: "Being much upset and craving for a healthier life, I abandoned all thought of becoming a physician, but felt most grateful for the enlarged insight into Nature that I had acquired through medical experiences." [13] His formal education was at an end.

* See Chapter 5 for a description of Braid's contributions to hypnotism.

The Measurement of Mind

At this stage of his life, Galton seemed likely to become a gentleman farmer or a member of the idle rich. His father had left him a sizable fortune so during 1845 and 1846 he could travel extensively in Egypt, the Sudan, and the Middle East, visiting places that were then little known to the Western world. Then he returned home and spent a few years riding, shooting, and socializing with other rich Englishmen. He had no regular outlet for his energy and curiosity, but contented himself with occasional expeditions and incidental adventures. He once tried to amuse himself with ballooning, a dangerous and not quite respectable activity. He found balloon flight itself quite delightful, and characteristically experimented on the causes of giddiness in himself. Landing was less enjoyable, however, as the balloon descended into the middle of a large country estate, belching stinking gas and nearly killing several sheep with its anchoring hook. Galton was too embarrassed to try another flight.

Even during this fallow period in his life, however, Galton was unlike most of the idle rich. Fascinated with gadgetry and the recently discovered phenomena of electricity, he constructed a miniature electrical laboratory in the drawer of his writing desk, and passed much time performing small experiments there. He even invented an electrical "telotype," or printing telegraph machine, the description of which constituted his first scientific publication in 1849. Soon after, he found a more organized outlet for his energies.

By 1850 Galton realized that occasional excursions and informal home experiments were insufficient to meet his craving for novelty. After consulting a professional phrenologist who recommended an active life, and reflecting on his considerable experience as a traveller, he turned his attention to the numerous "blank spots" in the world map of the time, primarily in the interior of Africa. He then consulted with the Royal Geographical Society, and at their recommendation outfitted and led a party to explore the interior of southwest Africa. He left England on April 5, 1850 and returned exactly two years later, after an arduous but successful exploration that effectively filled in one of those large blank spots on the map.

One of the things Galton liked best about the expedition—and one of the major reasons for its success—was that it enabled him to indulge his penchant for measurement. He mastered the sextant, the heliostat, and other navigational and surveying instruments, and returned home with several notebooks full of detailed readings and calculations of the African terrain. He found a rather more unorthodox use for his measuring skill when he encountered some native women who, he wrote home, had figures "that would drive the females of our native land desperate." Wishing to ascertain their measurements without risking a direct approach, Galton "sat at a distance with my sextant, and . . . surveyed them in every way and subsequently measured the distance of the spot where they stood—worked out and tabulated the results at my leisure." [14] For his geographical measurements, which yielded a highly accurate map, Galton was awarded the gold medal of the Royal Geographical Society in 1853. That year he also published an entertaining book about his expedition, entitled *Tropical South Africa,* which made him known to the general English public.

The African journey was a turning point in Galton's life, for it made his reputation as an explorer of the first rank, and also provided him with an entree into the governing circles of the Royal Geographical Society itself. Since he had considerable free time to give, he quickly became an officer of the Society. During the golden age of African exploration, he helped plan the expeditions of many renowned explorers of Africa and the Nile, including Burton, Speke, and Grant.

The Geographical Society was an ideal outlet for at least some of Galton's energy and enthusiasm, and for several years he occupied himself with a variety of tasks more or less closely related to travel and exploration. He wrote papers on technical aspects of travel in the wild and, following the English military disasters in the Crimean War, was commissioned to train troops in proper camping procedures. Galton also found time to invent several devices, including a hand-held heliostat for making triangulation measurements, a protective shield for soldiers in combat, and an unsuccessful "wave machine" whose purpose was supposed to have been the conversion of energy from ocean waves into more usable forms. In 1855 he published his second book, *The Art of Travel*. This popular work contained advice for travellers in the wild on such topics as clothing, bivouac, tents, drinking water, writing materials, the management of savages, and how to deal with the rush of an enraged animal. By 1856 Galton's inventiveness was widely recognized in scientific circles and he was elected to the prestigious Royal Society.

In the early 1860s Galton turned to a new subject of interest to travelers, and to almost everyone else besides: the prediction of weather. He had the idea to collect simultaneous weather information from many different places in the world, and write it all on a *weather map*. When he did so, and drew lines connecting points with the same barometric pressure (isobars), he discovered that they arranged themselves into roughly circular systems of low pressure ("cyclones") and high pressure ("anti-cyclones") that followed one another on a west-to-east course from one day to another. Today when weather reports mention "highs," "lows," and "approaching fronts," they follow procedures first set down by Galton.

Darwinian Theory and the Study of Hereditary Genius

Galton remained interested in meteorology and geography for the rest of his life, but in 1859 his primary attention was grasped by an event that shook the foundations of the scientific world: the publication of his cousin Charles Darwin's book, *On the Origin of Species*. Galton lost no time in taking a stand in favor of Darwin's controversial theory of evolution by natural selection. Within a few days of publication, he wrote to his newly famous relative to say, "Pray let me add a word of congratulations on the completion of your wonderful volume. . . . I have laid it down in the full enjoyment of a feeling that one rarely experiences after boyhood days, of having been initiated into an entirely new province of knowledge which, nevertheless, connects itself with other things in a thousand ways." [15]

Darwin's main thesis was that different species evolve because of the gradual "selection" of small variations within a species which are favorable to survival and propagation. Individuals possessing unfavorable small variations tend to die off and to reproduce less, whereas those with positive small variations transmit those characteristics to future generations. A basic assumption of the theory is the pre-existence of the small inheritable variations, or *individual differences,* among the members of a given species which can provide the basis on which natural selection can occur.

Darwin's *Origin of Species* clearly implied that human beings are animals subject to evolution by natural selection, though it did not emphasize the point. The work concentrated almost exclusively on animal species, and postponed the treatment of human beings until a later time. Galton immediately grasped the human implications of the theory, however, and a new guiding idea seized his imagination. It suddenly seemed of the greatest interest and importance to determine the inheritable characteristics that differentiate human beings from one another, and which therefore hold the key to the future evolution of the race. The determination of these differences, of course, was essentially a problem of *measurement,* and few people were more temperamentally suited to the task than Galton. His curiosity about human experience, his tendency to observe people with detachment and objectivity, and his passion for the gadgetry and techniques of measurement all combined to suggest a completely new field of investigation that was to dominate Galton's attention for years. He became seriously interested in psychological problems for the first time, and his efforts culminated in the publication of four books between 1869 and 1889 which made major original contributions to the psychology of individual differences.

As Galton pondered the range of potentially inheritable variations in human beings, he was forcibly struck by the observation that *eminence* seems to run in families. An obvious model for this, of course, was his own family. Several other eminent families also came quickly to mind, and Galton decided the issue could be settled by statistical tests. He made some rough calculations about the proportion of men in the general population who achieve sufficient eminence to be included in a dictionary of biography. Then he examined the family trees of various samples of eminent men to see how many of their relatives were also eminent.* His first rough tests showed that the proportion of eminent relatives of eminent men was much higher than the proportion of eminent men in the entire population. There could be no question about the statistical tendency for eminence to run in families.

Such evidence did not mean that eminence was necessarily or completely hereditary, of course, since members of the same family tend to have similar environments as well as similar hereditary backgrounds. Heredity or environment or both could be invoked to account for the findings. Galton was aware of this, but chose to emphasize the hereditary component. By so doing he involved himself in a controversy which persisted to the end of his life and which remains unresolved among psychologists today.

Galton's first systematic studies of eminent families appeared in an 1865 magazine article entitled "Hereditary Talent and Character," and then, in much more detail, in the 1869 book, *Hereditary Genius*. The main thrust of the book, and its two most original ideas, are stated in its opening sentences:

I propose to show in this book that a man's natural abilities are derived by inheritance, under exactly the same limitations as are the

---

* Galton omitted eminent women from his analysis, on the grounds that their relatives would be too difficult to track down.

form and physical features of the whole organic world. Consequently, as it is easy . . . to obtain by careful selection a permanent breed of dogs or horses gifted with peculiar powers of running . . . so it would be quite practicable to produce a highly gifted race of men by judicious marriages during several consecutive generations.[16]

The first original idea expressed here was the notion that "natural abilities" could be inherited just like physical characteristics such as height, weight, or skin color. The term "natural ability" was used by Galton in a general sense, but it clearly involved many factors that were psychological in nature. Though most people today have little trouble accepting the fact that intelligence, aptitudes, and character traits may be at least partially inherited, this was a novel idea in 1869, and one that surprised even Darwin. Galton's second original idea was that the overall quality of the human race can be improved—psychologically as well as physically—by paying judicious attention to breeding.

Inheritance of Natural Ability. Galton offered several lines of evidence in support of his hypothesis that natural ability is inherited like physical qualities. First, he showed that measurable intellectual characteristics tend to fall into *distributions* identical to those of inheritable physical traits. The Belgian statistician Adolph Quetelet (1796–1874) had already shown that measurements of physical characteristics such as height or weight fall into bell-shaped *normal distributions* if they are collected from many people. In such distributions many more people fall into the middle ranges of scores than at the extremes, and successive scores are more widely separated from one another at the extremes than in the middle range. If the heights of three hundred adult men are measured, and an average height of 70 inches is obtained, more individuals fall into the four-inch range between 68 and 72 inches than in the ranges between 60 and 64 inches, or between 76 and 80 inches (see Figure 7–1). Thus, the *difference* between the first and second tallest man, or between the first and second shortest, is likely to be much greater than that between the 149th and 150th in the overall distribution.

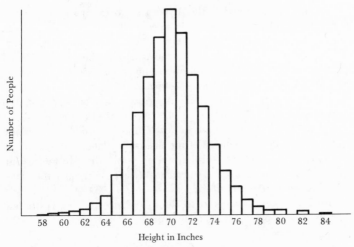

Figure 7–1 *An Example of Normal Distribution*

Galton showed how normal distributions were also found in measures of *intellectual* ability. As an example, he analyzed the examination scores of 200 candidates for mathematical honors at Cambridge University, which ranged from 7,634 points down to 237 points. The highest score was more than 2000 points greater than that of the second candidate, whereas the middle scores were all closely bunched about the 1000-point mark. Similar distributions are routinely found by teachers when they arrange their students' examination scores hierarchically. One or two students often stand head and shoulders above the rest, one or two do so poorly as to suggest that they had never attended the class, and many students are so closely bunched about the middle value that it is sometimes difficult to make reasonable distinctions among them.

The similarity between the distributions of measures of intellectual ability, and measures of known heritable qualities such as height or weight, did not prove that the intellectual abilities were also inherited or innate. But Galton felt it offered strong presumptive evidence, and he stated his case strongly:

I have no patience with the hypothesis occasionally expressed, and often implied, especially in tales written to teach children to be good, that babies are born pretty much alike and that the sole agencies in creating differences between boy and boy, and man and man, are steady application and moral effort. It is in the most unqualified manner that I object to pretensions of natural equality. . . . I acknowledge freely the great power of education and social influences in developing the active powers of the mind, just as I acknowledge the effect of use in developing the muscles of a blacksmith's arm, and no further. Let the blacksmith labour as he will, he will find there are certain feats beyond his power that are well within the strength of a man of herculean make, even although the latter may have led a sedentary life. . . .

This is precisely analogous to the experience that every student has had of the working of his mental powers.[17]

The heart of *Hereditary Genius* appears in the chapters examining the family trees of men who achieved eminence in various fields. Galton's analyses were refined versions of his earlier, rough attempts to compare the proportion of eminent relatives of eminent men with the proportion of eminent men in the entire population. He studied twelve separate groups: all the Judges of England between 1660 and 1865, statesmen, great military commanders, literary men, scientists, poets, musicians, divines, painters, outstanding classics scholars at Cambridge, champion oarsmen, and champion wrestlers.

With minor variations, the results were similar for all the groups, of which the Judges were the largest and most representative. An extremely large proportion of these men—almost 40 percent—had at least one eminent relative, and many had more than one. These eminent relatives were much more likely to be close than distant: relatives in the first degree (fathers, sons, or brothers) were more than four times as likely to be eminent as second-degree relatives (grandfathers, grandsons, uncles, or nephews), who in turn were four times more likely to be eminent than third-degree relations (great-grandfathers, great-grandsons, great-nephews, great-uncles, and first cousins). However, even the third-degree relatives showed a much higher proportion of eminence than that found in the general population.

These findings indicated a *general* transmission of eminence within the Judges' families, since the eminent relatives represented fields ranging from medicine and mathematics to diplomacy and the writing of biographies. But Galton also found that more than one Judge out of nine had a father, son, or brother who was also on the list of Judges. This was a figure extraordinarily higher than chance, suggesting that members of Judges' families shared specific legal and administrative ability as well as general ability.

Galton recognized that these were not *perfect* relationships, and that predictions about an individual would be risky if based only on information about family background. Nevertheless, he believed they showed a powerful hereditary factor. Every person, he argued, inherits from his or her parents a "natural ability" that is really the resultant of three components complexly interacting with one another: "Ability must be placed on a triple footing, every leg of which has to be perfectly planted. In order that a man should inherit ability in the concrete, he must inherit three qualities that are separate and independent of one another: he must inherit capacity, zeal, and vigor; for unless these three, or, at the very least, two of them are combined, he cannot hope to make a figure in the world." [18]

Even this formulation was something of an oversimplification, since the variable of "capacity" could itself be subdivided into many interacting physical and psychological components. Galton pointed out that "capacity" as a military commander, for example, required not only a brilliant tactical mind, but also the ability to survive battles, which was inversely related to one's physical size. Galton calculated that the probability of getting shot in combat varied as the square root of the product of one's height and weight. Thus, he accounted for the fact that so many of the world's great military figures—

Bonaparte, Nelson, and Wellington, for example—were short men. Their small stature was one part of their inherited capacity to succeed militarily.

With so many independently varying components of "natural ability," it was no wonder that eminence was transmitted irregularly from one generation to another. Virtually all of the offspring of eminent parents inherit some proportion of the necessary components of capacity, zeal, and vigor, but, unless they appear in the right combinations, eminence will be denied. Thus, the majority of these children do not attain the stature of their parents. Even so, however, they have a much greater chance of inheriting the right combination of characteristics than children of ordinary parentage, as Galton's statistics showed.

In sum, Galton made a plausible if not unassailable case that psychological characteristics were inherited like physical ones, and that the combinations of inherited variables accounted for the familial patterns of eminence. His arguments were convincing enough to impress at least one important reader. Shortly after *Hereditary Genius* was published, Charles Darwin wrote to say, "My Dear Galton, I have only read about 50 pages of your book . . . but I must exhale myself, else something will go wrong in my inside. I do not think I have ever in my life read anything more interesting and original. . . . You have made a convert of an opponent in one sense, for I have always maintained that, excepting fools, men do not differ in intellect, only in zeal and hard work." [19]

Much of Galton's subsequent attention—and of future generations of psychologists as well—was to be devoted to the questions of exactly *how* men differ in intellect and how those differences can be measured. The Anthropometric Laboratory of 1884, with its physiologically oriented tests of "intelligence," was one of the logical outcomes.

Eugenics. Galton's belief that people vary hereditarily in natural ability led logically to the second major theme of

Hereditary Genius, the idea that the human race can be made to evolve in more positive directions through the judicious regulation of breeding. He laid the foundations for a new science, unnamed in *Hereditary Genius* but later to be called *eugenics,* and defined as "the science of improving stock, which . . . takes cognisance of all influences that tend in however remote a degree to give to the more suitable races or strains of blood a better chance of prevailing speedily over the less suitable than they otherwise would have had." [20]

One of the first principles of a eugenic society was that men and women possessing the most desirable qualities should mate with each other. This followed from the experience of animal breeders, who had long known that desirable alterations in a breed could be produced by systematically selecting only the individual males and females who were strongest on the desired trait, and mating them to each other. When the process was repeated over many generations, the proportion of offspring showing the desirable trait increased until finally the entire breed possessed it.

As early as 1865, in his paper on "Hereditary Talent and Character," Galton had envisaged the day when valid tests would be devised to select the most promising young men and women, who would be offered special rewards by the state if they married each other. He half-humorously imagined an annual ceremony, "in which the Senior Trustee of the Endowment Fund would address ten deeply-blushing young men" to congratulate them on having taken the ten highest places of their years in a competition regarding "those qualities of talent, character, and bodily vigor, which are proved . . . to do most honour and best service to our race." A comparable process would have selected the ten young women scoring highest on "grace, beauty, health, good temper, accomplished housewifery and disengaged affections, in addition to noble qualities of heart and brain." The twenty young people would be scientifically paired up with one another. If they agreed to marry, the Queen herself would give away the brides at state weddings, the State would give each couple 5,000 pounds as a wedding present, and ample educational expenses for any offspring would be guaranteed.[21]

Galton realized that such a competition was highly fanciful in the 1860s but he hoped that something like it would be possible in the future. His subsequently developed intelligence tests were attempts to place assessment of natural ability on a scientific footing. Rather naively, Galton assumed that the State would not abuse such a selective breeding scheme, and that all citizens would appreciate its rationality and virtue sufficiently to comply.

Hereditary Genius was laced with some more down-to-earth analyses of human breeding propensities, and less fanciful suggestions for improvement. Galton noted, for example, that by a longstanding regulation, many of the most coveted academic fellowships in England were awarded only on condition that the winner did not marry. This officially sanctioned celibacy among the best academics inhibited the transmission of inherited academic ability to future generations, and Galton deplored it. (A few years later the policy was officially changed, to Galton's great satisfaction.) Galton also addressed the question of why so many families of the English nobility —supposedly the "best" families—tended to die out. The reason, he suggested, was that noble families naturally encouraged the most socially advantageous marriages for their sons, who accordingly often married heiresses. Heiresses, however, necessarily came from families with no *male* offspring to inherit the family wealth, that is, families that were relatively infertile. This relative infertility was inherited by the heiresses along with their wealth, so they had few children of their own to carry on the noble lines.

Some of Galton's sharpest barbs in *Hereditary Genius* were directed toward organized religion. His attitude reflected a general antagonism in the latter part of the nineteenth century between the Darwinians and the upholders of traditional religion. Darwin's theory had contradicted the orthodox theory of the "special creation" of all species by God, and many theologians were quick to heap abuse on evolutionary theory.* On the other side, many individuals felt that Darwin's theory exposed the dogmatism and narrow-mindedness of traditional religious authorities. Galton was among the latter, writing that the effect of *Origin of Species* on him was "to demolish a multitude of dogmatic barriers by a single stroke, and to arouse a spirit of rebellion against all ancient authorities whose positive and unauthenticated statements were contradicted by modern science." [22]

In *Hereditary Genius,* Galton was outspoken in his condemnation of the Church's historical influence on the genetic make-up of humanity. He attributed many of the pernicious customs of the so-called Dark Ages to the tradition of clerical celibacy. People of gentle or contemplative nature had no place else to go besides the Church, whose enforced celibacy ensured that they would not transmit their traits to future generations. The Church "acted precisely as if she had aimed at selecting the rudest portion of the community to be, alone, the parents of future generations. She practiced the arts which breeders would use, who aimed at creating ferocious, currish, and stupid natures. No wonder that club law prevailed for centuries over Europe." [23]

By the conclusion of *Hereditary Genius,* Galton's intention was clear: he hoped to replace traditional religious beliefs and practices with a new but essentially "religious" movement based on evolutionary science and eugenic principles. The anthropomorphic deities of the past were to be replaced by a pantheistic "over-soul," constituted by the totality of the organic universe and expressing itself through the evolution of ever-higher life forms. Human beings, with their intelli-

* The most celebrated confrontation between a theologian and an evolutionist occurred in 1860, when Samuel Wilberforce, the Bishop of Oxford, debated publicly with Darwin's champion, Thomas Huxley. The Bishop inquired derisively if Huxley claimed his descent from the monkey on his grandmother's or his grandfather's side of the family. Huxley replied he would rather have a monkey for an ancestor than be connected with a person (by implication, Wilberforce) who would use his great intellectual gifts to obscure the truth.

gence, were granted at least a dim understanding of the evolutionary mechanism of this great over-soul. Accordingly, the *religious* interests and activities of human beings could properly be redirected toward the general improvement of their species by eugenic science. Eugenics had become a religion for Galton, and he devoted the rest of his life to its pursuit with all the devotion, energy, and conviction of a religious zealot.

The Nature-Nurture Controversy

Though *Hereditary Genius* won the approval of Darwin, it was not universally well received upon publication. Much of its negative reception was due to its pro-evolutionary and sometimes shockingly anti-theological biases. Some people, however, also criticized it for its relative neglect of environmental factors in the creation of talent. Galton had rather blithely assumed that in "progressive" societies such as Victorian England, natural, inherited ability could always be expressed and rewarded. Thus he wrote, "If a man is gifted with vast intellectual ability, eagerness to work, and power of working, I cannot comprehend how such a man should be repressed. The world is always tormented with difficulties waiting to be solved—struggling with ideas and feelings to which it can give no adequate expression. If, then, there exists a man capable of solving those difficulties, or of giving voice to those pent up feelings, he is sure to be welcomed with universal acclamation." [24] This assumption, of course, ignored the great advantages enjoyed by members of the upper classes —Galton himself included—in the socially stratified society of Victorian England. Yet only if it were accepted could the evidence of *Hereditary Genius* be interpreted as lending unambiguous support to Galton's hereditarian theory.

One person who distrusted this assumption was the Swiss botanist Alphonse de Candolle (1806–1893). Like Galton, de

Candolle came from a distinguished scientific family. Unlike Galton, however, he was more impressed with environmental than hereditary factors as determinants of successful families. To test his view, he collected biographical data on a large group of eminent scientists, and in 1872, published a book entitled *History of the Sciences and Scientists over Two Centuries*. While he cited Galton and conceded that heredity plays a certain role in the creation of scientific excellence, he also provided statistical data showing that great scientists tended to come from countries with moderate climates, democratic governments, tolerant religious establishments, and thriving commercial interests. Here was clear evidence of an environmental effect.

De Candolle sent Galton a copy of his book, which, understandably, touched a raw nerve or two. Galton responded with a long letter defending himself and criticizing aspects of de Candolle's work: "You say and imply that my views on hereditary genius are wrong and that you are going to correct them; well, I read on and find to my astonishment that so far from correcting them you re-enunciate them. . . . I feel the injustice you have done to me strongly, and one reason that I did not write earlier was that I might first hear the independent verdict of some scientific man who had read both books. This I have now done, having seen Mr. Darwin whose opinion confirms mine in every particular." By the time he had reached the conclusion of his letter, however, Galton had cooled down. De Candolle, after all, had not rejected the hereditary hypothesis outright, but merely suggested that it had to be augmented by environmental considerations. Galton ended the letter on a conciliatory note: "I feel, now that I have come to the end of this letter, that I have done little else than find fault, but I beg you to be assured that my general impression of the book is of another kind. I feel the great service you have done in writing it, and shall do what I can to make it known, as it ought to be, in England." [25]

Galton's letter brought a prompt and courteous reply from

de Candolle: "If there escaped from me, in the 482 pages of my book, one phrase, one word making it possible to doubt my respect for your impartiality, your character, and your talent for investigation, it could only have been in error and contrary to my intentions. You have always sought the truth." The essence of the difference between them, he went on, was not disagreement about the facts themselves, but about their interpretation. "I have had the advantage of coming after you," he wrote. "It was not difficult for me to confirm with new facts the influence of heredity, but I never lost sight of the other causes, and the remainder of my researches convinced me that they are generally more important than heredity, at least among men of the same race." [26] The heredity-environment question was here clearly put, and in a much more amiable manner than would often be the case with later partisans of both sides.

De Candolle's book and letters stimulated Galton to undertake his own study of scientists in an effort to sort out some of the effects of heredity and environment in the production of scientific talent. The result, in 1874, was *English Men of Science: Their Nature and Nurture,* another milestone in the historical development of the psychology of individual differences. This study was the first attempt to use the *self-questionnaire method* to investigate psychological issues. Galton's unprecedented strategy was simple: he devised an extensive questionnaire asking for detailed information about personal background, and sent it to almost 200 Fellows of the Royal Society who had achieved distinction for scientific work. It requested information ranging from the racial, religious, social, and political backgrounds of the respondents and their parents, to their hair color and the size of their hats. Some questions were explicitly psychological, asking respondents to rate themselves and their close relatives on such qualities as "energy of mind," "retentiveness of memory," "studiousness of disposition," or "temperament, if distinctly nervous, sanguine, bilious, or lymphatic." Galton also asked his subjects to assess their educational experiences in detail, with special emphasis on influences toward scientific development. Finally, there was a series of questions that Galton regarded as the heart of his questionnaire: "Can you trace the origin of your interest in science in general and in your particular branch of it? How far do your scientific tastes appear to have been innate? Were they largely determined by events after you reached manhood, and by what events?" Galton hoped to resolve the heredity-environment issue for once and for all from the answers to these questions.

Although the length of the questionnaire was "alarming," to use Galton's own description, and touched on many personal and sensitive issues, most of the scientists completed it without complaint. In Galton's eyes the most significant feature of their responses was that a majority declared that their taste for science had been innate. "As far back as I can remember, I loved nature and desired to learn her secrets," wrote one. Other typical responses were, "I was always observing and inquiring, and this disposition was never checked or ridiculed," and "[I had] a natural taste for observing and generalizing, developed by noticing the fossiliferous rocks which happened to occur in the neighbourhood of the school where I was." [27] These rather naive and unsubstantiated responses were sufficient to confirm Galton's belief that his scientist subjects had been *born* with their tastes and aptitudes for science. Hence (of course) their traits were probably hereditary.

Galton's data did lead him to make one concession to de Candolle. When he analyzed the descriptions of the scientists' educational experiences, he found they were more likely to castigate their educations than to praise them, with most of the complaints censuring the narrowness of their formal training. The minority of subjects who praised their educations almost always mentioned breadth as the most positive feature. Furthermore, a disproportionate share of the positive comments came from Scottish scientists who also constituted a disproportionate share of the total sample of scientists. The educational system in Scotland was notably broader and more progressive than the English, so Galton drew a rather unsurprising conclusion: if England wished to produce more scientists, she ought to reform and broaden her educational system, bringing it more in line with that of Scotland. Galton was here admitting that environmental factors could augment or facilitate innate predispositions toward science. He no longer believed that hereditary scientific talent would inevitably manifest itself, no matter what environmental obstacles were placed in its way. He still maintained that innate aptitude was a necessary predisposing factor, however, which might or might not be fully expressed, depending on the environmental supports or hindrances.

Galton's data analyses were naive, and they certainly did not conclusively settle the issues as Galton thought they would. The real virtue of *English Men of Science* lay not in what it proved, but in its demonstration that the statistical analysis of questionnaire data was a *potentially* valuable approach to psychological questions.

English Men of Science was also notable for a permanent contribution to the language of science. The phrase "nature and nurture" was introduced in the subtitle of the book, and formally defined early in the text:

The phrase "nature and nurture" is a convenient jingle of words, for it separates under two distinct heads the innumerable elements of which personality is composed. Nature is all that a man brings with himself into the world; nurture is every influence that affects him after his birth. The distinction is clear: the one produces the infant such as it actually is, including its latent faculties of growth and mind; the other affords the environment amid which the growth takes place, by which natural tendencies may be strengthened or thwarted, or wholly new ones implanted.[28]

The phrase caught on, and ever since 1874 biologists and psychologists have used it to differentiate innate developmental factors from environmental ones.

The Measurement of Mind

Studies of Human Faculty

In the ten years immediately following the publication of *English Men of Science* Galton engaged in an astonishingly wide variety of activities related to heredity, eugenics, and individual differences, which culminated in *Inquiries into Human Faculty and Its Development*. Published in 1883, this book reflected the man himself—his versatility, his breadth of interests, and his passion for measuring. He fairly described the book in his opening paragraph:

My general object has been to take note of the varied hereditary faculties of different men, and of the great differences in different families and races. . . . The subject is, however, so entangled with collateral considerations that a straightforward step-by-step inquiry did not seem to be the most suitable course. I thought it safer to proceed like the surveyor of a new country, and endeavour to fix in the first instance as truly as I could the position of several cardinal points.[29]

The explorer-surveyor analogy was apt, for *Human Faculty* —like *The Art of Travel*—was a handbook full of helpful hints and suggestions for those who wished to follow in Galton's footsteps. This time, however, the terrain was psychological rather than geographical. The book took up more than twenty different topics, ranging from "variety of human nature" to "statistical studies of the efficacy of prayer." Among those which have been most influential for psychology were *anthropometry, mental imagery, associations,* and *twin studies.*

Anthropometry. Although Galton's Anthropometric Laboratory was still a year in the future when *Human Faculty* was published, the preparatory work had all been completed, and was reported fully. He described his theory—already noted at the beginning of this chapter—that intelligence must be closely related to sensory acuity and general physiological functioning. He also described some of the specific tests that were shortly to be included in his laboratory to measure sensory acuity.

He gave extended treatment to the whistle—now known as

"Galton's whistle"—whose pitch could be adjusted and thus used to measure sensitivity to shrill sounds. After describing its manufacture, he gave the results of some informal experiments he had conducted with it. "It is an only too amusing experiment," he wrote, "to test a party of persons of different ages, including some rather elderly and self-satisfied personnages. They are indignant at being thought deficient in the power of hearing, yet the experiment quickly shows that they are absolutely deaf to shrill notes which the younger persons hear acutely, and they commonly betray much dislike to the discovery." [30]

Galton described another experiment, in which he hid one of his whistles at the tip of a hollow walking stick, with a rubber handle at the other end which he could squeeze to sound the whistle. He liked to test the hearing of various animals by unobtrusively placing the whistle near their ears and squeezing the handle. If they betrayed any reaction he concluded that they had heard the sound. He discovered that cats and small dogs were exceptionally sensitive to high pitches, but laconically confessed that "my attempts on insect hearing have been failures." [31]

Galton's style was lighthearted, but he saw a serious purpose behind these tests of sensory acuity. They were his first faltering steps toward the development of easily administered tests that could accurately detect "natural ability"—and that would ultimately be useful in his ideal eugenic society. Though they failed to achieve their ultimate purpose, since intelligence turned out not to be highly correlated with sensory acuity, they nevertheless provided the germinative idea that eventually led others to invent more valid tests of intelligence or ability.

Mental Imagery. Another of the seminal sections of *Human Faculty* dealt with variations in people's capacity for mental imagery. Galton's curiosity had been piqued by published popular accounts of people with photographic visual memories, who could scrutinize their mental images of things much as if they were real objects. Here was a clear example of a mental ability—presumably hereditary, of course—which varied greatly among different people, and which could be investigated statistically. Naturally, Galton composed a long questionnaire that asked each subject to "Think of some definite object—suppose it is your breakfast-table as you sat down this morning—and consider carefully the picture that rises before your mind's eye." Then came a long series of detailed questions dealing with such characteristics of the image as its *illumination* (Was the image dim or clear, its brightness comparable to the original scene?), *definition* (Are all of the objects on the table well defined at the same time, or is the place of sharpest definition more contracted than in a real scene?), *coloring* (Are the colors of the objects distinct and natural?), and *apparent location* (Does the image seem located in the head, in the eyeballs, in front of the eyes, or in the position corresponding to actually perceived reality?). Other questions dealt with the subject's general facility in imagining scenery, numbers and dates, faces, sights, sounds, smells, and other sensations.

When the results were in from many subjects, Galton found even more variability than he had anticipated. He was particularly astonished by the replies of several of his scientist friends, who reported that they had virtually no visualizing capacity at all, and—supposing everyone else to be like them—that they were amazed to be asked about such an obviously non-existent quality. One scientist wrote, "It is only by a figure of speech that I can describe my recollection of a scene as a 'mental image' which I can 'see' with my 'mind's eye'. . . . I do not see it . . . any more than a man sees the thousand lines of Sophocles which under due pressure he is ready to repeat." [32]

Some other subjects were at the other extreme, reporting that their images were indistinguishable in most qualities from perceptual reality. Most people, of course, fell between these two extremes, reporting images that were distinctly "visual" in quality, but that fell somewhat short of the vividness of real scenes. One average subject reported, "Fairly clear. Brightness probably at least one-half to two-thirds of original. Definition varies very much, one or two objects being much more distinct than the others." Another said, "I can recall any single object or group of objects, but not the whole table at once." [33]

Galton concluded that this highly variable "visualizing faculty" was determined in each individual by both nature and nurture. Family resemblances, plus subjects' reports that they had "always" been either high or low in visualizing ability convinced him of the hereditary component. But he also conducted some informal experiments showing that people could be trained to increase their visualizing capacity to a degree, and he suspected that at least part of the scientists' poverty of visual imagery was caused by their having accustomed themselves to long periods of highly abstract thought. These considerations suggested that nurture interacted with nature to produce each person's final visualizing tendency.

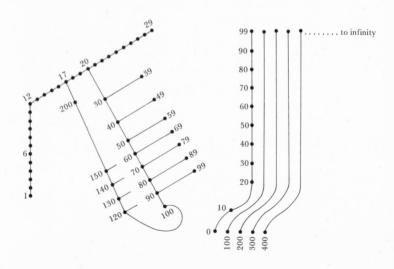

Figure 7–2 *Two Typical Number Forms* [34]

The Measurement of Mind

Some of the most fascinating variations in visual imagery lay in certain people's conceptions of numbers. For some individuals, the different numerals were not just abstract concepts, but were imagined in highly particular ways—a different color for each numeral, for example, or a different location in imaginary space. About one man in thirty, and one woman in fifteen, reported highly individualized "number forms" in which every imagined number occupied a specific location in a well-developed system. Such number forms were more easily drawn than described verbally, and two typical ones are reproduced in Figure 7–2. In each case, when the person thought of a specific number, it always occupied a position in imaginary space corresponding to the notation of the figures.

Galton believed that number forms, like the visualizing faculty generally, were the result of both nature and nurture. There were several cases where members of the same family had similar number forms, and this seemed evidence for a hereditary factor. Another observation suggested a nurture factor, however. Despite the great variability among the forms, most of them reflected in some way the peculiarities of the English nomenclature for numbers. As Galton noted:

We speak of ten, eleven, twelve, thirteen, etc., in defiance of the beautiful system of decimal notation in which we write those numbers. What we see is one-naught, one-one, one-two, etc. . . . The conflict between the two systems creates a perplexity, to which conclusive testimony is borne by these numerical forms. In most of them there is a marked hitch at the 12. . . . The run of the lines between 1 and 20 is rarely analogous to that between 20 and 100, where it frequently first becomes regular. The 'teens frequently occupy a larger space than their due.[35]

Galton thought the irregularities in the English nomenclature were "barbarous," and that arithmetic could be learned earlier and more easily by children if the 'teens could be given a system of names as regular as their written notation. Thus "on-one" might be substituted for eleven, "on-two" for twelve, "on-three" for thirteen, and so on. Bad as the English system was, Galton deplored the French even more, where a number such as ninety-eight could be rendered as *quatre-vingt-dix-huit* —literally, "four-twenties–ten–eight." Galton imagined that the number forms of Frenchmen must be truly something to behold.

Galton's studies of mental imagery also included several case histories of people prone to visions, hallucinations, or phantasmagoria. These, like his other studies, established clearly how much variability there was in the ways different individuals imagined things. Subsequent research has confirmed Galton in this finding, and shown that great variability is also characteristic of other imaginative products such as dreams and daydreams. The study of such fantasy material is a major research activity today, and Galton's work on mental imagery must be recognized as one of its foundations.

Twin Studies. Galton provided the foundation for yet another major research tradition with a chapter in *Human Faculty* entitled "History of Twins." He solicited information from and about many different pairs of twins, particularly concerning their similarity to each other at various periods throughout their lives. His analysis was unsophisticated, but it nevertheless revealed two general classes of twins. First, there were those whose lives and personalities had been very similar to one another from virtually the moment of birth, sometimes in spite of their having been separated and subjected to different environmental effects. Second, there were twin pairs who showed marked divergence of character from early childhood onwards, even though they had been reared under conditions of strict equality. Galton recognized that these two kinds of twins represented two degrees of biological similarity. Twins of the first type developed from a single fertilized ovum, which split into identical halves giving rise to two genetically identical individuals. Today these are referred to as *monozygotic* or *identical twins*. The second type of twins developed from separate ova which were separately fertilized. These twins—called *dizygotic* or *fraternal twins* today—were not genetically identical, but bore only the same similarities to one another as ordinary brothers and sisters.

Galton drew a predictable conclusion from these data: "There is no escape from the conclusion that nature prevails enormously over nurture when the differences of nurture do not exceed what is commonly to be found among persons of the same rank of society and in the same country."[36] How else could one account for the persistent similarity of the genetically identical monozygotic twins, or the persistent dissimilarity of the non-identical dizygotic twins? In spite of the simplistic nature of Galton's analysis, this work started an important research strategy known as the *twin study method*. With it, comparisons between samples of monozygotic and dizygotic twins are used to determine whether specific traits are inherited or acquired. Monozygotic twins are very similar to one another in terms of both heredity and environment, while dizygotic twins are highly similar only in environment; thus, if monozygotic twins are more similar to each other on a particular characteristic than a matched sample of dizygotic twins, the difference may be attributed to the greater hereditary similarity of the monozygotic twins. If, on the other hand, monozygotic and dizygotic twin pairs show equal degrees of similarity, the characteristic in question is probably not hereditary. The twin study method has been used by modern behavior geneticists in attempts to assess the hereditary components of many psychological characteristics, including IQ, hypnotizability, and susceptibility to various mental illnesses.

Associations. At least one of the innovative psychological investigations reported in *Human Faculty* dealt with a phenomenon that was admittedly *not* hereditary, but that was produced almost exclusively by nurture. This was the store of *associations* among ideas that each person develops from experience.

In studying associations, Galton served as his own first subject by examining the variety of his fleeting thoughts and associations as he took a routine stroll along London's Pall Mall:

I scrutinised with attention every successive object that caught my eyes, and I allowed my attention to rest on it until one or two thoughts had arisen through direct association with that object; then I took very brief mental note of them, and passed on to the next object. I never allowed my mind to ramble. The number of objects I viewed was . . . about 300. . . . It was impossible for me to recall in other than the vaguest way the numerous ideas that had passed through my mind; but of this, at least, I am sure, that samples of my whole life had passed before me, that many bygone incidents, which I had never suspected to form part of my stock of thoughts, had been glanced at as objects too familiar to awaken the attention. I saw at once that the brain was vastly more active than I had previously believed it to be, and I was perfectly amazed at the unexpected width of the field of its everyday operations.[37]

A few days later Galton repeated the experiment, and was surprised to find that many of the same associations recurred the second time around. He remained impressed by the mind's constant and often unnoticed activity, but realized that the store of associations was not so large as his first experiment had led him to believe: "The actors in my mental stage were indeed very numerous, but by no means so numerous as I had imagined. They now seemed to be something like the actors in theatres where large processions are represented, who march off one side of the stage, and, going round by the back, come on again at the other." [38]

Next, Galton experimented more systematically as he invented the *word association test*. He wrote seventy-five stimulus words on separate pieces of paper, randomized the order, and permitted himself to glance at them one by one. Each time he noted the two or three first thoughts that came to mind, and recorded them on a separate sheet of paper. He found this to be "repugnant and laborious" work, but persevered until he had gone through the entire list on four widely separated occasions. Then he statistically analyzed his total list of 505 separate associations gleaned from his 300 trials. The 505 responses contained only 289 different associations, because several ideas recurred on two, three, or even all four of the times he went through the list. This confirmed Galton's impression from the early experiments that the mental stock of associations is relatively limited, and that "the roadways of our minds are worn into very deep ruts." [39]

Two of Galton's findings about his associations anticipated discoveries which Freud was to confirm several years later with his closely related *free association method*. A surprisingly high proportion of the associations, especially the repeated ones, dated from childhood. This suggested a greater importance of childhood experience in determining adult mental life than Galton had expected. Even more striking was the embarrassing nature of many of the associations. Galton would not publish verbatim accounts of his associations because "they lay bare the foundations of a man's thoughts with curious distinctness, and exhibit his mental anatomy with more vividness and truth than he would probably care to publish to the world." [40] This was undoubtedly part of the reason he found the experimental procedure to be so laborious and repugnant, as his more intimate associations inevitably aroused the *resistance* that Freud would later document so fully. While he did not pursue these studies, there is a hint in *Human Faculty* that Galton perceived the existence of an unconscious lying behind his peculiar associative processes: "Perhaps the strongest of the impressions left by these experiments regards the multifarious-ness of the work done by the mind in a state of half-uncon-sciousness, and the valid reason they afford for believing in the existence of still deeper strata of mental operations, sunk wholly below the level of consciousness, which may account for such mental phenomena as cannot otherwise be ex-plained." [41] Once again, Galton had shown his ability to antic-ipate and initiate psychological ideas that would soon capture the imagination of the world.*

* Freud is known to have subscribed to the journal in which Galton first published his association studies, in 1879. Though he never referred to them in his own writings, they remain possible as a minor source of his later ideas on free association and resistance as described in Chapter 6.

Correlation and Regression

Human Faculty was the last of Galton's major works addressed explicitly to psychological issues, but it was not the last of his contributions to the emerging science of psychology. In 1888 he published a paper entitled "Co-relations and their Measurement," and in 1889 a book entitled *Natural Inheritance,* which described some new mathematical ideas that were to revolutionize biological and psychological research.

Until the appearance of these works, scientists had been unable to state mathematically the degree of relationship between two imperfectly correlated variables. Historically, this inability had not significantly hindered the development of the *physical* sciences, most of whose laws had been expressible as straightforward mathematical relationships between variables. The speed of a freely falling body, for example could be calculated by multiplying the time the body had been falling by the acceleration due to gravity, a constant. The relationships among speed, time, and the gravitational constant were all straightforward and immediately comprehensible. In biology and psychology, however, observed variables usually related to one another only partially and incompletely. Observations showed that tall fathers were likely to have tall sons, for example, but this was not always the case; sometimes a tall father had a short or an average-sized son. It was not possible to write an equation giving every son's height as a fixed proportion of his father's. Many other imperfect relationships of this type had been observed or hypothesized in the history of biology and psychology. Several of them have been noted in this book, where variables were described as *tending* to be associated with one another: aphasia tended to be associated with left frontal brain damage; hypnotizability tended to be enhanced by the contagion effect; intelligence tended to be associated with sensory acuity (or so Galton thought), and so on. Obviously these were imprecise statements, and up until 1889 they had to remain imprecise because there was no way of giving mathematical description to the relative strengths of the hypothesized tendencies.

Galton was concerned with this problem because of his intense interest in determining the precise laws of inheritance. For example, he knew that inherited characteristics were more highly correlated among close relatives than distant ones—that fathers and sons were more similar to one another than were uncles and nephews—but he lacked a way of stating the relationships precisely.

As was his wont, Galton began his search for a solution by measuring and counting, obtaining an empirical data base from which to work. He planted peas of varying sizes, then measured the sizes of the offspring peas.* He badgered his friends into doing the same thing, and sending him their results. Later, he encouraged families to undergo the tests and measurements of the Anthropometric Laboratory. In sum, he collected thousands of measures from relatives of varying degrees, and then spent countless hours scrutinizing his data, trying to see what patterns might be revealed.

After some trial and error procedures, Galton learned to cast his data in the form of *scatter plots,* where the two correlated variables were marked off on perpendicular coordinates, and individual pairs of scores were plotted at the appropriate intersections. Figure 7–3 is a reproduction of one of Galton's scatter plots showing the relationship between the heights of 314 adult children and those of their parents. Each parental value was the average of mother and father, with all females' heights multiplied by 1.08 to make them comparable to males'.) The numbers in the various cells represent the number of observed cases for each possible combination. Thus the 2 in the lower left hand corner indicates that there were two children between 63″ and 64″ who had parents between 65″ and

---

* It was by the merest of circumstances that Galton chose to experiment with a plant similar to that used by Gregor Mendel (1822–1884) in his great studies of inheritance in the 1860s. Mendel's studies had been published in obscure journals, and did not become known to Galton or other workers in genetics until the turn of the century.

Children's Heights (Mean = 68.0")

Parents' Heights (Mean = 68.1")	63"	64"	65"	66"	67"	68"	69"	70"	71"	72"	73"
72"						1	2	2	2	1	
71"				2	4	5	5	4	3	1	
70"	1	2	3	5	8	9	9	8	5	3	
69"	2	3	6	10	12	12	2	10	6	3	
68"	3	7	11	13	14	13	10	7	3	1	
67"	3	6	8	11	11	8	6	3	1		
66"	2	3	4	6	4	3	2				
65"											
Mean Height of Parents in Each Column	67.2	67.3	67.4	67.6	67.9	68.2	68.4	68.8	69.1	69.3	

Figure 7–3 *One of Galton's Scatter Plots*

66". The 3 immediately above it shows there were 3 children between 63" and 64" with parents between 66" and 67", and so on for the rest of the table.

Regression Analysis. After a long study of his scatter plots, Galton came to a simple but fundamental insight: all of the data representing a less than perfect correlation between two variables showed a characteristic that he called *regression toward the mean*. This rather forbidding sounding expression simply meant that extreme scorers on one correlated variable tended to have less extreme scores on the second. This is illustrated by the values in Figure 7–3. Consider the eleven cases in the far left-hand column, representing all the children between 63" and 64". Assuming an average height for them of 63.5", they deviate from the overall children's mean of 68.0" by 4.5". Now regard the parents' heights of those same eleven children. Assuming that there are two parental values of 65.5", three of 66.5", and so on, the mean parental value for that column is 67.2"—only 0.9" less than the overall

The Measurement of Mind

parents' mean of 68.1". This deviation is in the same direction as the children's, but it is less extreme. The parental scores have "regressed" toward the mean of the population.

A similar phenomenon is revealed by the other columns. For example, the eighth column from the left represents thirty-four children between 70" and 71". The children's average deviation is 2.5" above the overall mean. Their parents' average height of 68.8" is also above the overall parental average, but by only 0.7"—once again showing the regression.

Regression toward the mean occurs in countless other relationships besides that between parents' and children's heights. Students who do exceptionally well on one psychology examination, for example, are likely to do well on the next one also, but not as well, on the average, as on the first. Conversely, students who do very poorly on the first exam will tend to improve somewhat on the second. Horse breeders know that the offspring sired by the Triple Crown winner, Secretariat, will be fast runners, but their average speed will

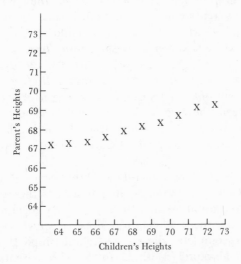

Figure 7-4 *Regression Line Computed for Figure 7-3*

not match his. Top professional athletes in one sport tend to be talented in other sports as well, but their skill in those sports is not as great, on the average.

It is essential to note that regression toward the mean refers to *average* tendencies in *populations* of paired variables, and it does not mean that an exceptional rating on one variable is *never* associated with one even more exceptional on the other. Tall fathers sometimes do have sons taller than themselves; indeed, they are much more likely than short fathers to have exceptionally tall sons. Horse breeders certainly know that Secretariat is more likely than a run-of-the-mill horse to sire exceptionally fast offspring. That is why they are willing to invest millions of dollars in him. But on the average, regression toward the mean always occurs.

Galton recognized yet another important mathematical quality of the data in his scatter plots. If the number of cases was sufficiently large, the means of the successive columns always created an approximately straight line when plotted across the graph. Figure 7-4 shows this for the data of Figure 7-3; the *x*s represent the parental means, as reported in Figure 7-3, for each of the columns of children. The line along which the *x*s lie is known as the *regression line*.

One of Galton's great insights occurred when he recognized that the *slope*, or steepness, of a regression line can be, under certain conditions, an index of the strength of the relationship between the two variables. This becomes clear after considering two ideal cases: a perfect relationship between the variables, and the complete absence of relationship between them.

First, assume a perfect relationship, where every child's height is exactly the same as its parents'. If these values are plotted on a graph, as in Figure 7-5a, they form a perfectly diagonal line, the mathematical slope of which is 1.0. Now consider a complete absence of relationship. If children's height has absolutely nothing to do with parental stature, then *all* groups of children—short, average, or tall—will have parents whose average height approximates the mean for

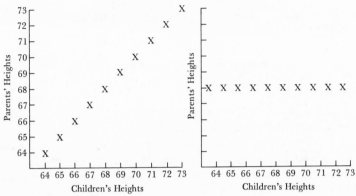

Figure 7–5 *Ideal Cases of Regression Lines*

the total parents' group. These parental averages will form a perfectly horizontal regression line, coinciding with the value of the total group's mean. This line, which is represented in Figure 7–5b, has a mathematical slope of o.o.

Galton realized that under certain conditions—when the two variables are expressed in the same units and show equal degrees of variability—the slope of the regression line for positively correlated variables must lie between these two extremes, and be an index of the strength of the relationship. If the relationship is strong, the line approaches the diagonal and has a slope close to 1; if the relationship is weak, the slope approaches zero.

There still remained several difficulties to be overcome before these ideas could be widely applicable. It was necessary to deal with cases where the units and variabilities were different for the two variables, for example, and to provide a mathematically exact method of computing the slopes of the regression lines. Galton himself could provide only partial solutions for these difficulties. Final success had to await the mid-1890s, when a young English statistician named Karl Pearson (1867–1936) read Galton's work on regression and was inspired to take up the remaining challenges.

Coefficient of Correlation. Pearson succeeded brilliantly, and devised a relatively simple computing formula to yield a *coefficient of correlation* varying between +1 and −1 for pairs of variables. The interpretation of these coefficients is the same as for the slope of regression lines, with weak relationships indicated by values close to zero, strong ones by those approaching plus or minus one. Negative values indicate negative relationships, when high scores on the one variable are associated with low scores on the other.

Pearson employed the symbol r to designate the coefficient of correlation, to indicate its foundations in Galton's regression analysis. Together with several closely related statistical measures of association, "Pearson's r" has become one of the most widely used of all statistical tools in psychological research. Hundreds of thousands of correlation coefficients have been reported between psychological variables, lending a precision to psychological studies that was undreamed of before Galton.

Besides providing valuable information in themselves, correlation coefficients have provided the basis for a whole new series of powerful multivariate statistical techniques for examining complex interactions among many different variables at the same time. These techniques would not be possible without the high-speed data-processing capacity of modern computers, but they rest firmly on the foundations laid by Galton's regression analysis. Thus Galton, who had begun his psychological career with the rather crude empiricism of *Hereditary Genius,* capped it off with a methodological contribution of great precision and sophistication. Many contemporary investigators regard regression analysis as Galton's greatest gift to psychology.

Galton's Place in Psychology

Galton was sixty-seven when *Natural Inheritance* was published. Though his formal psychological work was at an end, he scarcely became inactive in his old age. In fact, his energy and versatility were manifest again in the 1890s as he pioneered the founding of yet another new discipline. His interest in individual differences had naturally led him to seek characteristics that could *identify* specific individuals conclusively. Accordingly, he developed the first workable system for classifying and identifying fingerprints—an innovation that was eventually adopted by Scotland Yard and then by most other police agencies around the world.

If there was a major disappointment for Galton to live with in old age, it was the ironic fact that he had never had children of his own. Even though he had married according to the best eugenic principles—his wife came from a family nearly as distinguished as his own—here was one caprice of nature that his science could not have anticipated.

Even so, Galton had the consolation of seeing his intellectual descendants prosper. Karl Pearson founded a new journal entitled *Biometrika* in 1901, which carried on Galton's innovating traditions in biological statistics. Galton was pleased to act as consulting editor, and he occasionally contributed articles. Furthermore, a small but avid band of followers supported Galton's eugenics movement. More than anything else, this personal "religion" dominated his declining years as he wrote and spoke frequently on the scientific principles of race betterment. At the age of eighty-six Galton wrote his autobiography, *Memories of My Life,* where he recalled with relish and humor his mutifaceted and long life. He died three years later on January 17, 1911.

Few men have had greater impact on modern psychology, as scientists continue to involve themselves in the ideas and issues he originated. Twin studies, questionnaire studies, correlational studies, and investigations into imagery and associations are the lifeblood of many modern psychologists, to say nothing of the vast industry that concerns itself with the testing of intelligence. Even Galton's controversies continue unabated, as psychologists still hotly debate the nature-nurture question. There is now little doubt that Galton overemphasized the role of heredity in determining individual differences, prevented as he was by many of the biases of his class from appreciating the helps and hindrances of the social environment. But there is equally little doubt that heredity plays a substantial role. The question is, *how* substantial, and how may its effects be disentangled from those of the environment? Modern psychologists differ in their answers to this question, just as Galton and de Candolle differed one hundred years ago. Despite the progress that has been made, the facts remain difficult to interpret and it is likely to be many more years before the question is conclusively answered. Thus, quite apart from his continuing influence on geography, meteorology, biology, statistics, and criminology, Francis Galton remains a central figure in the progress of modern psychology.

Suggested Readings

For more on Galton's life, see his own *Memories of My Life* (London: Methuen, 1908); Karl Pearson's monumental *The Life, Letters and Labours of Francis Galton* (Cambridge, England: The University Press, 3 Vols., 1914–1930); and D. W. Forrest's *Francis Galton: The Life and Work of a Victorian Genius* (London: Paul Elek, 1974).

Galton's psychological ideas appear mainly in his three lively books, *Hereditary Genius* (Gloucester, Mass.: Peter Smith, 1972), *English Men of Science* (London: Frank Cass & Co., 1970), and *Inquiries into Human Faculty and its Development* (London: J. M. Dent & Sons, 1907). More detailed information about Galton's contributions to correlation and regression analysis are found in his own *Natural Inheritance* (London: McMillan, 1889), Volume III of the Pearson biography, and Chapter 5 of Helen M. Walker's *Studies in the History of Statistical Method* (Baltimore, Williams & Wilkins Co., 1929).

8

Psychology as the
Science of Behavior:
Ivan Pavlov and John B. Watson

At the turn of the present century, the Russian physiologist Ivan Petrovitch Pavlov (1849–1936) was on the horns of a dilemma. He had just completed a monumental series of studies on the physiology of digestion that would win him a Nobel Prize, and he was looking for new scientific challenges. Some incidental observations he had made in the course of those studies seemed to point to a new and promising area, but Pavlov was uncertain about its scientific propriety.

The new idea was to study a class of responses that Pavlov initially called "psychic secretions." His earlier research had concerned itself only with *innate* digestive responses that occurred in response to clear-cut and measurable *physical* stimuli, such as the salivation of a dog whenever food powder or dilute acid was placed in its mouth. He could not help but notice, however, that many digestive responses were *learned,* and occurred in the presence of *psychological* stimuli. The watering of a dog's mouth at the sight of its keeper as its customary mealtime approached was the clearest example. Pavlov knew that he had already developed a series of procedures and apparatuses that could enable him to study and measure these psychic secretions with the same precision he had achieved on the innate responses. But he was worried by the nature of the scientific company he might have to keep if he plunged into this new venture. The study of psychic secretions seemed bound to have connections with psychology, and Pavlov was disdainful of the introspection-based theories of academic psychology. He thought of himself as a hard-headed, completely scientific *physiologist,* and was reluctant to contaminate his work by associating it with questionable doctrines about unverifiable subjective states. "It is still open to question," he wrote, "whether psychology is a natural science, or whether it can be regarded as a science at all." [1]

Finally, in 1902, Pavlov saw his way to a solution. His compatriot Ivan M. Sechenov (1829–1905) had years before written a book entitled *Reflexes of the Brain* which argued that all behavior could be accounted for in terms of an expanded reflex concept. Acquired reflex processes in the cortex of the brain could presumably become superimposed on innate reflexes lower in the nervous system, thus exerting control over them. The cortical reflexes were hypothesized to be the neurological underpinnings of such psychological phenomena as thinking, willing, or deciding. After pondering Sechenov, Pavlov realized that psychic secretions could be interpreted as the result of new, cortical reflexes becoming attached to the innately given neural circuitry of the basic digestive reflexes.

From this new point of view, everything could be described in proper physiological terms, and embarrassing references to subjective psychological states could be dropped altogether. Psychic secretions could be renamed *conditioned* (or *conditional*) *reflexes* to emphasize their acquired and variable character; by contrast, the innate digestive responses could be called *unconditioned reflexes.* Observed relationships between conditioned and unconditioned reflexes could form the basis of inferences—not about vague psychological states, but about potentially observable physiological processes in the brain.

Pavlov formally banned all psychological terminology from his laboratory, threatening to fire anyone who discussed findings in subjective terms, and spent the rest of his long life studying conditioned reflexes. To his dying day he maintained that he was not a psychologist, but a physiologist studying the brain.

Inevitably, however, psychologists began to take an interest in Pavlov's work. Prime among them was the young American professor John Broadus Watson (1879–1958) who, like Pavlov, had grown suspicious of the unverifiable nature of introspective psychology. In 1913 Watson electrified his colleagues by asserting that the proper subject matter for psychology was not the abstract concept of the "mind," but objective, observable *behavior* instead. Shortly thereafter, he realized that Pavlov's conditioned reflex concept could be applied to responses other than digestive ones, and could be an ideal tool for the objective analysis of learned behavior in general. Armed with this new conceptual weapon, Watson created the school of *behaviorism* that was to dominate American psychology for many years, and that remains a major force today.

The present chapter deals with the biographies of Pavlov and Watson. Though different from one another in many respects, both were effective advocates of their behavioristic visions who pursued their ideas with single-minded energy and zeal. Each was a powerful personality who swept others along with his enthusiasm, and who exerted a lasting influence on the intellectual life of his country.

Ivan Pavlov: Early Life and Education

Ivan Pavlov was born on September 27, 1849, in the central Russian farming village of Ryazan. His father was the village priest and his mother the daughter of a priest, but the family's life differed little in its external respects from that of the other peasant families in the town. At the age of ten, Pavlov suffered a serious fall, which led to a prolonged period of ill health. Since his family had to work the fields, he was placed under the care of his godfather, the abbot of a nearby monastery. Here, Ivan was encouraged to read, and at first he always rushed to tell his godfather about any book he had just finished. Instead of giving the boy an immediate audience, the godfather always insisted that he write down his observations on the book so they could be examined and commented on at leisure. This strategem not only bought the abbot time free from interruption, but also provided excellent training in systematic observation and reporting for the young Pavlov.

In his formal education, Pavlov benefitted from the educational reforms of Czar Alexander II, which guaranteed that gifted but poor students could receive proper educations. Pavlov received complete primary and secondary educations in ecclesiastical schools, and in 1870 he was permitted to enroll in the University of St. Petersburg as a student in the natural sciences. His choice of subject had been partly determined by his reading a translation of G. H. Lewes's *The Physiology of Common Life*. This standard physiological text fascinated Pavlov, particularly by its treatment of the digestive tract. "How does such a complicated system work," [2] he asked himself, and he was embarked on the scientific quest that would eventually win him the Nobel Prize.

Pavlov's most influential professor at St. Petersburg was a mercurial young physiologist named Ilya Cyon (1843–1912). Cyon had been trained in Leipzig, where he was assistant to Carl Ludwig, one of the leaders of the mechanist movement in physiology. Cyon imbued Pavlov with a firm belief in physiological mechanism, as well as an appreciation for the importance of precise experiments. Pavlov was an excellent student, and was asked to become Cyon's assistant. The plan fell through, however, when Cyon was dismissed from the university for his political activities. Pavlov was offered the job as assistant to Cyon's successor, but he refused it because he did not respect the new man's scientific integrity.

After completing his undergraduate work, Pavlov went on for a degree in medicine. He supported himself (and after 1881, his wife as well) through several poorly paying assistantships. He also found time to conduct several independent experimental studies, which were so impressive that he was asked in 1878 to become director of a new experimental laboratory attached to a clinic in internal medicine. This was extraordinary, since Pavlov had not yet completed his own doctoral thesis. Nevertheless, his organizational and experimental abilities were already apparent, and he guided many fellow students through experiments on the effects of different drugs on the heart and vascular system. Finally in 1883, after five years at the laboratory, Pavlov finished his own thesis on the nerves of the heart. He then studied and travelled abroad for two years, spending some time in Leipzig with Carl Ludwig.

Even though Pavlov had outstanding credentials, jobs were scarce for young Russian scientists when he returned home. For several years he had to conduct his research from subordinate and ill-paid positions. Not until he was past the age of 40 did he obtain a post which provided him with the

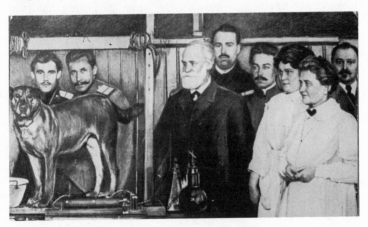

9. Ivan Pavlov and co-workers in his laboratory at the Military Medicine Academy, 1911. *Tass from Sovfoto*

scientific independence he needed. In 1890 he was appointed professor at St. Petersburg's Military-Medical Academy, where he was to remain for most of the rest of his life and win worldwide fame.

Pavlov's Laboratory

Ivan Pavlov showed two distinctly different faces to the world, depending on whether he was inside or outside his physiological laboratory. Outside, he was an impractical, absent-minded, and often sentimental man whose misadventures sometimes aroused the wonder of his friends. Inside, he was a vigilant, implacable, and superbly efficient administrator who aroused not only wonder, but also respect and fear in those who worked under him.

In private life Pavlov was notoriously careless about money even though he often lived just above the poverty line. Many months he simply forgot to pick up his salary. Once, after he had just won an academic promotion which brought with it a badly needed cash bonus, Pavlov lent an unscrupulous acquaintance most of the sum before he even got home. The money was never seen again, After this, all family financial affairs were conducted by Pavlov's wife, and he was seldom allowed to carry more than loose change. One of the few times he did carry much money was on a visit to the United States, made without his wife. All of his money—more than $800 in small bills—was jammed into a bulky wallet that protruded visibly from his jacket pocket. When Pavlov ventured onto the crowded New York subway, the predictable felony occurred. Fortunately for him, he was already world famous and the guest of the Rockefeller Institute, which replaced his funds.

Sometimes Pavlov's impracticality took a sentimental turn. When he was engaged, he spent almost all of his available money on luxuries for his fiancée—candy, flowers, theater tickets, and such. The only practical gift he bought her was a new pair of shoes, which she badly needed for a trip she was planning. She arrived at her destination and opened her trunk, to find only one shoe! Upon writing to Pavlov about the mystery, she received this answer: "Don't look for your shoe. I took it as a remembrance of you and have put it on my desk." [3]

If negligence, sentimentality, and impracticality characterized Pavlov's personal life, they were absolutely banned from his laboratories. In his pursuit of science he overlooked no detail. Though he often lived uncomplainingly in poverty, he spared no effort to ensure that his laboratory was always equipped and his experimental animals well fed. He was punctual in his arrival at the laboratory, perfectionistic in his experimentation, tyrannical in his control, and unhesitating in docking or firing workers who failed to meet his standards.

One of the most famous Pavlov stories concerns a worker who was late to the laboratory one day during the Russian Revolution, because he had to dodge skirmishes in the streets. Believing that devotion to science should supersede all other values, Pavlov did not regard that as a proper excuse. According to some versions of the story he fired the worker, though it is more probable he simply issued a reprimand. Less extreme manifestations of this same attitude occurred almost every month, as Pavlov would become irritated when his workers had to take time off to collect their pay.

In spite of his often unreasonable demands, Pavlov did inspire great loyalty among those workers who remained in his laboratory. Whatever else might be said, he was always honest in his reactions. So long as his workers were conscientious and careful, there were no long-term recriminations. Perhaps most important of all, his assistants realized that Pavlov never demanded more of others than of himself, and that his quirks were the result of a single-minded devotion to his science.

Unquestionably the most remarkable aspect of Pavlov's laboratory was its organization. Despite his troubles in looking after the necessities of private life, Pavlov ran a large and efficient laboratory that would be the envy of any administrator. Experiments were performed systematically by the thousand, according to a simple but ingenious scheme. Each time a new worker came into the laboratory, he would not be given a new or independent project to work on, but instead be assigned to replicate a series of experiments that had already been performed by Pavlov's other workers. In a single stroke, the new person learned first-hand about the work already in progress, and provided Pavlov with a check on the reliability of results already in. If the replication were successful, all was well and good and the new worker was ready to move on to something new. If it were not, a new replication by a third party would be done to clarify the situation. Because of this system, workers tended to know exactly what their co-workers were doing and could fill in for one another if necessary.

Pavlov's role in the laboratory was that of general planner and administrator. He designed the experiments, and assigned them to specific workers. He also liked to work on the experiments himself, and since he was familiar with all of their details he frequently took over for his workers when they took lunch breaks.

When he was an old and famous man, Pavlov wrote an article for the Soviet youth movement in which he described the secret of his own scientific success: "This is the message I would like to give the youth of my country. First of all, be systematic. I repeat, be systematic. Train yourself to be strictly systematic in the acquisition of knowledge. First study the rudiments of science before attempting to reach its heights. Never pass on to the next stage until you have thoroughly mastered the one on hand." [4] Someone who knew Pavlov only non-professionally might understandably have been incredulous of such advice from him. Those who worked with him in the laboratory, however, knew that he had accurately described the secret of his own success.

The Physiology of Digestion. During his first decade in the St. Petersburg laboratory, Pavlov set out to solve the mystery that had intrigued him since secondary school: the complicated workings of the digestive system. In many respects, his success in this venture was like Pierre Flourens's success in investigating the brain. Both men devised or perfected techniques for studying physiological functions in living and nearly normal organisms, which were effective because of their great surgical virtuosity. Originally, most physiological research had been performed simply by operating on an experimental animal to expose the organ under study. Often the animal was already dead, as in Helmholtz's studies of the nerves in frogs' legs, and in other cases the organ was simply observed in the still-living animal. While these procedures revealed some important information, they also had obvious limitations. Newly operated upon animals with their organ systems exposed were in a highly traumatized state, and there was no guarantee that their physiological functions were the same as in normal animals. Digestive functions, which are notoriously susceptible to the effects of stress, were especially difficult to study this way. Pavlov's problem, then, was to replace these *acute preparations,* in which organs were investigated immediately after being surgically exposed, with *chronic preparations,* in which the organs could be made permanently observable and be studied after the animals had recovered from surgical trauma. In the case of the normally well-concealed digestive organs, this was no mean feat.

Pavlov knew, however, that at least one spectacular chronic preparation of the digestive system had already been achieved, as the result of an almost incredible accident. In 1822, a young French-Canadian trapper named Alexis St. Martin suffered a terrible gunshot wound to his stomach. He was tended by the physician William Beaumont (1785–1853), who assumed the wound was fatal but patched him up as best he could. Surprisingly, St. Martin recovered and went on to live an almost normal existence. The only unusual thing about him was that the hole in the wall of his stomach never closed up, but remained for the rest of his life as a "window" through which the inside of his stomach could be seen. In gratitude for Beaumont's surgical skill, St. Martin agreed to serve as an experimental subject. He allowed the physician to observe his digestive processes, and even to insert instruments for collecting and measuring the digestive substances. Until Pavlov, Beaumont's observations of St. Martin remained the single greatest source of knowledge about the normal digestive processes.

In the 1890s Pavlov sought to replicate Beaumont's studies on a more controlled basis, through chronic preparations of different parts of the digestive tracts of dogs. Others had tried this before, without notable success. Pavlov succeeded, for two major reasons. First, Pavlov was among the first to recognize the importance of preventing post-operative infection through the use of aseptic surgical techniques. At a time when many humans were still dying from infections contracted in unsanitary surgical wards, Pavlov went to extreme lengths to assure the antiseptic cleanliness of his operations. Operations on the digestive tract were especially dangerous sources of possible infection, but Pavlov's methods ensured that most of his animals lived, whereas most of his predecessors' animals had died.

The second factor in Pavlov's success was his technical virtuosity as a surgeon. He was made uncomfortable by the sight of blood, and so always tried to perform his operations with the absolute minimum of physical trauma to the structures involved. Sure-handed and precise, he perfected a particularly delicate surgical preparation known as the *gastric fistula,* a channel leading from the inside of a digestive organ to the outside of the body through which various digestive products could be collected.

Using fistulas, Pavlov was able to study the functions of virtually every part of the digestive system. In his systematic way, he conducted hundreds of experiments in which the stimuli impinging on the different parts of the system were varied, and the resulting secretions were collected, measured, analyzed—and sometimes even bottled and sold as medicines to provide extra revenue for the laboratory. These were the studies that won him the Nobel Prize for physiology in 1904, and they are still cited as authoritative in modern textbooks of physiology.

Conditioned Reflexes

By the time Pavlov became a Nobel laureate, his primary interest had already shifted from digestion per se to conditioned reflexes; in fact, his first public mention of that term occurred in his Nobel address. He soon put his familiar research strategy to use in this new field, devoting the rest of his life to thousands of studies which systematically varied the four basic components of the conditioned reflex.

The four components were labelled by Pavlov the *unconditioned stimulus,* the *unconditioned response,* the *conditioned stimulus,* and the *conditioned response.* Before any conditioning occurred, the unconditioned stimulus and response were united in the innate unconditioned reflex. For example, food or acid in the mouth was an unconditioned stimulus which automatically elicited the unconditioned response of salivation. The conditioned stimulus—say the sight of the animal keeper, or the sound of a tone in an experiment—originally failed to elicit any salivary response, but after it had been paired with the unconditioned stimulus a number of times, it elicited salivation even in the absence of the unconditioned stimulus. In mentalistic terms, one could say that the conditioned stimulus had been "associated" with the unconditioned stimulus, and so came to elicit a response similar to the unconditioned response. In Pavlov's laboratory, of course, such terms had been banished. But Pavlov could express the relationships among the concepts objectively, in terms of the magnitudes of the unconditioned stimuli and responses, the numbers of pairings between the conditioned and unconditioned stimuli, the conditions under which the pairings took place, and so on.

Consider a simple Pavlovian experiment. The unconditioned stimulus was a certain amount of dilute acid on a dog's tongue, which had been shown by repeated trials to elicit a certain average number of drops of saliva as an unconditioned response. The conditioned stimulus was a tone of a certain pitch and loudness, which was sounded a certain number of times and immediately followed each time by the acid. Then, in the crucial test trial, the tone was sounded but not followed by the acid. The dog salivated, and the number of drops was taken as a measure of the strength of its new conditioned reflex.

Within this simple design there was room for the systematic variation of many factors, and the precise calculation of many laws of conditioning. For example, the numbers of pairings of conditioned with unconditioned stimuli prior to the test trial were varied, and as expected, few pairings produced weaker responses than many. The interval between the conditioned and unconditioned stimuli was varied, and it was found that the strongest and quickest conditioned responses occurred when the interval was very short. If the conditioned stimulus *followed* the unconditioned stimulus, however—even by a very short interval—no conditioned reflex at all could be produced.

Generalization and Differentiation. In one series of experiments Pavlov investigated the effect of a test stimulus that was somewhat different from the original conditioned stimulus. He discovered that if an animal were tested with a stimulus that was similar to the conditioned stimulus—say a tone of a slightly higher or lower frequency than that which had been paired with food during the conditioning—a response occurred, but it was weaker than it would have been in response to the original conditioned stimulus. The more dissimilar the test stimulus was, the weaker the response. This phenomenon is known as *generalization*, since the subject generalizes its conditioned response from one stimulus to other, similar ones.

Repeated generalization tests led to further developments. For example, a dog was repeatedly fed following the sounding of a certain musical tone. On the first generalization trial a tone one-half an octave lower was sounded, and a substantial salivary response occurred. Thereafter, the two tones were randomly sounded on different trials, with the original tone always being "reinforced" by the immediate presentation of food, and the lower tone never being reinforced. Gradually, the generalized response to the lower tone decreased, until it finally

disappeared altogether. In Pavlov's terminology, the conditioning procedures had led to a *differentiation* * between the two
stimuli. That is, the animal had learned not only to respond
positively to one stimulus, but also to inhibit the generalization of the response to a similar stimulus.

Experimental Neurosis. Some of Pavlov's most intriguing
findings occurred when he attempted to test the limits of his
animals' ability to differentiate. He discovered that while
it often required many trials to establish the first differentiation, it was easy to sharpen it after it had been established.
Thus, in one study, a differentiation was established in a dog
between the flashed image of a circle on a screen, which was
always followed by reinforcement, and a flashed ellipse, which
was never followed by reinforcement. The ellipse was quite
oblong. Then, after the differentiation was strongly established, the ratio between the ellipse's axes was gradually reduced, making it more and more circle-like. The animal
quickly learned to discriminate these new stimuli from the
circle—up until a dramatic breaking point. When the ratio
was so reduced that the ellipse was almost circular, the dog
became extremely agitated. Whereas it had previously been
placid and had submitted to the restraining harnesses of the
experimental apparatus with no difficulty, it now made frantic
efforts to escape and became very difficult to handle. The experimenter tried returning to some of the earlier differentiation
trials that the animal had previously mastered easily, but there
was no alleviation of the symptoms. All of the earlier differentiation conditioning had disappeared completely, and the
dog remained highly agitated. Only after it was given a long
rest and treated with much patience was the original, easy
differentiation re-learned. The breakdown in the dog's behavior became known—perhaps misleadingly—as an *experimental neurosis.*

Other experiments demonstrated other conditions under

* Most English-speaking psychologists today use the term *discrimination*
instead of differentiation, but the concept is identical to Pavlov's.

which experimental neuroses could be produced. In one, a dog had been conditioned with great difficulty to salivate when an electric shock to one of its rear feet was the conditioned stimulus. Originally, the dog had responded to the shock by struggling in its harness and trying to escape the situation. After many reinforcements with food, however, it began to accept the shock calmly, and immediately began salivating when it was administered. On the crucial trial, the shock was applied to a different part of its leg from that to which it had become accustomed. This stimulus elicited a much stronger avoidance response than the animal had ever shown before, even to the earliest shocks before the conditioning had become established. All of the earlier conditioning disappeared, and the animal required several months to recover from its experimental neurosis. In sum, Pavlov showed that experimental neuroses were likely to occur whenever an animal was subjected to an unavoidable conflict between two strong but incompatible response tendencies, like salivating or suppressing salivation at the ellipse, or tolerating or pulling away from the shock to the new part of the leg.

Pavlov's Theory of the Brain

Pavlov attempted to account for all of his findings in a speculative and rather complex theory of the brain and its functions. Following Sechenov, he argued that *un*conditioned reflexes are mediated by connections between sensory and motor nerves at the spinal and lower brain centers of the nervous system. Conditioned reflexes supposedly occurred when neural pathways in the *cortex* became part of the circuitry, establishing connections between certain stimuli and responses that had not been interconnected before. Crude evidence for the importance of the cortex was provided by animals whose cortexes were completely removed after they had already acquired a number of conditioned reflexes. These animals, who were kept alive by attentive keepers for up to four and a half years, retained their unconditioned reflexes.

Their conditioned reflexes disappeared with their cortexes, however, and no amount of training could make them return.

Pavlov's belief that the cortex was the site of conditioned reflexes naturally involved him in the localization of function question, for it became only logical to ask if different kinds of conditioned reflexes were localized in different specific regions of the cortex.* In deciding the question, he became briefly embroiled in one of the most spectacular controversies of his career. His antagonist was a colleague at the Military Medical Academy, named Vladimir Bechterev (1857–1927).

The trouble began when Bechterev's students ablated the portion of a dog's cerebral cortex which, when electrically stimulated, had produced a salivary response (just as stimulation of the motor strip produced a motoric response). They reported that all previously acquired conditioned salivary responses were lost following removal of this "salivary center," and that no new ones could be produced. Pavlov was initially pleased to learn of this experiment, since it was consistent with his own view of the importance of the cortex in conditioned reflexes. But when Pavlov tried to replicate the study, he found that the dog regained a full capacity for conditioned salivary reflexes if given a few days to recover from the operation. The Bechterev experiments had apparently not allowed the dog sufficient recovery time before testing. Pavlov concluded that the salivary center, however efficacious it might be in producing salivation upon electrical stimulation, was *not* a necessary component of conditioned reflexes involving salivation.

Pavlov began attacking Bechterev vigorously in print, until finally a public test was arranged between the two sides. The salivary centers were removed from two dogs in Bechterev's laboratory, and after a few days the animals were presented in a public demonstration—placed in front of a rotating glass drum with meat inside. The sight of the meat elicited not a drop of saliva, so the Bechterev forces claimed that condi-

* See Chapter 2 for the general details of the localization of function question.

tioned salivary reflexes had been removed. However, Pavlov immediately saw that meat inside a glass drum was a very weak conditioned stimulus for these dogs. One of his assistants has described what happened next:

Pavlov rose from his seat and firmly demanded a weak solution of hydrochloric acid. He had a resolute appearance, with his lips set and his brows knitted. When he was given the acid, . . . he poured [it] into the dogs' mouths several times. This produced an abundant salivary secretion. After the secretion had stopped, the mere sight, smell, or splash of the acid in a test tube caused the secretion of saliva, that is, a conditioned salivary reflex to the acid was formed . . . notwithstanding the absence of the cortical salivary centers. After this, Pavlov did not pay much attention to the proceedings and soon left.[5]

The dramatic Bechterev episode indicated that there was not a single cortical location necessary for all conditioned salivary reflexes, but it did not completely deter Pavlov from adopting the localizationist position. While there was clearly no cortical *salivary* center required for the reflexes, there just as clearly *were* necessary *sensory* centers for different kinds of conditioned reflexes. For example, all reflexes involving visual conditioned stimuli were entirely absent following complete removal of the visual center of the occipital cortex; auditory reflexes similarly disappeared following removal of the auditory areas of the temporal lobes. Thus, Pavlov could and did argue that different conditioned *stimuli* result in the arousal of different specific centers in the sensory cortex, even though the conditioned *response* did not have to originate from a single specific location.

Excitatory and Inhibitory Processes. Pavlov believed that there were two separate kinds of processes occurring in the various sensory areas of the cortex to produce conditioning. The one process was *excitatory,* and occurred in the acquisition and generalization of conditioned responses. The other was *inhibitory,* and occurred when a conditioned response was suppressed, as in differentiation training. Excitatory processes were aroused and strengthened by the repeated reinforcement of a conditioned stimulus through the presentation of the unconditioned stimulus; inhibitory processes were aroused by repeated non-reinforcement.

To account for the phenomena of generalization, differentiation, and experimental neuroses, Pavlov made two further assumptions about the structure and function of the brain. First, he assumed that the specific sensory locations representing similar stimuli are close to one another on the cortex. Second, he assumed that whenever excitation or inhibition is aroused in a particular location, it spreads out in a "wave" over nearby centers. Like a wave in water or air, its strength dissipates as it gets farther from the center. Pavlov called this hypothetical cortical phenomenon, which has never been actually observed, *irradiation*.

The irradiation of excitation and inhibition presumably caused the generalization and differentiation of conditioned reflexes. In generalization, a stimulus similar to the conditioned stimulus arouses excitation in a cortical center close to that for the conditioned stimulus. The excitation irradiates until, in a somewhat weakened state, it arouses the center for the conditioned stimulus, which in turn triggers a somewhat weakened response. If the similar stimuli are not reinforced, however, their centers begin to irradiate surrounding areas with waves of inhibition instead of excitation. As differentiation increases, the portion of the cortex surrounding the center for the true conditioned stimulus becomes increasingly irradiated with inhibitory potential. The final state has been almost poetically described as follows: "When a [differentiation] is firmly established, only a small region of the brain corresponding to the conditional stimulus will produce a response. Inhibition lies over the rest of the brain like winter over the empty plains of central Russia, limiting all activity to the lonely stockades." [6]

It would be wrong to think, as the winter image above might suggest, that the inhibition-irradiated areas are inert. Pavlov thought of them as fields of potentially highly active forces, which under the conditions of the experimental neurosis can have a disruptive effect on learning and behavior. An experimental neurosis occurs when a stimulus which cannot be avoided arouses strong excitation and inhibition at the same time; that is, its cortical position lies on a "boundary" between two nearby and very powerful centers of excitation and inhibition. Pavlov envisaged the resulting neurophysiological events as a *rupture* of the boundary, so that the entire surrounding area becomes inundated with an indiscriminate mixture of both excitation and inhibition. Instead of being confined within their boundaries, and thus producing the precise and regular effects of generalization and differentiation, the two forces conflict with one another in the same area and produce disorganized behavior whenever their centers are stimulated.

Human Psychiatric Disorders. In the course of his work on experimental neuroses in dogs, Pavlov made an observation that determined his major interest for the last few years of his life. He noted that there were striking individual differences among dogs in the specific symptoms of their experimental neuroses. Some dogs—especially those who had been naturally very active before the experiments—became hyperexcited in their neuroses, snapping, chewing, howling, and clawing in an indiscriminate manner. Other dogs—mainly those whose normal dispositions had been relatively placid—developed neuroses whose major symptoms were excessive lethargy and apathy. Pavlov concluded that these two "types" resulted from innate differences in the balance between excitatory and inhibitory processes in their brains. In one type, excitation naturally predominated, and the rupture led to a relatively indiscriminate dominance of excitation. In the other type, the opposite occurred.

In 1929, though past the age of eighty, Pavlov began to consider the implications of this work for the understanding of psychiatric disorders in humans. He familiarized himself with the varieties of psychiatric illness, and then attempted to account for them in terms of excesses and deficiencies in excitation and inhibition, the weakening of cortical cells, and the other variables he had found to be related to experimental neuroses. The therapies he prescribed for these conditions were strictly physical in nature, consisting mainly of regimens intended to rest or exercise the brain cells presumably at fault. Pavlov was also intrigued by the therapeutic potential of certain chemical substances, especially bromides, which he thought could rejuvenate injured or exhausted neurons. This work was influential in the development of several organically-based therapeutic programs in the Soviet Union.

Pavlov continued to be active in this work until February 21, 1936 when he fell ill following a full day at work. As his symptoms worsened and developed into pneumonia, he made systematic observations about his mental functions even with a high fever and a racing pulse. On the afternoon of February 27, he remarked to a consulting neuropathologist, "My brain is not working well, obsessive feelings and involuntary movements appear; mortification may be setting in." [7] One hour after making this final scientific observation, Pavlov died.

Pavlov's Reputation and Influence

By the time of his death Pavlov was a national hero in the Soviet Union, with even a town named in his honor. His final attitude toward his government was correspondingly grateful, though this had not always been the case. Just after the Revolution, when times were hard for scientists and Pavlov's Nobel Prize money had been confiscated by the State Bank, he did not hesitate to speak out against the Bolsheviks. Characteristically, he complained much more bitterly about his scientific hardships than about his personal loss of wealth. In the following years, he was investigated by the secret police, and lampooned in a state-sanctioned play. The government gradually recognized his value, however, both as a prestigious representative of Soviet science and as the promulgator of a new and properly materialistic theory that could become the foundation of a Marxist psychology. Pavlov was provided with increasingly generous research funds, and his attitude toward the government warmed correspondingly. By the 1930s, he was an avid supporter of the government, and conditioned-reflex theory was the official psychological doctrine of the Soviet Union. His theories had by now also been appreciatively noted in the United States, where they were an integral part of J. B. Watson's behaviorism.

It is perhaps ironic that Pavlov's greatest impact was on Soviet and American *psychology,* since he maintained to the end of his life that he was a physiologist, and that his work was of no interest to psychologists. The psychologists he had in mind, however, were those who studied the subjective states of consciousness. Little did he imagine a breed of psychologists who would cast all subjective phenomena to the winds, and concern themselves exclusively with the observable relationships between measurable stimuli and behavioral responses. These new psychologists did not feel constrained to speculate about the cortical underpinnings of their observed data, as Pavlov did, but recognized that objective techniques like his could be used to establish *behavioral* laws that would stand by themselves. This viewpoint, as championed by John B. Watson, was the foundation of the behaviorist movement that was to dominate American psychology for many years.

John B. Watson: Early Life and Education

The father of American behaviorism was born on January 9, 1878 near Greenville, South Carolina. Named after an eminent local minister, John Broadus, Watson was reared in a highly religious, fundamentalist household, but at an early age he developed a rebellious streak that was to become a permanent part of his character. In spite of mediocre high school grades, he gained admission at the age of sixteen to Greenville's Furman University where he proved himself to be an able and occasionally hard-working student. Following his mother's wishes, he was scheduled to enroll in Princeton Theological Seminary after graduating from Furman in 1899, until a peculiar circumstance intervened. During Watson's final term

10. John Broadus Watson (1878–1958). *The Bettman Archive, Inc.*

one of his favorite teachers announced that any student who dared to hand in an essay with the pages backwards would fail his course. As Watson later described it, "Although I had been an honor student the whole year, by some strange streak of luck, I handed in my final paper of sixteen pages in Civics backwards." [8] The teacher kept his word, and the next year saw Watson doing an extra year at Furman instead of a first year at seminary. As recompense, he was graduated in 1900 with a master's rather than a bachelor's degree.

During that final year at Furman, Watson's mother died, resulting in the sudden disappearance of external prods toward the ministry. Perhaps because of this, and perhaps because of a genuine shift in his interests, Watson's ambitions took a more secular turn. He had become interested in philosophy and psychology, and decided to attend graduate school in those two (not yet academically divided) subjects. An added motive was a desire to upstage the professor who had flunked him. The older man had taken a year's sabbatical to study psychology, and Watson resolved to make his teacher come to *him* for instruction one day.* Watson looked into both Princeton and the University of Chicago, then settled on the latter mainly because of its more lenient classical language requirements.

At Furman, Watson had been attracted to the philosophical side of psychology, and he expected that his most influential teacher at Chicago would be the well-known philosopher-psychologist, John Dewey (1859–1952). But Dewey turned out to be a great disappointment; "I never knew what he was talking about then, and unfortunately for me, I still don't know," Watson wrote many years later in his autobiography.[9] He had little more success with the traditional introspective methods of Wundtian experimental psychology. A fellow student recalled, years later, that Watson never learned to give consistent introspective reports, and speculated that this failure may have provided part of his motivation to create a purely objective psychology.[10] Watson himself partially corroborated this assessment, writing, "I hated to serve as a subject. I didn't like the stuffy, artificial instructions given to subjects. I was always uncomfortable and acted unnaturally." [11]

If the philosophical and introspective aspects of psychology came hard to Watson, there was one emerging area in which he could excel. Some of the professors associated with the psychology program at Chicago approached psychology from a *biological* perspective, and used animals rather than human beings as their subjects. One of these professors was Jacques Loeb, a German biologist who had developed the concept of *tropism* to account for the movement of plants (toward light,

* There was a sad aftermath to this story. Eight years later the old teacher, whom Watson genuinely liked, actually did apply to become his research student. His eyesight failed before arrangements could be completed, however, and shortly thereafter he died.

water, etc.), and who was concerned at Chicago with finding a similar, reflex-like concept to account for animal behavior. Another was the neurologist H. H. Donaldson, who conducted studies on the nervous system of the white rat. As a country boy who was both familiar and comfortable with animals, Watson found the study of animal behavior to be one psychological specialty in which he did not feel disadvantaged.

Donaldson became especially important to Watson, lending practical as well as intellectual support. On learning that Watson had to support himself by taking part time jobs, Donaldson hired him as keeper of his large colony of white rats. As Watson became intimately familiar with the behavior of these tame creatures, he realized that they would make ideal subjects for his doctoral thesis research. Under the direction of Donaldson and the psychologist James Angell, Watson conducted a study showing that increasing complexity in the behavior of young rats was associated with increasing growth of the myelin sheaths around the nerve fibers of their brains. Donaldson lent Watson $350 so he could publish this thesis, which appeared in 1903 under the rather unbehavioristic-sounding title, *Animal Education: The Psychical Development of the White Rat.*

Watson was an exceptionally energetic student, obtaining his Ph.D. in three years and becoming the youngest University of Chicago student ever to earn that degree. His achievement was all the more remarkable since he had to hold several part-time jobs to support himself. In addition to being a rat keeper, he was also an assistant janitor, waiter, library assistant, and laboratory assistant. During his final year he paid the price of overwork with a breakdown in which he suffered from severe insomnia. For a stretch of time he had to go to sleep with the light on, only to wake up at three in the morning with anxiety attacks that could only be dissipated by ten-mile walks. The symptoms finally disappeared after a vacation.

Upon graduation, Watson received several job offers in both psychology and neurology, the most attractive of which was to remain at Chicago as an assistant in experimental psychology. Two years later he was made an instructor, and two years after that he was about to be promoted to assistant professor when suddenly his professional advancement was startlingly accelerated. An associate professorship at Johns Hopkins University became vacant, and Watson was offered the position at the then substantial salary of $2,500 per year. When Watson hesitated slightly in the hopes that Chicago would raise its offer to an associate professorship, Hopkins increased its offer to a full professorship at $3,500. Even though Watson had been happy at Chicago, this was more than he could refuse. He set off for Baltimore at the age of twenty-nine, to assume an important position at one of America's major universities.

The Founding of Behaviorism

Once at Johns Hopkins, Watson's professional luck continued to hold good. In 1909, the psychology department's chairman became involved in a scandal and had to resign. Watson, as a full professor, inherited the leadership of the department as well as the editorship of a prestigious journal, the *Psychological Review*. At age thirty-one, Watson found himself in a position to mold the future shape of his department, and to publish his point of view before a wide audience. He took full advantage of these opportunities, pressing the president of the university almost immediately to sever the psychology department's ties to philosophy, and to strengthen those with biology.

At first, Watson lived in a kind of uneasy alliance with traditional introspective psychology, teaching courses along the lines of James and Wundt while conducting his own research on animals. He grew increasingly uncomfortable, however, as people asked him what bearing his animal work had on "real" psychology, the study of human consciousness. Watson was embarrassed by this question. "I was interested in my own work and felt it was important," he wrote, "and yet I could not trace any close connection between it and psychology as my questioner understood psychology." [12] Finally, Watson decided on a characteristically bold course of action. He would no longer accommodate himself to the demands of traditional psychology, but rather would insist that psychology redefine itself so as to offer a major position to his own specialty. He expressed this opinion in a strongly worded article in 1913 entitled "Psychology as the Behaviorist Views It," which he promptly published in the *Psychological Review*.

The essence of Watson's message was contained in his opening paragraph:

Psychology as the behaviorist views it is a purely objective natural science. Its theoretical goal is the prediction and control of behavior. Introspection forms no essential part of its methods, nor is the scientific value of its data dependent upon the readiness with which they lend themselves to interpretation in terms of consciousness. The behaviorist, in his efforts to get a unitary scheme of animal response, recognizes no dividing line between man and brute. The behavior of man, with all of its refinement and complexity, forms only a part of the behaviorist's total scheme of investigation.[13]

Three features of this statement were striking. First and foremost, Watson decreed that behavioristic psychology must be purely objective, ruling out all subjective data or interpretations in terms of conscious experience. Whereas traditional psychology employed objective observations of behavior to supplement introspective data, Watson argued that they ought to become the sole subject matter of psychology. For him psychology became the "science of behavior" rather than the traditional "science of conscious experience."

The second striking feature of Watson's statement was the new and highly practical set of goals it prescribed for psychology. Whereas traditional psychologies sought to *describe and explain* conscious states, Watson's goals were to *predict and control* overt behavior. Concepts such as Wundt's elements of consciousness or James's stream of thought meant not a whit to Watson, not only because they were "subjective" but also because they did not lend themselves to immediately useful purposes in the control of behavior.

Third and finally, Watson wished to eradicate the traditional distinction psychologists had drawn between human beings and animals. Following from Darwin's recognition that different species have evolved from common ancestors, Watson argued that the similarities among different species were just as important to emphasize as their differences. In Watson's behaviorism even the distinctive human characteristic of language did not matter much once subjective states had been ruled out by psychology. Studies of the behavior of rats, pigeons, apes, and flatworms took on new importance because of the continuity of all life forms.

Watson restated and expanded upon these views in his 1914 textbook, *Behavior: An Introduction to Comparative Psychology*, and met with a receptive audience among American psychologists. The following year he was elected president of the American Psychological Association. His presidential address dealt with his recent "discovery" of Pavlov's conditioned reflex theory, and suggested that the conditioned reflex could become the foundation of a full-scale *human* psychology encompassing everything from habit-formation to emotional disorders. Whereas his behaviorism had been at first little more than a point of view, it promised to become a full-fledged program of research with apparently limitless horizons.

Later Life and Career. Just as Watson's career was at its zenith, his life was adversely complicated by the First World War. He was drafted and assigned to run an examining board for aviators, but he soon found the rigidity of military existence too much for his independent temperament. "Never have I seen such incompetence, such extravagance, such a group of overbearing, inferior men," he wrote of professional soldiers.[14] Just as the war ended, Watson was about to be assigned to a dangerous intelligence mission in the army, apparently as a punishment for some form of insubordination. He was happy to return to Johns Hopkins and civilian life.

Watson immediately took up where he had left off in 1915, and began extending behaviorist principles to human psychology. His expanded horizons were evident in the new text he published in 1919 entitled *Psychology from the Standpoint of a Behaviorist*. Whereas his earlier text had been limited to *comparative* psychology—a sub-branch of psychology restricted to the comparative studies of differing species of animals—the new book purported to be a *general* psychology text. Watson tried to show here how subjects such as thought, language, personality, emotional disorders, and child development could be dealt with behavioristically. Later in 1919, Watson began some highly influential (and controversial) work on the conditioning of emotional responses in human infants, and seemed on the verge of completely dominating academic psychology.

Then, in the autumn of 1920, Watson's academic career ended even more abruptly than it had begun. Watson, who was married, became involved in an affair with his graduate student Rosalie Rayner, which terminated in divorce from his first wife and remarriage to Miss Rayner. The affair would hardly seem noteworthy today, but in the Baltimore of 1920 it was front-page scandal material. The Johns Hopkins administration concluded that it could not appear to condone such behavior and retain respectability as a co-educational institution. Watson was forced to resign.

Suddenly cut off from an important academic career, the resilient Watson went to New York to pursue business connections. He soon obtained a trial position with the J. Walter Thompson advertising agency. With characteristic vigor, he did a door-to-door survey among poor people in the south to determine the market there for rubber boots, peddled a well-known brand of coffee in Pittsburgh, and worked part time as a clerk in Macy's Department Store to learn about consumer attitudes. As he later put it, "I began to learn that it can be just as thrilling to watch the growth of a sales curve of a new product as to watch the learning curve of animals or men." [15] Not surprisingly, he was quickly successful in this lucrative profession and by 1924 he was a highly paid vice-president of the company.

Watson, however, did not immediately give up all psychological work. During his first years in New York, he lectured on behavioristic psychology at the New School for Social Research, and in 1924 he published his lectures under the title *Behaviorism*. This successful book was more engagingly written and more flamboyant in tone than anything he had written before and achieved a great popular success. A review in *The New York Times* proclaimed that *Behaviorism* marked "a new epoch in the intellectual history of man." [16]

As Watson became further removed from the staid halls of academe and more intimately involved in the world of advertising, his psychological writings naturally reflected the change. He wrote articles for popular magazines rather than scholarly journals, and gave them catchy titles such as "Feed Me on Facts," "The Weakness of Women," "The Heart or the Intellect," and "Are Parents Necessary?" Most of these articles took a frankly practical tone, and offered advice on such topics as child-rearing, personality improvement, or sex education. In 1928, Watson and his wife published *Psychological Care of the Infant and Child,* a guide to child-rearing along behaviorist lines. As the first child-rearing guide to achieve great popular success, this book opened up a whole new genre in American publishing.

Despite their popularity, these later works were never more than a sideline for Watson. As time went on he became increasingly more absorbed in advertising, and when he revised *Behaviorism* in 1930 it marked the end of his involvement in psychology. At the age of fifty-one, Watson had completed one of the most spectacular careers in the history of the discipline and become a full-time businessman. He remained active in advertising until his retirement in 1946. He died in 1958.

Watson's Behaviorist Writings

Watson's first behaviorist textbook, *Behavior,* was relatively limited in its scope. Explicitly subtitled as an introduction to comparative psychology—that is, the study of similarities and differences among various animal species—the book was mainly devoted to considerations of infra-human animals. Only in its opening chapter, which was a verbatim reprinting of the famous "Psychology as the Behaviorist Views It," and in a short chapter entitled "Man and Beast," did Watson hint at his larger ambitions. In fact, Watson in 1914 lacked the conceptual tools to apply behaviorism to more than a few problems in human psychology. Thus *Behavior* was hardly perceived as a revolutionary text by most psychologists, in spite of the radical prescriptions of its opening chapter.

But even though *Behavior* was generally perceived as just a compendious account of animal psychology, it contained the seeds of several ideas that would later assume importance in the behavioristic analysis of human psychology. One of these was a consideration of the relation between *instinct* and *habit,* the two most important units of behavior. Both were defined as sequences of concatenated reflexes, but the instinctual sequences are inherited while the habitual ones are acquired by experience. A bird builds its nest according to the instinctual patterns of its species, whereas an architect designs a house according to particular habits and customs acquired through personal experience. Even among the relatively more instinct-driven lower animals, however, Watson noted that innate, instinctual tendencies become quickly overlaid by experiential factors. The "pecking instinct" of a newly hatched chick becomes more accurate with experience, for example. At first, only about one-fifth of the pecks actually strike a grain on the ground; after a week, four-fifths are successful. Thus instincts, even simple ones, become modified by experience and assume some of the attributes of habits. Watson concluded: "That instincts are overlapped and obscured by later habits is unquestionable." [17] A few years later he would extend this point radically in his analysis of human behavior, arguing that innate factors are so completely overlaid by experience as to be negligible.

Another idea that would later assume importance in Watson's behaviorism was the notion that even such "mental" phenomena as *images* or *thought* could be dealt with as chains of muscular or glandular responses—that is, as habits like any other acquired animal behavior. Watson hotly denied that images and thoughts are anything more than various low level muscular responses in various parts of the body. When we "imagine" something, there is no internal, ephemeral "picture" that is mysteriously presented to the mind; instead there are small movements of the eye which produce an illusion of actually seeing: "Concurrently with the faintly articulated word apple there arise associated kinaesthetic impulses in the eye muscles. If these latter are strong, one can see how the fiction of visual imagery might arise." [18] Thought is much the same. Watson cited some suggestive (though admittedly inconclusive) evidence to suggest that the tongue and larynx make very\small movements when we think about something |that are similar to the larger movements made when we say its name. Thought thus becomes simply the perception of these very small responses. Like imagery, it becomes potentially explainable in terms of small but observable overt behaviors.

Another point briefly made in *Behavior* foreshadowed another later Watsonian preoccupation. After discussing the cases of animals trained to perform extraordinary feats, Watson noted that no valid comparison could be drawn between them and human beings until careful observations have been made on *human* development. "Unfortunately," he wrote, "neither the behavior of the chimpanzee nor that of the child has been subjected to sufficient analysis to make comparison feasible. . . . It is quite obvious that the behaviorist has no right to be content until the newly born chimpanzee and the newly born child are brought up side by side and subjected to the same training." [19] The study of child development would later become an important part of Watson's program.

Conditioned Reflexes. In spite of these hints of future developments, Watson in 1914 knew he was ill-prepared to carry out all of the provisions of his behaviorist manifesto. He freely admitted as much as he opened his presidential address to the American Psychological Association in 1915:

Since the publication two years ago of my somewhat impolite papers against current methods in psychology I have felt it incumbent upon me before making further unpleasant remarks to suggest some method which we might *begin* to use in place of introspection. I have found, as you easily might have predicted, that it is one thing to condemn a long-established method, but quite another thing to suggest anything in its place.[20]

His problem, in short, was to find an objective investigative technique that had as much relevance to human psychology as introspection was supposed to have.

By the time of his presidential address, Watson believed he had finally discovered just such a technique: the conditioned reflex method of Pavlov and Bechterev. None of the Russians' work had yet been directly translated into English, and when he wrote *Behavior,* Watson was familiar with only the barest outlines of Pavlov's work. By 1915, however, he had heard more extensive reports of conditioning methods, and realized that they could be applied to human as well as animal subjects. His presidential address was devoted to a description of some early experiments. He told how his student Karl Lashley had devised a removable salivary fistula that could be fitted inside the cheek of human subjects and used to measure their unconditioned and conditioned salivary reflexes.* He also described an apparatus which administered mild shock to a human subject's finger or toe, and measured the strength of

* A few years later Lashley, stimulated partly by the Pavlov-Bechterev dispute, made the important contributions to the localization of cortical function debate that are described in Chapter 2.

the withdrawal reflex. By pairing a neutral conditioned stimulus with the shocks, conditioned withdrawal responses could be elicited and measured.

As Watson clearly saw, the real significance of these experiments was not simply that people, like dogs, could be conditioned to salivate or to withdraw their toes in response to inherently neutral stimuli. What was significant was the implication, once the basic ability of humans to be conditioned was demonstrated, that different kinds of conditioned reflexes could explain many different varieties of human behavior. By stressing this point, Watson made his own most original contribution to the conditioning literature. Pavlov, of course, saw himself as a physiologist, and was more interested in the brain than in the behavior of his animal subjects. One type of response—salivation—was as good as any other for drawing the speculative physiological inferences that interested him, and so he did not concern himself with other kinds of responses. Watson, on the other hand, was seeking a general principle that could account for many different kinds of behavior, and he realized that Pavlov's conditioned reflex could be employed as a *model* for many other kinds of responses as well. In particular, he realized that human *emotions* could be conceptualized as glandular and muscular reflexes which, like the salivary reflex, become associated with many and sundry conditioned stimuli. Thus, the conditioning model potentially provided a non-introspective means of studying a complicated and important area of human psychology.

Human Emotions. Watson just hinted at these implications in his 1915 presidential address, but when *Psychology from the Standpoint of a Behaviorist* was published in 1919, he had developed them more fully. This textbook marked a major expansion of the behaviorist program, because from its opening sentences it was an unabashedly *human* psychology: "Psychology is that division of natural science which takes human activity and conduct as its subject matter. It attempts to formulate through systematic observation and experimentation the laws and principles which underlie man's reactions." [21] True to its promise, the text goes on to analyze several important and exclusively human characteristics in behavioristic terms.

Watson directly applied Pavlov's conditioned reflex theory in his treatment of human emotions, actually carrying out part of the recommendation he had made in 1914 by basing his theory on observations of human infants. His first step was to try to determine which aspects of human emotional response are innate—that is, what kinds of "emotional" behaviors may be observed in infants and what kinds of stimuli elicit those behaviors. These would correspond to the Pavlovian unconditioned reflexes. On the basis of his observations, Watson concluded that there were just three kinds of unconditioned emotional response, each one elicited by a specific and surprisingly restricted range of stimuli.

The first of the three innate emotions seemed to be a *fear* response. Behaviorally, this response was characterized by "a sudden catching of the breath, clutching randomly with the hands . . . , sudden closing of the eye-lids, puckering of the lips, then crying." [22] In very young infants, only two kinds of stimuli were found to be effective in eliciting this response. The first was a sudden loss of support, as when the infant was dropped (and caught without any actual physical harm being done) or when its covers were suddenly jerked beneath it. The second type of fear-producing stimulus was a loud and unexpected sound.

The second basic infantile emotional pattern was a *rage* response: "The body stiffens and fairly well-coordinated slashing or striking movements of the hands and arms result; the feet and legs are drawn up and down; the breath is held until the child's face is flushed." [23] The only stimulus Watson could find that would elicit this response in a newly born infant was a physical hindering of its movements: "Almost any child from birth can be thrown into a rage if its arms are held tightly to its sides; sometimes even if the elbow joint is clasped tightly between the fingers the response appears; at times just the placing of the head between cotton pads will produce it." [24]

Watson called the third unconditioned infantile emotion *love*, and noted that it was similar to the Freudian conception of polymorphously perverse *sex*. "The original situation which calls out the observable love responses seems to be the stroking or manipulation of some erogenous zone, tickling, shaking, gentle rocking, patting and turning on the stomach across the attendant's knee. The response varies. If the infant is crying, crying ceases, a smile may appear, attempts at gurgling, cooing, and finally, in older children, the extension of the arms, which we should class as the forerunner of the embrace of adults." [25]

As nearly as Watson could tell, these three responses, and the restricted range of stimuli that produced them, constituted the sum total of the innate human emotional predilections. Everything else, including such supposedly "instinctive" emotional responses as fear of the dark or love of one's mother were interpreted as the result of *conditioning*. Watson's debt to Pavlov was clear as he wrote, "When an emotionally exciting object stimulates the subject simultaneously with one not emotionally exciting, the latter may in time (often after one such joint stimulation) arouse the same emotional reaction as the former." [26] All the complications and complexities of adult emotional experience were explained as nothing more than conditioned responses based on three relatively simple unconditioned emotional reflexes.

Conditioned Emotional Reactions. When he wrote his 1919 textbook, Watson had little firm experimental support to back up his theory of adult emotions. The theory was plausible, but he had not actually produced a clear-cut conditioned emotional response in the laboratory. He lost little time in remedying this deficiency, however, and published his results the next year in a paper entitled "Conditioned Emotional Reactions." Written with Rosalie Rayner, his student and wife-to-be, this article recounts one of the most famous and controversial case histories in the entire literature of psychology.

Essentially, the article is a description of Watson's and Rayner's attempts to produce a conditioned fear response in an eleven-month old child they called "Albert B." The purpose of the experiment was to see if Albert could be conditioned to fear a white rat, a stimulus that initially evoked his interest and enjoyment rather than fear. The unconditioned fear stimulus subsequently paired with the rat was the sudden sound of a steel bar struck violently with a hammer just behind Albert's head. Watson and Rayner described the first conditioning trial as follows:

1. White rat suddenly taken from the basket and presented to Albert. He began to reach for rat with left hand. Just as his hand touched the animal the bar was struck immediately behind his head. The infant jumped violently and fell forward, burying his face in the mattress. He did not cry, however.
2. Just as the right hand touched the rat the bar was again struck. Again the infant jumped violently, fell forward and began to whimper.

In order not to disturb the child too seriously no further tests were given for one week.[27]

A week later the rat was again presented to Albert and, not surprisingly, received a less enthusiastic response than the week before. Albert did not cry or respond strongly otherwise, but kept his distance from the animal. Then, on five successive occasions Watson and Rayner placed the rat close to Albert and followed with the noise behind his head. When the rat was presented alone after this, a full-fledged fear response was evident: "The instant the rat was shown the baby began to cry. Almost instantly he turned sharply to the left, fell over on his left side, raised himself on all fours and began to crawl away so rapidly that he was caught with difficulty before reaching the edge of the table." [28]

Five days later the next test was performed. On the first trial the rat alone produced immediate whimpering and withdrawal. Then, to test for the generalization of the conditioned fear, Watson and Rayner presented a series of other furry stimuli—a rabbit, a dog, a seal coat, cotton wool, and a Santa

Claus mask. Each of these produced a noticeable avoidance response though less strongly than the rat. Finally, Watson put his own head down to see if Albert would play with his gray-ing hair. The result had a touch of poetic justice: "Albert was completely negative. Two other observers did the same thing. He began immediately to play with their hair." [29]

On a later test day, Watson and Rayner inexplicably wanted to "freshen" Albert's response to the rabbit and dog, and so clanged the bar after the presentation of these two stimuli whose only previous negative response had come from gen-eralization. The fear response to the rat was similarly fresh-ened, and Albert was then tested in a room different from the one in which all previous conditioning experiments had occurred. He showed marked fear responses to all the stimuli, indicating that his acquired emotional responses were not re-stricted to the situations and circumstances surrounding the initial conditioning. Finally, after a month with no trials at all, Albert was once again presented with the Santa Claus mask, the fur coat, the rat, the rabbit, and the dog, with no clanging bar. Crying and pronounced signs of fear were pro-duced by every stimulus.

Incredibly—at least from the present-day standpoint regard-ing research ethics—that was the last time Watson and Rayner saw Albert. He left the hospital permanently three days after these tests, with no attempt having been made to de-condi-tion the fears that had been so spectacularly produced. Wa-son and Rayner's discussion of these circumstances seems pe-culiarly insensitive, and hardly geared to convince parents to volunteer their children as subjects in future behavioristic research:

Our own view . . . is that these [fear] responses in the home environ-ment are likely to persist indefinitely, unless an accidental method for removing them is hit upon. . . . Had the opportunity been at hand we should have tried out several methods, some of which we may mention. (1) Constantly confronting the child with those stimuli which called out the responses in hopes that habituation would come in. . . . (2) By trying to "recondition" by showing objects calling out fear responses (visual) and simultaneously stimulating the erogenous zones (tactual). We should first try the lips, then the nipples and as a final resort the sex organs. (3) By trying to "recondition" by feeding the subject candy or other food just as the animal is shown. . . . (4) By building up "constructive" activities around the object by imitation and by putting the hand through the motions of manipulation.[30]

In their concluding section, Watson and Rayner poked fun at the psychoanalyst who might some day be asked to cure Albert's phobia:

The Freudians twenty years from now, unless their hypotheses change, when they come to analyze Albert's fear of a seal skin coat . . . will probably tease from him a recital of a dream which upon their analysis will show that Albert at three years of age attempted to play with the pubic hair of the mother and was scolded violently for it. . . . If the analyst has sufficiently prepared Albert to accept such a dream when found as an explanation of his avoiding tendencies, . . . Albert may be fully convinced that the dream was a true revealer of the factors which brought about the fear.[31]

The "Little Albert" case, for all its importance as a demonstration of the reality of conditioned emotional responses, was symptomatic of changes soon to come in Watson's writing habits. Shortly after its publication, Watson was stripped of his academic credentials, and he embarked on his second career in advertising. As he began to direct his psychological writings as well as his advertising copy to a mass audience, he used similar techniques in both. One expert on Watson's writings has noted that his post-1920 psychological works were "interesting, forceful, and assertive, but . . . also propagandistic, sometimes simplistic, and occasionally unscholarly. They seem to betray a mischievous pleasure in shocking their audience . . . by questioning cherished beliefs regarding child-rearing, marriage, religion, and so on." [32] As the Little Albert case clearly shows, many of these characteristics were already present in Watson before he left academia, and so cannot be attributed solely to his new environment.

In any case, Watson did become an immensely popular psychological writer during the 1920s, producing two influential books, *Behaviorism* and *Psychological Care of Infant and Child,* as well as a series of magazine articles.

Behaviorism. The most polished of Watson's later popular writings was *Behaviorism,* which treated all of his favorite subjects with more completeness and flair than ever before. The theory of emotions was given great emphasis, illustrated by the case of Little Albert and further enlivened by naturalistic observations of children's behavior when their parents fight or make love in their presence. A discussion of personality disturbance described a hypothetical dog which was first behaviorally conditioned to sleep in an ash can, foul its own bed, salivate constantly, and run away from small animals, before being deconditioned of these symptoms and retrained into a blue ribbon winner.

Watson also attempted to account behavioristically for the psychoanalysts' concept of *unconscious thought.* In a chapter entitled "Do We Always Think in Words?" Watson suggested that "unconscious thought" exists, but is far from the mysterious metaphysical entity he accused the psychoanalysts of fostering. Consistent with his earlier writings, Watson defined conscious thought as a series of vocal or sub-vocal verbal responses—the thinker literally talking to himself. Each verbal response serves as a stimulus calling forth one or more new responses which in turn serve as new stimuli, so that thinking proceeds in a chainlike fashion. All of the new responses in the chain need not be verbal, however; they can also be kinaesthetic or visceral, and often include emotional reactions. These non-verbal emotional responses serve as links in the chain of thought in the manner of the verbal responses, and may call forth in turn new responses of any variety. To the extent that the responses are nonverbal, thought is experienced as "unconscious;" to the extent they are verbal, the thought seems conscious.

Psychology as the Science of Behavior

Another new feature in *Behaviorism* was its *radical environmentalism*, the assertion that experiential factors are of overwhelmingly greater importance than hereditary ones in determining human behavior. (Indeed, if Watson felt the ground rumble beneath his feet as he wrote this book, it was probably the ghost of Francis Galton rolling over in his grave.) Watson's view had taken several years to develop. In 1914, he had argued that both instinct and habit were important, but noted how difficult it was to find an example of an instinct unmodified by experiential factors. By 1919, he had buttressed this position by asserting that there were only three innate human emotions, and that the complexity of human emotional life came entirely from conditioned reflexes built upon those simple foundations. Now he carried his argument a step further. Since the innately given foundations of behavior are so often obscured or modified by learned complications, Watson argued that one may safely disregard virtually *all* innate factors in accounting for individual differences in the behavior of adults. He admitted that there are differences in people's physical makeup, but denied that they could account for significant psychological differences. The most significant factors affecting individual differences, Watson believed, were early experiences rather than innate predispositions: "We draw the conclusion that there is no such thing as an inheritance of *capacity, talent, temperament, mental constitution,* and *characteristics.* These things . . . depend on training that goes on mainly in the cradle. . . . A certain type of structure, plus early training—*slanting*—accounts for adult performance." [33]

The major practical implication of this view, of course, is that an individual's character can be completely molded if one exerts complete and proper control over the crucial developmental experiences. One of Watson's most quoted passages boldly proclaimed this belief:

Give me a dozen healthy infants, well-formed, and my own specified world to bring them up in and I'll guarantee to take any one at random and train him to become any type of specialist I might select—doctor, lawyer, artist, merchant-chief and, yes, even beggar-man and thief, regardless of his talents, penchants, tendencies, abilities, vocations, and race of his ancestors.[34]

Needless to say, Watson could offer no conclusive proof in favor of his hypothesis. The best he could do in *Behaviorism* was to offer it up as an article of faith, much as Francis Galton had offered the contrasting view in *Hereditary Genius*.

Psychological Care of Infant and Child. Watson's environmentalism had one enormously practical effect, implying as it did that the rearing of children could be greatly improved by carefully controlling their conditioning experiences. Watson was unable to carry out his experiment with the twelve healthy infants, but he was soon able to influence the development of many more children indirectly through advice contained in his last psychology book, *Psychological Care of Infant and Child.* Here he strongly urged parents to take direct and frankly manipulative control of their children's environments, and expressly opposed the "progressive" educational methods of his old intellectual nemesis, John Dewey. Dewey, said Watson, espoused a "doctrine of mystery" which teaches that "there are hidden springs of activity, hidden possibilities of unfolding within the child which must be waited for until they appear and then be fostered and tended." But Watson held that really "there is nothing from within to develop." [35] All that is necessary is to control the child's environment so its conditioned reflexes develop properly.

Psychological Care of Infant and Child contains descriptions of the basic behaviorist studies of fear, rage, and love, and offers many practical suggestions about how to minimize the development of inappropriate conditioned emotional reactions. Thus, the home should be set up to minimize the occurrence of banging doors and other sudden loud sounds that could create fear responses, and children should be dressed in loose clothing to prevent unnecessary rage responses. Above all, children should never be stimulated into "love" responses on occasions when they ought to be developing self-reliant behaviors. Nothing drew Watson's scorn more severely than the coddling of children, the rewarding of their ineffective behavior with hugs, kisses, and other signs of solicitude. "When I hear a mother say, 'Bless its little heart' when it falls down, or stubs its toe, or suffers some other ill, I usually have to walk a block or two to let off steam," he grumbled.[36]

Watson encouraged parents to treat children "as though they were young adults" rather than coddle them, and offered a few suggestions that seem faintly humorous today. "Let your behavior always be objective and kindly firm," he urged. "Never hug and kiss them, never let them sit in your lap. If you must, kiss them once on the forehead when they say good night. Shake hands with them in the morning. Give them a pat on the head if they have made an extraordinarily good job of a difficult task." [37]

Few child-care experts today would endorse such a spartan approach, and most would argue that children actually need a certain amount of physical affection. But disagreements over points like this ought not to obscure the general message of Watson's book (which contains many sensible suggestions about how to encourage self-reliant behavior). He himself admitted that there is no single ideal way to bring up a child, and that desirable specific behaviors may differ widely from place to place or from time to time. Any habitual response can be evaluated only in the context of the culture in which it occurs. What is general, however, is the fact that parents or others charged with the upbringing of children can exert much more purposeful and effective control over the outcome than they usually do, whatever specific outcome they may desire. They need only to be familiar with the principles of conditioning, and then analyze their children's environments intelligently.

Such an approach to child rearing was a beautiful fulfillment of the general behaviorist program Watson had outlined in 1913. It began with systematic observations of the overt behavior of children until their responses to various specific situations could be predicted in advance. Then the environment was modified so as to control the responses, eliminating some and strengthening others at the will of the parent. Children, whose environments could be more or less completely controlled, and who lacked the verbal sophistication to complicate matters with mentalistic accounts of their psychological processes, turned out to be as ideal as subjects for behavioristic research as the animals that had originally inspired it.

Needless to say, the consequences of such research are immensely greater when children are its subjects, and its conduct is properly a subject of vigorous debate. But the scientific principles Watson espoused are exactly the same for rearing children and studying animals, and it was in his child-rearing recommendations that Watson came closest to realizing his vision of psychology as an applied science of human behavior.

Watson's Place in Psychology

John B. Watson was a flamboyant personality who liked to make his points by exaggeration and overstatement, and whose arguments often lacked delicacy or precision. Accordingly, it is not surprising that many of his major ideas have been toned down or refined by subsequent generations of psychologists. Most would now agree, for example, that children are not so easily conditioned into paragons of virtue; that heredity cannot be overlooked to the extent that Watson suggested; that emotional development entails more than just the building of conditioned reactions upon only three basic responses; and that language and thought are not just simple chains of verbal, visceral, and kinaesthetic reflexes. Further, while the conditioned reflex is still recognized as a major unit of learned behavior, post-Watsonian learning theorists have realized that its usefulness is confined to the explanation of relatively passive responses elicited by specific external stimuli. The more active learned responses with which an organism manipulates or operates upon its environment have required that Pavlovian conditioning be supplemented by another model of learning, generally called *instrumental* or *operant conditioning.**

Despite these changes, however, psychologists still follow Watson's lead in many different ways. Many contemporary introductory psychology textbooks define their subject as the science of *behavior,* and insist that its data be properly objective. The study of learning and conditioning in humans as well as in animals remains one of psychology's most important sub-areas. Large numbers of psychologists continue to take the prediction and control of behavior as their paramount goal, using "behavior modification" techniques to influence the responses of disturbed children or adults. These techniques are the direct descendants of Watson's conditioning and de-conditioning experiments on children, and have become major rivals of the "psychodynamic" approaches that stem more directly from Freud. Child-rearing manuals continue to proliferate, instructing parents how to bring their children up according to the most up-to-date principles.

Perhaps most of these things would have happened in the normal course of events even if Watson had never appeared on the scene. But he certainly hastened their occurrence, and lent a vitality and power to the objective psychology movement that it might otherwise have lacked. Watson assessed his own contribution to psychology at the conclusion of his autobiography, written several years after he had already left the field. "I still believe as firmly as ever in the general behavioristic position I took overtly in 1912," he wrote. "I think it has influenced psychology." [38] He was not being immodest.

Suggested Readings

The standard account of Pavlov's life is B. P. Babkin's *Pavlov: A Biography* (Chicago: The University of Chicago Press, 1949). A shorter biography, accompanied by a discussion of Pavlov's

* See Chapter 9.

physiological work, is *Ivan Pavlov* by Elizabeth and Martin Sherwood (Geneva: Heron Books, 1970). Pavlov's own descriptions of his work on conditioned reflexes are included in his *Lectures on Conditioned Reflexes* (New York: Liveright, 1928) and *Conditioned Reflexes: An Investigation of the Physiological Activity of the Cerebral Cortex* (New York: Dover Publications, 1960).

Watson's short but lively autobiography is included in the third volume of Carl Murchison (ed.), *A History of Psychology in Autobiography* (Worcester, Mass.: Clark University Press, 1936). Further biographical details are provided in two articles from the *Journal of the History of the Behavioral Sciences:* David Bakan's "Behaviorism and American Urbanization" (*2:* 5–28, 1966) and Paul G. Creelan's "Watsonian Behaviorism and the Calvinist Conscience" (*10:* 95–118, 1974). Any of Watson's own writings cited in the text are to be recommended. The 1967 reissue of *Behavior: An Introduction to Comparative Psychology* (New York: Holt, Rinehart and Winston, 1967) includes an excellent introduction by Richard J. Herrnstein, and *Behaviorism* (New York: Norton, 1970) is the most engaging and readable of his textbooks.

9

Modern Pioneers:
Jean Piaget and B. F. Skinner

If any one generalization is possible from the preceding chapters, it is that the early pioneers of psychology were an extremely diverse lot, both collectively and as individuals. Psychology has never had a Newton, a single towering figure whose thought has dominated the entire field and given direction to everyone else's work. Instead, it has been created by a large number of people whose psychological inclinations have been informed and enriched by a great variety of interests in other fields such as mathematics, philosophy, physics, physiology, linguistics, genetics, anthropology, or sociology.

This diversity is still clearly reflected by today's psychologists. The American Psychological Association, the largest professional and scientific organization for psychologists, recognizes formally through its divisional structure nearly forty different psychological specialty areas. These include such varied fields as evaluation and measurement, physiological and comparative psychology, developmental psychology, personality and social psychology, psychology and the arts, clinical psychology, industrial and organizational psychology, educational psychology, consumer psychology, philosophical psychology, the experimental analysis of behavior, history of psychology, community psychology, psychotherapy, hypnosis, and humanistic psychology. Psychology's continuing tendency to merge with other widely varying disciplines is illustrated by the current prominence of such hybrid specialties as psycholinguistics, psychopharmacology, psychohistory, and neuropsychology.

Another continuous aspect of psychology's diversity has been its joint status as an applied as well as a theoretical science. From its very beginnings, practical utility and abstract theorizing have complemented one another. Solutions to concrete medical problems have suggested general psychological theories, just as philosophical conceptions of the mind have had practical implications for surgical techniques, psychotherapies, or advertising practices. Today, thousands of professional psychologists work in primarily applied settings as psychotherapists, diagnosticians, industrial consultants, or educational specialists. Others work mainly as researchers or academicians, producing and disseminating new psychological knowledge. Their functions may be quite distinct and separate, but both the practitioner and the scientist must be aware of what the other is doing. The most influential psychologists manage to keep a foot in each camp.

Psychology's historical and continuing diversity makes it extremely unlikely that its future will be dominated by a single individual or point of view, any more than its past has been. Those psychologists of the 1970s who will be remembered as pioneers after fifty or a hundred years will most likely be a varied group of men and women with broad individual interests, who made contributions with practical as well as theoretical implications.

It is impossible to predict who all of those individuals will be, of course. Many are probably relatively obscure today, the implications of their work yet to be recognized. Nevertheless, it seems fitting to conclude this book on pioneers of psychology with brief sketches of two modern psychologists who will undoubtedly be remembered and influential well into the future. They represent very different approaches to psychology, one being a developmental psychologist interested in children's thought processes, the other a behaviorist who has extended and strengthened the explicitly non-cognitive approach of Pavlov and Watson. Each, however, has conducted an extensive program of systematic and ingenious research which has captured the imagination of large numbers of followers. And each has effectively communicated to the general public something of the practical implications of his work. They will surely be joined by others, but it seems safe to say that the Swiss developmental psychologist Jean Piaget, and the American behaviorist B. F. Skinner, number prominently among the select group of psychology's pioneers for tomorrow.

Jean Piaget: Early Life and Career

Jean Piaget was born on August 9, 1896 in Neuchâtel, Switzerland. His father was an academic who wrote extensively on medieval literature and the history of his home region. His mother was intelligent and kindly, but also prone to emotional disorders. Piaget reports that he coped with the resulting tumult in his family's emotional atmosphere by identifying with his father and forgoing play for serious intellectual work. Even as a child he produced prodigious amounts of independent scientific work. When, as an adult, he was asked how he could write so much—his publication rate among psychologists discussed in this volume is second only to Wundt's—he replied, "Fundamentally I am a worrier whom only work can relieve." [1]

Piaget's earliest works, which included a pamphlet describing his invention of a combination wagon-locomotive, and a small handwritten book entitled "Our Birds," were written primarily for his private amusement. He broke into print in a local natural history journal at age ten, however, with a description of a partly albino sparrow. During his early teens Piaget volunteered his part-time assistance to the director of the Neuchâtel natural history museum, whose specialty was malacology, the study of mollusks. By the time his mentor died in 1911, Piaget had absorbed much of his expertise, and he soon became the world's youngest internationally known malacologist. Between the ages of fifteen and nineteen he published twenty-one articles on the subject in various scientific journals. His readers assumed he was much older, and one offered Piaget a mollusk curator's job. He had to decline because he still had two years of high school remaining.

Though Piaget later regarded his malacological works as "premature," and "far from being accomplished feats," they gave him a very firm grounding in the principles of scientific method and observation. This, he felt, stood him in good stead when he was temporarily obsessed by the "demon of philosophy" as a late adolescent. Religious doubts and philosophical questions seemed resolvable when brought into connection with biology. As Piaget later wrote:

> I recall one evening of profound revelation. The identification of God with life itself was an idea that stirred me almost to ecstasy because it now enabled me to see in biology the explanation of all things and of the mind itself. . . . The problem of knowing (properly called the epistemological problem) suddenly appeared to me in an entirely new perspective and as an absorbing topic of study. It made me decide to consecrate my life to the biological explanation of knowledge.[2]

Piaget eagerly began to study philosophical systems that attempted to integrate biology with epistemology, most notably the "creative evolution" of the French philosopher Henri Bergson. This was disappointing, however: "Instead of finding science's last word therein, . . . I got the impression of an ingenious construction without an experimental basis: Between biology and the analysis of knowledge I needed something other than a philosophy. I believe it was at that moment that I discovered a need that could be satisfied only by psychology." [3] At that point Piaget had only a vague idea of what formal psychology was, but his biological and philosophical interests had conspired to create his life's ambition: the development of an adequate psychological theory explaining how people come to know about their world.

Piaget's conversion to the formal study of psychology was not immediate, however. Following receipt of his baccalaureate degree in 1915, a bout of ill health forced him to spend a year recuperating in the mountains. During that time he read some psychology, including William James, but his major intellectual undertaking was the writing of a philosophical novel entitled *Recherche*. Though far from a literary or philosophical masterpiece, it was published in 1917. After his year in the mountains, Piaget entered the doctoral program in natural science at his home university of Neuchâtel. This school offered no psychology, but Piaget took courses in zoology, embryology, geology, chemistry, and mathematics while writing a thesis on the mollusks of the region. He completed his doctorate in 1918. At the age of twenty-two he was an internationally recognized malacologist, an amateur philoso-

11. Jean Piaget. *Yves De Braine from Black Star*

pher, and a published novelist. He now proceeded to seek his training in psychology.

At first he went to Zurich, where he learned something about Freud and psychopathology, and attended lectures by Freud's erstwhile follower Carl Jung. He found little opportunity to conduct challenging research there, however, and so a year later he went to Paris to work at the Sorbonne. A fortuitous meeting there with Theodore Simon (1873–1961), who had earlier assisted Alfred Binet (1857–1911) in the development of the first workable intelligence test, set in motion the events that led Piaget to discover his life's work.

When Piaget met him, Simon had moved from Paris to the city of Rouen, but he remained the nominal director of the pedagogical laboratory associated with a Paris grade school where he and Binet had conducted many of their experiments. Simon suggested that Piaget might like to use the laboratory to standardize a series of reasoning tests for children that had recently been developed in England. Piaget was not particularly excited by the proposed research, but the opportunity to be his own master in a large laboratory seemed too good to refuse. He soon found that this seemingly pedestrian task, involving the testing of children's intelligence, led to some very exciting questions.

Intelligence Testing

To understand Piaget's accomplishments in Simon's laboratory it is necessary first to trace briefly the history of the intelligence testing movement. The *idea* of intelligence testing, of course, had been introduced by Francis Galton, as described in Chapter 7. Galton's own tests, based on the incorrect hypothesis that intellectual differences would be reflected in sensory and physiological differences, were failures. People who did well on tests of reaction time, sensory acuity, line bisection, or color naming did not manifest consistently high intelligence in real life situations. In Galton's wake the concept of an intelligence test seemed potentially useful, but the actual development of a valid instrument remained one of the major unsolved problems of applied psychology.

Binet and Simon were among those who addressed themselves to this problem. Unlike Galton and most other workers in the area, they were interested in devising a test for the intelligence of children rather than adults. The French government had recently instituted mandatory universal education, which meant that retarded children who previously would never have entered the school system at all, now had to be provided with special programs. It was suddenly of the greatest practical interest to have a test that would help to identify those children so they could be started on their special education as early as possible. Binet and Simon thus started out with the relatively straightforward aim of devising a test to differentiate retarded from normal children.

Unlike Galton, Binet and Simon began experimenting with tests that seemed to directly require complex mental functions —tests of memory, of vocabulary, or of logical reasoning, for example. As they systematically administered these tests to hundreds of children already clearly identified as retarded or normal, they came to a simple but brilliant insight. On many tests, the retarded children differed from the normal ones not by *what* they did, but by the *age* at which they could first do it. Retarded children could typically indicate their right hands or left ears on request, for example, but usually not until they were nine or ten years old. Normal children, on the average, could perform the same task at age seven.

Thus Binet and Simon discovered that age could be the crucial variable in measuring intelligence. Intelligence could be thought of as something that grows with age, so that older children are, on the average, more intelligent than younger ones. By experimenting with large numbers of children of varying ages, it was possible to identify tests to serve as standards for each age. A five-year-old's standard, for example, might be any test passed by fifty percent of five-year-olds, but a smaller proportion of four-year-olds and a larger proportion of six-year-olds.

Such standards were based on *average* figures, of course, and individual children deviated above and below the average. Bright children could pass tests standardized at levels above their actual ages, while dull children had difficulty with those standardized below. By giving large numbers of tests, an approximate *mental age* could be calculated for each child based on the difficulty of the tests he passed. This could be compared with the child's actual or *chronological age* to determine his intelligence. Binet and Simon argued that if the mental age were two years or more below the chronological age, and there was independent evidence to suggest intellectual difficulty (a very important qualification that Binet and Simon stressed heavily), a child was likely to require special education.

Binet and Simon published their first scale of intelligence in 1905, followed by more extensive revisions in 1908 and 1911. In 1912, the German psychologist William Stern (1871–1938) introduced the concept of the *intelligence quotient* or *IQ*, calculated by taking the ratio of a child's mental age to his chronological age and multiplying it by 100. Thus, average children whose mental and chronological ages were the same, had IQs of 100; brighter children had IQs greater than 100, slower children less than 100, with the deviations in either direction proportional to the degree of brightness or slowness. Intelligence—at least in children—now seemed quantifiable, and a new era in research seemed at hand. Intelligence tests on the Binet-Simon model proliferated, and among the new products were the Burt reasoning tests which Piaget was asked to standardize in Simon's laboratory.

Genetic Epistemology

The Binet-Simon-Burt approach to testing suggested—though it certainly did not prove—that intelligence was something that varied primarily *quantitatively* with age. That is, older children could perform more tasks more quickly than younger children of roughly the same native ability, suggesting that

346

intelligence grows linearly with age in much the same way that physical stature does. As Piaget began testing large numbers of children, however, he realized that this was only a very small aspect of the story. He summarized his early discoveries as follows:

From the very first questionings I noticed that though Burt's tests certainly had their diagnostic merits, based on the number of successes and failures, it was much more interesting to try to find the reasons for the failures. Thus I engaged my subjects in conversations patterned after psychiatric questioning, with the aim of discovering something about the reasoning processes underlying their right, but especially their wrong answers. I noticed with amazement that the simplest reasoning task involving the part in the whole [finding the part common to two wholes] . . . presented for normal children up to the age of eleven or twelve difficulties unsuspected by the adult.[4]

Piaget had learned that on reasoning tasks, older children and adults did not just think faster and more than younger children; they also thought in entirely different ways. Older children had cognitive abilities that enabled them to understand problems and concepts in ways that were completely beyond the capacity of younger children. In short, intelligence varied qualitatively with age, as well as quantitatively.

Piaget realized that the systematic working out of qualitative changes in children's intelligence was an approach to the epistemological question that interested him so much. By learning how children understand the world, and how their thought processes gradually mature and become more like adults', he could come to grips with the nature of human knowledge. Piaget named this study *genetic epistemology*, and he has pursued it tirelessly for more than fifty years.

In 1921, shortly after the publication of his first findings from his Paris laboratory, Piaget was invited to become director of studies at the J. J. Rousseau Institute in Geneva. He accepted, and has remained in Geneva ever since—attracting students and co-workers from all over the world and producing hundreds of studies in genetic epistemology.

These works describe studies of children ranging in age

from earliest infancy to late adolescence. Piaget devised scores of ingenious tasks for his subjects to perform—in areas as diverse as rattle play, language use, moral judgment, the conception of numbers, space perception, algebra, and the conception of dreams and fantasies—and then he meticulously observed the ways children of different ages performed them. For each task he found evidence of *stages of development,* of systematic and qualitative differences between the way younger and older children conceptualized and attacked the problems.

This vast corpus of work cannot be summarized in a few pages, but its general nature may be hinted at by a very brief consideration of the four major *stages of cognitive development* that Piaget believes characterize intellectual life from infancy through adolescence. Each successive stage is marked by cognitive structures permitting the solution of problems that were impossible earlier. Thus the stages are definable in terms of tasks that children can and cannot do. The following are some typical examples.

The sensory-motor stage. Piaget labelled the first stage of intellectual development, lasting from birth to approximately two years of age, the *sensory-motor period.* As the name implies, the child's intelligence in this stage is much more concerned with elementary sensory and motor activities than it is with abstract "thought" in the adult sense of the word. Before objects can be thought about in any mature sense, the child must learn how they strike the senses and how they can be manipulated.

A major task which the child must complete before moving beyond the sensory-motor period is the attainment of a sense of *object constancy*—the knowledge that objects have continuing existences even when they are outside immediate sensory awareness. Children under the age of approximately eight months illustrate the lack of a sense of object constancy when an adult places a favorite toy under a blanket or other cover. Even though the children watch the adult hide the toy, and even if they were playing energetically with it before it was hidden, they typically make no purposeful effort to remove the cover and regain the object. From a child's point of view, the toy has simply dropped out of existence since it dropped out of immediate sensory awareness. As is evidenced by enjoyment in games such as peek-a-boo, the appearance, disappearance, and reappearance of objects take on a special fascination as the child begins to master the notion of object constancy.

This sense of object constancy is acquired gradually, in an increasing variety of situations, as children gain more mastery over their own bodies and learn how to manipulate objects actively. As they learn to make the objects disappear and reappear through their own efforts—by *reversing the operations* which had led to appearance or disappearance—the sense of a stable universe of continuously existing objects becomes a possibility. Now that objects are recognized as permanent, it becomes possible to *name* them, to indicate their continuing existence by a word which can always represent them. With the acquisition of a sense of object constancy, and with the rudiments of language enabling them to express and symbolize the continuing existence of objects, children are ready to move on to the next stage of intelligence.

The preoperational stage. This second stage of cognitive development lasts from approximately two years of age until approximately seven years. Though children in this stage recognize the constancy of objects, they are strikingly unable to grasp the constancies of other, more abstract properties such as quantity or volume. Consider the following example. A preoperational child is given two lumps of clay to play with, and asked to remove bits from the larger one until both seem exactly the same size. Then the experimenter takes one of the equal lumps and breaks it up into many pieces and places them in a pile. The child is now asked which has more clay, the remaining lump or the newly created pile. The preoperational child, noting that the pile takes up more space and *looks* bigger, usually responds that there is more clay there. In

Piaget's terms, such a child has failed to recognize that there is *conservation of quantity,* regardless of the shape of the clay.

Besides showing that preoperational children may be tricked into believing that they get larger portions of favorite foods merely by cutting them up into many small pieces, experiments like this show that young children do not think about abstract properties such as quantity in the same way that adults and older children do. Older children are not just better with numbers, or capable of handling bigger numbers; they make their judgments of quantity on an entirely different basis. The younger children are guided by the way things look, by the immediate perceptual qualities of the substances to be judged. The key to the older children's conception is the knowledge that reversal of operations can re-transform quantities back into their original sizes and shapes. They are able to transcend the immediate appearance of things, and recognize that the same quantity may manifest itself in many different guises.

Stages of Concrete and Formal Operations. Children in Piaget's third stage, the *stage of concrete operations,* share the adult's conception of quantity, but still remain tied to the immediately given situation in other ways. There are still conceptual and reasoning problems which they cannot solve successfully until they enter the *stage of formal operations,* at the age of eleven or so. The difference between these two final stages of intelligence is illustrated in the following situation.

The subject is presented with four flasks numbered one through four, each filled with an identical looking transparent liquid, and a smaller flask containing another clear liquid labelled "g." The subject is told that by adding a few drops of g to some combination of the liquids in flasks one through four, a yellow-colored liquid can be produced. The task is to experiment with the liquids until the proper combination is discovered.

In actuality, "g" is potassium iodide, which produces a yellow precipitate when mixed with oxygenated water in an acid solution. Flask 1 contains dilute sulfuric acid and flask 3 contains oxygenated water, so the combination of g + 1 + 3 yields the yellow color. Flask 2 contains water, and flask 4 contains thiosulfate, a chemical base which neutralizes sulfuric acid. The presence or absence of liquid 2 has no effect on the reaction, while the presence of 4 neutralizes the color reaction altogether. Thus g + 1 + 2 + 3 is the only other combination capable of producing the color.

Given enough time, concretely operational children discover the color-producing combinations just as the formally operational children do. The difference lies in the way they go about the task, and the conclusions they are able to draw from their experimentation. The younger children typically proceed in an unsystematic manner, trying out different combinations randomly until finally hitting on one that produces the desired color. The task is then finished, as far as they are concerned. The older children, by contrast, understand at once that there are a limited number of *possible* combinations which can be investigated systematically and completely. Thus they may start by adding g to each of the four liquids individually, discovering that no single chemical will produce yellow with g. Then they may try each of the six possible combinations of *two* chemicals with g (1 and 2, 1 and 3, 1 and 4, 2 and 3, 2 and 4, 3 and 4), in the course of which they discover a correct combination.

Even after finding a correct solution, however, formally operational children may not be satisfied. Realizing that there are only a few more possible combinations (four mixtures of three chemicals, and one of all four), they may proceed to try them out as well. After exhausting all the possibilities, they are in a position to generalize about the nature of the chemicals. They will know that 1 + 3 is the crucial combination, but that 4 can neutralize it while 2 makes no difference at all. They have proceeded in a methodical manner which has enabled them to draw the maximum number of correct inferences from their observations. The formally operational child has finally developed the cognitive structures and strategies that permit logical reasoning like an adult's.

From these and many other observations, Piaget has clearly shown that rational, adult, scientific thinking, and the knowledge which proceeds from it, is but the end point of an extensive developmental process. The human mind does not immediately or automatically think that way, but first must pass through several intermediate stages. At the beginning, human thinking is tied to the immediate present of sensory and bodily experience. Only gradually does it come to deal with imagined rather than immediately given concepts, such as memories of objects when they are physically absent, the variety of possible shapes into which a fixed quantity of clay may be formed, or a complete matrix of combinational possibilities for a group of chemicals.

The most general conclusion Piaget draws from his research is that human knowledge, in whatever developmental stage, is an *active* process which transforms the data of the external world:

I find myself opposed to the view of knowledge as a passive copy of reality. . . . I believe that knowing an object means acting upon it, constructing systems of transformations that can be carried out on or with this object. Knowing reality means constructing systems of transformations that correspond, more or less adequately, to reality. The transformational structures of which knowledge consists are not copies of the transformations in reality; they are simply possible isomorphic models among which experience can enable us to choose. Knowledge, then, is a system of transformations that become progressively adequate.[5]

In seeing knowledge as the result of an active mind which transforms reality, Piaget partakes of the psychological tradition going back to Kant. In specifying how the mind's transformational processes develop with age and experience, he enriches that tradition, and in so doing begins a new one of his own.

Piaget's Influence on Education

Inevitably, Piaget's demonstration that the child's mind is not a miniature replica of the adult's, but develops in that direction in specifiable stages, has been of great interest to educators. Piaget himself, while admitting that he is no pedagogue, has argued that schools could do a better job in instilling an experimental frame of mind in their pupils by providing them with developmentally appropriate problems and challenges. Thus, while it will do little good to try to teach pre-operational children the formal, hypothetico-deductive reasoning of adult sciences, it is possible to facilitate their learning about conservation of quantity by providing opportunities to manipulate and transform the shapes and appearances of varying substances. As Piaget summarizes, "It is a matter of presenting to children situations which offer new problems, problems that follow on one another. You need a mixture of direction and freedom." [6]

The American psychologist Jerome Bruner has attempted to show how some of these ideas can be applied in the classroom. According to Bruner, the ideal teaching technology is one which moves the student smoothly from *doing something* with the materials under study, to appreciating their *perceptual* qualities, and culminates by teaching an appropriate *symbolic language* for dealing with them abstractly. This progression, of course, roughly parallels the development from sensory-motor through operational levels of intelligence.

One of the programs Bruner describes as conforming to this pattern is used to teach mathematics. Children are presented with a set of cut-out patterns labelled x^2, x, and 1, as illustrated in Figure 9–1a. They are encouraged to play with these forms, to put them together to create different shapes. As they do so, they will naturally produce squares like those in Figures 9–1b and 9–1c. Thus they come to "know" the pieces, both in terms of what to do with them and in terms of the appearance of the arrangements which make different shapes.

353

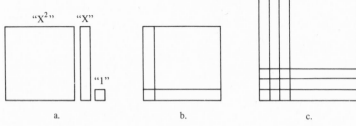

"X²" "X"

"1"

a.   b.   c.

Figure 9–1

After this, they begin to learn about some of the relationships among the *names* of the shapes. As they do, they naturally learn the fundamentals of algebraic quadratic equations. From figures like 9–1b, they learn that a square whose sides are x plus 1 long is made up of one x^2, two xs, and one 1; in other words, $(x + 1)^2 = x^2 + 2x + 1$. From figure 9–1c, they learn that $(x + 3)^2 = x^2 + 6x + 9$. And from the totality of their experience with many different constructed squares, they may acquire a knowledge of the general rule that $(x + a)^2 = x^2 + 2ax + a^2$.

The degree to which learning can be accelerated by techniques like these remains an open question, with Piaget and Bruner coming down on different sides. Piaget believes that intellectual development is closely tied to biological and social development as well. Therefore, while intellectual growth can be nurtured and facilitated like the physical growth of a child, it cannot be accelerated beyond a certain natural and biologically fixed limit. Bruner, for his part, believes in greater intellectual flexibility in children and his cognitive theory differs somewhat from Piaget's to reflect this difference. For him, if eight-year-olds can be taught quadratic equations, then other even greater educational wonders may be in store if educators can only develop sufficiently ingenious teaching techniques.

Thus, the question of how rapidly intellectual development can be accelerated is currently unanswered, and awaits further research. But whatever the results of that research may be, teachers will learn something useful. Either they will have new and effective methods for accelerating learning, or they will have a better appreciation of the limits to their pupils' understanding. In either case, they will have improved their ability to speak the language of the child. Piaget's pioneering demonstrations of the existence and importance of that language are a practical contribution which will keep him in the forefront of educational theory for years to come.

B. F. Skinner: Early Life and Influences

Burrhus Frederic Skinner was born on March 20, 1904 in the small railroading town of Susquehanna, Pennsylvania. His father was a primarily self-taught lawyer who never attended college and went to law school for only one year before passing the final examinations. He was a gifted speaker, both in the courtroom and on the political stump in support of the Republican party. At one time he had hopes of being elected a judge, but his tendency to take on (and win) unpopular court cases in his private practice ruined any chances he might have had. He wrote a highly regarded textbook on workmen's compensation law and always provided well for his family—yet Skinner reports that his father secretly thought of himself as a failure in life.

Skinner describes his mother as having been "bright and beautiful." A Susquehanna native like her husband, she was popular, a good singer, and ranked second in her high school class. Concerning her rather strict notions of propriety, Skinner later wryly summarized, "I was taught to fear God, the police, and what people will think. As a result, I usually do what I have to do with no great struggle." [7]

As a boy in Susquehanna, Skinner showed both musical and mechanical aptitudes. He enjoyed listening to opera on the family Victrola, played the piano and saxophone, and earned pocket money while in high school by playing in a dance ensemble. He was also skilled at building things, from wagons to Rube Goldberg contraptions. One of his more successful creations as a young boy was inspired by his mother's constantly reminding him to keep his room neat: "A special hook in the closet of my room was connected by a string-and-pulley system to a sign hanging above the door to the room. When my pajamas were in place on the hook, the sign was held high above the door and out of the way. When the pajamas were off the hook, the sign hung squarely in the middle of the door frame. It read 'Hang up your pajamas!' " [8]

Skinner's earliest intellectual ambitions were literary. Inspired by a sympathetic teacher, he came to take writing seriously. Like Piaget, he saw his first work in print at the age of ten, a poem entitled "That Pessimistic Fellow." Most of his other boyhood work remained unpublished, including an extensive private journal; a morality play featuring the characters Greed, Gluttony, Adventure, Jealousy, and Youth; and a melodramatic novel about the love affair between a young naturalist and the daughter of a dying trapper.

Skinner did well at Susquehanna High School, and in 1922 he became the first member of his family to attend university when he enrolled in Hamilton College. He took a wide variety of courses there, including biology and a philosophy course taught by one of Wundt's former students, but he took no psychology. His favorites remained English and literature. His literary ambitions intensified as he wrote regularly for the college newspaper and literary magazine, and published a series of pieces in the Hamilton humor magazine under the pen name of Sir Burrhus de Beerus.

Skinner was something of a practical joker at Hamilton, and once conspired with a friend to perpetrate the hoax that Charlie Chaplin would speak on campus. After observing the disappointed crowds who had gathered, they wrote an editorial in the campus newspaper declaring that "no man with the slightest regard for his alma mater could have done it." [9] During his senior year, Skinner publicly parodied the speech teacher, subverted the traditional oratory contest by submitting a farcical speech, and decorated the hall for his class day exercises with caricatures of the faculty.

There was another, serious side to Skinner's college career, however, as he worked very hard to improve his writing. The summer before his senior year he attended a writers' workshop at Middlebury College where Carl Sandburg and Robert Frost were among the guest faculty. Frost was sufficiently impressed with Skinner to suggest that he send him some of his work for close analysis. Skinner complied, and toward the end of his senior year he received a letter from Frost saying, "You are worth twice anyone else I have seen in prose this year." [10] Skinner now had do doubts about his vocation: he would become a professional writer.

Following graduation from Hamilton, he returned to his parents' home, built himself a study in the attic, and tried to write. The experience was an unmitigated disaster, later referred to by Skinner as his "Dark Year." The atmosphere at home was difficult, and his father was going through an unsuccessful period and feeling particularly depressed. Skinner himself felt isolated, having few friends or colleagues with whom to discuss ideas. And worst of all, he could think of nothing important to write about. He read great literature, but found little to say about it. He tried to write about writing, but that seemed empty. As he later summarized, "The truth was, I had no reason to write anything. I had nothing to say, and nothing about my life was making any change in that condition." [11] He considered consulting a psychiatrist, and finally was driven to seek both distraction and remuneration by abstracting several thousand legal decisions that had been handed down by the Anthracite Board of Conciliation.

Fortunately, a more satisfactory resolution was gradually developing. First came the realization that literature was not the only or the perfect route to truth about human behavior. Skinner was struck by a critic's comment about one of the novelist Thackeray's characters, to the effect that "Thackeray didn't know it, but she drank." Skinner reflected that writers may often portray characters accurately, but with no insight as to *why* they should behave as they are portrayed. Only a scientific approach to behavior could provide that insight.

357

At about this time behaviorism was coming to popular attention. Watson's *Behaviorism* had just been published, and the first English translation of Pavlov's *Lectures on Conditioned Reflexes* was about to appear. Bertrand Russell, one of Skinner's favorite writers, discussed behaviorism in his latest philosophy text. Russell did not fundamentally agree with Watson—in fact, he later told Skinner he thought he had "demolished" behaviorism in these writings—but he did take him seriously and concluded that Watson's theory "contains much more truth than most people suppose, and I regard it as desirable to develop the behaviourist method to the fullest extent." [12] Skinner was led to read Watson's *Behaviorism,* where he found much with which he could agree. He began to suspect that the behaviorist approach could explain many curiosities of animal and human behavior that had previously fascinated him, such as the performances of trained pigeons or the lecturing idiosyncrasies of a former teacher.

Skinner reached a symbolic turning point when he read an article by H. G. Wells about Pavlov and the British dramatist G. B. Shaw. The redoubtable Shaw had just published an intemperate attack on Pavlov, labelling him a scoundrel and a vivisectionist whose habit was to boil babies alive just to see what happens. Wells expressed his personal admiration for both men, and concluded by posing a hypothetical question: Pavlov and Shaw are drowning on opposite sides of pier; you, on the pier, have but one life belt to throw; to which side would you throw it? The question posed thus, Skinner had little trouble deciding on what *his* answer would be. He resolved to enter graduate school to study behavioristic psychology, and was accepted at Harvard for the autumn of 1928.

Operant Conditioning

Harvard's psychology department was hardly a hotbed of behaviorism when Skinner arrived, but its atmosphere was stimulating and tolerant. He found some graduate students who shared his views, and faculty who allowed him to go his own way. Skinner spent the next eight years at Harvard, as graduate student, postdoctoral fellow, and finally as a Junior Fellow in the prestigious Society of Fellows. During those eight years he laid the groundwork for a whole new kind of behavioristic analysis.

A major part of Skinner's early success was his development of an ingeniously simple piece of laboratory apparatus, which has since come to be known as the "Skinner box." It made possible an exhaustive series of systematic experiments on a kind of behavior he called *operant conditioning*. Thus in many ways the Skinner box became for Skinner what the salivary reflex apparatus had been for Pavlov. Skinner has told the story of how he came to invent his box in a delightfully tongue-in-cheek article entitled "A Case History in Scientific Method." [13] According to this account, four "unformalized principles of scientific practice" were the secret to his success. The box was the end result of a long series of less successful experiments which had been abandoned in mid-course, thus illustrating the importance of the first principle: "When you run into something interesting, drop everything else and study it." The box was a highly automated device, requiring little or no active participation by the experimenter after the animal subject was placed inside. This illustrated his second principle, the realization that "some ways of doing research are easier than others." Some of the most useful aspects of the device were the unintended consequences of improvising with some cast-off parts, illustrating principle three: "Some people are lucky." Skinner's final principle was the assured fact that "apparatus sometimes breaks down." Some of his more interesting experiments were suggested by the accidental malfunctioning of his apparatus.

At least of equal importance to these "unformalized principles" was a major guiding idea. Skinner very much admired the precision Pavlov had brought to the study of conditioned salivary reflexes, and he appreciated Watson's attempts, as described in the preceding chapter, to extend the concept of conditioned reflexes into his explanations of emotional behavior. But Skinner felt that something was still lacking from this approach. "I could not . . . move without a jolt from salivary reflexes to the important business of the organism in everyday life," he wrote.[14] He knew that there was more to behavior than the relatively passive acquisition of reflexive responses. He sought a behavioristic method of studying the way intact and normally functioning organisms *actively* operate on the environment, learn to manipulate it, and, to a certain degree, to control it. The Skinner box was an ideal tool for studying this kind of learning, which he came to call operant conditioning.

Just what was this marvellous device? In its usual form, as illustrated in Figure 9–2, it was a cage large enough to hold a white rat comfortably, with a lever-bar mounted on one wall near a food tray. Pressure on the lever activated a mechanism which caused a food pellet to drop into the tray, and which also recorded the response on a *cumulative record* kept outside the box. The cumulative record was made by a pen point contacting a roll of paper moving beneath it at a constant rate. Each bar press caused the pen point to rise by a

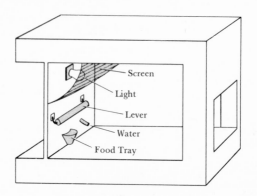

Figure 9–2 *The Skinner Box* [15]

small fixed amount, so that cumulative records resembled mathematical *curves* whose steepness was a measure of the rate of responding. If the rate was low, there were few or no elevations of the pen and the record was relatively flat, as in the left hand portion of the sample curve illustrated in Figure 9–3. As the rate increased, the slope became steeper as in the right hand portion.

Figure 9–3 is a typical record produced by a hungry but untrained rat when first placed in the box. Its initial rate of bar pressing is usually between one and ten responses per hour. That is, it occasionally makes the response, but its occurrence is almost "accidental." It does not take long for the rate to increase dramatically following the first *reinforcements* with food, however. A rapid and steady rate of responding is quickly established, which continues for as long as the rat remains hungry.

Obviously, there is nothing particularly important about a lever-pressing rate in itself, nor is there anything extraordinary about these typical acquisition curves. The significance of the lever pressing response is its easy measurability, which makes it a convenient laboratory representation of *any* learned response which, in Skinner's terms, "operates on the environment" so as to produce some particular end. Further, response rates may be studied as functions of many other conditions besides the one where every single response is reinforced with food. The *contingencies of reinforcement*—that is, the rela-

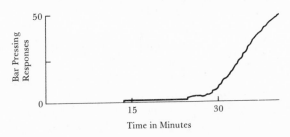

Figure 9–3 *A Cumulative Record of Response Acquisition*

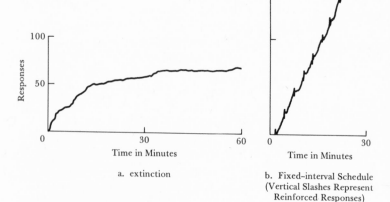

a. extinction

b. Fixed–interval Schedule
(Vertical Slashes Represent
Reinforced Responses)

Figure 9–4 *Two Typical Cumulative Records*

tionships between the occurrence of the response and the presence or absence of the food pellets—can be systematically varied by the experimenter in many different ways, thus approximating the various contingencies that operate with other reinforcers in the real world.

For example, after a response has been regularly reinforced and a steady rate established, the experimenter may suddenly withhold the food altogether. (This was one of the conditions Skinner first observed after the food dispensing mechanism accidentally jammed.) The result is an *extinction curve* like that reproduced in Figure 9–4a, which represents the responses of a previously conditioned rat whose reinforcement is suddenly withheld. At first, there is a very high rate, partly because the animal is no longer pausing between responses to eat the food, and partly because there seems to be an "emotional" or "frustrated" activation of the response. Then there is a slowing of the response rate, followed by a series of progressively diminishing, wavelike bursts. Finally, the curve flattens out almost completely, indicating that the response is seldom made any longer; that is, it has been "extinguished." Despite the wavelike, emotional distortions, the overall trend of the cumulative record approximates a regular, negatively accelerating curve.

Another kind of variation in the contingencies of reinforcement involves providing food at only some of the times when the lever is pressed. On a *fixed-interval reinforcement schedule,* for example, reinforcement comes only after there has been a specified, mandatory wait between successive reinforcements, regardless of how many responses are made in the interim. On a three-minute schedule, the first response is reinforced, but no further reinforcement follows until the first response after three minutes have passed. Under these conditions a scallop-shaped cumulative record appears, as in Figure 9–4b. Responding decreases immediately following each reinforcement, then gradually increases in intensity as the end of the interval approaches.

On a *fixed-ratio reinforcement schedule,* reinforcement comes only after a certain number of responses have been made—after every fourth response, or every tenth, or any other number the experimenter decides upon. Skinner found that rates took longer to stabilize under these conditions, but tended to level off at the same slope as for regular reinforcement. He also found that it was possible to increase the ratio gradually, starting off by reinforcing every second response, for example, then every fourth response, then every eighth, and so on—doubling the ratio each time the rate rose to the level of the one-in-two ratio. In one of his experiments, a rat continued to respond at a high rate when only every 192nd response was reinforced. This clearly suggested that organisms may be conditioned to work harder and harder for progressively diminishing rewards—a principle that unscrupulous employers may be tempted to exploit in real life, and that vigilant employees attempt to resist.

Another kind of reinforcement schedule—closely approximating many other real life situations—provides *intermittent reinforcement,* where the intervals and the ratios between reinforced and unreinforced responses vary randomly. A Skinner box programmed to provide intermittent reinforcement thus resembles a Las Vegas slot machine. Intermittent schedules can produce high and regular rates of responding which are strikingly resistant to extinction. That is, responding goes on much longer after reinforcement has been cut off completely than would have been the case if the previous reinforcement had been regular and predictable. The rat in the box, like the slot machine player in Las Vegas, has no way of predicting accurately when the next reinforcement will come. But the occasional and irregular reinforcements they do receive nurture a constant hope that the "next" response will be a rewarded one. Rat and player alike may become hooked, and respond long past the point of diminishing returns.

Skinner published the results of these and many other experiments using his box in *The Behavior of Organisms* (1938), his first book. This work clearly established operant conditioning as a kind of learning equal in importance to, but distinctly different from, the Pavlovian conditioned reflex. In the Pavlovian situation—referred to as *respondent conditioning* by Skinner—a new stimulus-response connection is created; in operant conditioning, a response that already exists in the subject's behavioral repertoire is strengthened or weakened by altering the reinforcement contingencies. In respondent conditioning the response is *elicited* by the conditioned stimulus, whereas in the operant situation the subject must *emit* the response before any conditioning can take place. In the respondent situation the conditioned and unconditioned stimuli may be precisely defined; in operant conditioning it is impossible to define with any precision the stimuli which give rise to the responses. The strength of respondent conditioning is typically measured by response latency or response magnitude, while that of operant conditioning is measured by response rate. In sum, Skinner demonstrated a properly behavioristic method for studying an entirely new range of learned responses. Whereas Watson had promised somewhat more than he could deliver with the techniques available to him, Skinner felt that behaviorism was now ready to take its place as a complete psychology.

The Applications and Implications of Skinnerian Psychology

After laying the foundations for the study of operant conditioning at Harvard, Skinner assumed faculty positions at Minnesota in 1936 and Indiana in 1945. In 1948 he returned to Harvard, where he has remained. During this time he has attracted a large number of followers who have sought to apply the findings and techniques of Skinnerian psychology to a wide variety of experimental and practical situations, and who have joined with him to create a separate division of the American Psychological Association devoted to the "Experimental Analysis of Behavior." Skinner himself has been increasingly concerned with the practical applications and philosophical implications of operant conditioning.

One of his first concerns after leaving Harvard was to determine how the concepts of operant conditioning might be extended to the analysis of complex behaviors, instead of the simple response of bar-pressing he had previously studied. His working hypothesis was that complex behaviors may be thought of as chains of simple behaviors. He sought a method by which he could efficiently build up complex responses by systematically reinforcing longer and longer chains of individual simple responses.

A necessary first step was the development of a reinforcer that could be easily administered to an animal subject without interfering with the flow of its behavior. Skinner found he could do this by subjecting his animals to respondent conditioning, repeatedly pairing an easily produced neutral stimulus such as the click from a toy clicker with a primary reinforcer such as food. After a sufficient number of pairings, the clicks by themselves became effective *secondary reinforcers,* as demonstrated by the fact that conditioned animals would maintain a high degree of Skinner box responding when reinforced only by clicks.

With this simple but effective reinforcer, Skinner could progressively "shape up" complicated chains of responses in

12. B. F. Skinner with one of his subjects. *Ken Heyman*

animals. To train a pigeon to peck at a certain spot on the wall, for example, he began by sounding the clicker each time it turned partially toward that location. It quickly became oriented toward the spot, and Skinner could now withhold reinforcement until the pigeon began to extend its head more precisely. Once this response was established, reinforcement would await an actual peck at the spot. After this highly specific response was once emitted and reinforced, it was no problem to build it up to a high rate. By patient shaping like this, Skinner was able to train animals to perform highly complex and "artificial" acts. In one of his best known examples, he even trained pigeons to "play ping-pong," rolling a ball with their bills back and forth to each other across a table.

Ping-pong playing pigeons may seem frivolous, but they provided an effective and dramatic example of the kind of highly complex responses that can be produced by the efficient use of operant conditioning. Further, as a good behaviorist, Skinner believed that the principles found effective in shaping animal behavior could also be applied to humans. While visiting his daughter's fourth grade class in 1953, he had the sudden inspiration that techniques like those which had produced ping-pong playing in pigeons could be used to produce more efficient classroom learning in children. The result was the development of *programmed instruction,* an educational technique in which a complicated subject such as mathematics is broken down into simple, stepwise components which may be presented to a student in order of increasing difficulty. At first, the student is presented with an easy question about the very simplest component, and then learns immediately whether his answer is right or wrong. Skinner believes that the knowledge that one has answered a question correctly is a powerful secondary reinforcer in our society, so the correct response is strengthened. If the program has been carefully and properly designed, this correct response provides the basis necessary for responding correctly to the next, slightly more difficult question. In stepwise fashion, then, the student gradually proceeds to a mastery of a complicated subject. Occasional incorrect responses that may occur are followed by reviews and supplementary instructions that provide the small amount of information required for a correct response on the second try.

One advantage of programmed instruction is that it may be self-administered by students, sometimes in automated devices known as *teaching machines.* Thus students are free to proceed at their own individual pace. Many programs have been developed for subjects at all levels of difficulty, from elementary schools through medical school. While it is now clear that they are not an educational panacea capable of replacing traditional teacher-student relationships, they have nonetheless proved to be valuable additions to the teachers' resources.

Skinner has been consistently attuned to the philosophical as well as the practical implications of his work. He realized very early that when *negative reinforcers*—consequences that an organism will work to avoid or escape from—are considered along with positive ones, then virtually *all* behavior is controlled by the contingencies of reinforcement that occur constantly in the environment. The notion of behavioral freedom is thus an illusion. When we believe we are behaving "freely," Skinner argues, we are merely free of negative reinforcement or its threat; our behavior is nonetheless determined by the pursuit of things that have been positively reinforcing to us in the past, and consists of responses that have previously been positively reinforced. When we perceive other people as behaving "freely," we are simply unaware of the reinforcement histories and contingencies that govern their behavior.

In 1948, Skinner presented some of these ideas in a utopian novel entitled *Walden Two*. This book—which finally established Skinner as a writer of commercially successful fiction —describes a society in which negative reinforcement has been completely abandoned as a means of social control. Knowledge and application of conditioning principles have made positive reinforcement a supremely powerful controller of behavior. Children, rigorously conditioned from birth onwards by exclusively positive reinforcement, inevitably grow up to be cooperative, intelligent, sociable, and—according to Frazier, the society's creator—happy. Frazier expresses the society's rationale, and the paradoxical role of "freedom" within it, in a conversation with a skeptical visitor. "When a science of behavior has once been achieved," he remarks, "there's no alternative to a planned society. We can't leave mankind to an accidental or biased control. But by using the principle of positive reinforcement—carefully avoiding force or the threat of force—we can preserve a personal sense of freedom." The visitor interrupts, "But you haven't denied that you are in complete control. You are still the long-range dictator." Frazier responds, "As you will. In fact, I'm inclined to agree.

When you have once grasped the principle of positive reinforcement, you can enjoy a sense of unlimited power. It's enough to satisfy the thirstiest tyrant. But it's a limited sort of despotism, and I don't think anyone should worry about it. The despot must wield his power for the good of others. If he takes any step which reduces the sum total of human happiness, his power is reduced by a like amount." [16]

Walden Two has been a highly controversial work, with many readers condemning its happy yet highly controlled society as totalitarian. Others have responded positively to Skinner's vision, however, and there have even been a few small-scale attempts to create actual societies like Walden Two. As usually happens with such attempts, the groups have lacked the resources or the influence to provide a real test of the underlying principles.

In more recent years Skinner has continued to speak out provocatively about the dilemmas of social control in our present society. His controversial and best-selling *Beyond Freedom and Dignity* (1971) has repeated his argument that behavioral freedom is an illusion. In it he has also pointed out that the doctrine of "autonomous man" upon which so many of our society's institutions are based has deleterious consequences. Under this doctrine, we "credit" a person more for good behavior if we do not know the contingencies that produced it, than if we do. That is, a person who is perceived to do something good "of his own free will" is more to be praised than one who does it because he has to. The dark and obverse side of this position is that if a person is to be credited for good behavior, then he must be *blamed and punished* for his "freely" produced bad behavior. In other words, one rarely emphasized consequence of the assumption that people are free is the *requirement* that punishment or the threat of punishment must constantly be employed as negative reinforcers. As Skinner summarizes: "Under punitive contingencies a person appears to be free to behave well and to deserve credit when he does so. Nonpunitive contingencies generate the same behavior, but a person cannot be said to be free, and the contingencies deserve the credit when he behaves well. Little or nothing remains for autonomous man to do and receive credit for doing." [17]

Since the autonomy of autonomous man is only apparent, the receipt of personal "credit" seems to Skinner a very small recompense for the constant exposure to punishment. Further, his experiments show that behavior may be more efficiently and effectively conditioned with positive than with negative reinforcement. Thus he argues that we should abandon our illusory beliefs in behavioral freedom, forthrightly accept the inevitability of control, and set ourselves to designing environments in which people's behavior will be directed toward socially desirable ends by the exclusive means of positive reinforcements. This was the key to Skinner's imaginary utopia in *Walden Two,* and he now argues that it is the key to the salvation of our real society as well.

Skinner's theory does not bear directly on the classic political question of *who* should seize the control, of course, or under which conditions and toward which socially desirable ends. But he has argued that as the power of operant techniques becomes known, *someone* will inevitably seize it. Since psychologists are likely to have just as enlightened values as any other groups, and have specialized knowledge of human nature besides, Skinner has urged them not to be shy about participating in the shaping of policies of control.

Skinner's assertions about the ubiquity of environmental control, and the desirability of openly seizing it, have made him at once the best known and the most controversial of American psychologists. He was awarded a place in the 1970 revision of *The 100 Most Important People in the World Today,* and a 1975 survey showed him to be the best known scientist in the United States.[18] Recognition does not always imply approval, however, and just as Skinner has many admirers and followers, so has he frightened or enraged others with his pronouncements. He has reported how he was made poignantly aware of his darker reputation one evening after attending a private concert at a friend's home. The musicians were young, their music delightful, and Skinner had mused as he listened to them that *this* was precisely the sort of thing he had envisaged as part of the good life in *Walden Two*. As he left, and spoke warmly to his hostess about the young conductor who had done so well, she replied, "You know, he thinks you are a terrible person. Teaching machines . . . a fascist."[19] Such is perhaps the inevitable price of raising difficult questions. As partial recompense, Skinner has the satisfaction of knowing that thousands of psychologists and other workers daily apply his ideas and techniques to real problems in areas as diverse as education, the behavioral modification of chronically hospitalized mental patients, or testing the effects of drugs. Like Jean Piaget and the earlier generations of psychology's pioneers, B. F. Skinner has both produced knowledge that is useful, and raised issues about human experience and conduct that have a continuing fascination.

Suggested Readings

Piaget's autobiography (translated by Eleanor Duckworth) is included in *Jean Piaget: The Man and His Ideas* by Richard I. Evans (New York: Dutton, 1973). Also included in that volume are transcripts of an interview with Piaget, his own general article entitled "Genetic Epistemology," and several interpretive articles about him. An excellent and comprehensive overview of Piaget's massive corpus is John H. Flavell's *The Developmental Psychology of Jean Piaget* (New York: Van Nostrand, 1963). To get the flavor of Piaget's work from primary sources, the reader might start with *The Moral Judgment of the Child,* 2nd edition, translated by Marjorie Gabain (Glencoe, Illinois: The Free Press, 1948); *Play, Dreams and Imitation in Childhood,* translated by C. Gattegno and F. M. Hodgson (New York: Norton, 1951); and his book co-authored with Barbel Inhelder, *The Growth of Logical Thinking from Childhood to Adolescence,* translated by A. Parsons and S. Seagrim (New York: Basic Books, 1958). Bruner's method of teaching quadratic equations is fully described in Chapter 24 of his *Beyond the Information Given* (New York: Norton, 1973).

Skinner's brief autobiography is contained in *A History of Psychology in Autobiography*, Volume 5, ed. E. G. Boring and Gardner Lindzey (New York: Appleton-Century-Crofts, 1967); the account of his early years is greatly amplified in his recent *Particulars of My Life* (New York: McGraw-Hill, 1976). His early studies with the Skinner box are described in his *The Behavior of Organisms: An Experimental Analysis* (New York: Appleton-Century-Crofts, 1938). He has written engagingly on the applications and implications of his theories in *Science and Human Behavior* (New York: Macmillan, 1953) and *Beyond Freedom and Dignity* (New York: Bantam/Vintage, 1971). For a succinct analysis of Skinner's influence see Norman Guttman's "On Skinner and Hull: A Reminiscence and Projection," in *American Psychologist* (32: 321–328, 1977).

Notes

Chapter 1. The Foundations of Modern Psychology

1. René Descartes, *Discourse on Method,* in *Discourse on Method and Meditations,* ed. and trans. Laurence J. Lafleur (New York: Library of Liberal Arts, 1960), pp. 7–8.

2. Ibid., p. 5.

3. Julian Jaynes, "The Problem of Animate Motion in the Seventeenth Century," in Mary Henle, Julian Jaynes and John J. Sullivan, eds., *Historical Conceptions of Psychology* (New York: Springer, 1973), pp. 166–179.

4. Descartes, *Discourse,* p. 9.

5. Quoted in Jack R. Vrooman, *René Descartes: A Biography* (New York: G. P. Putnam's Sons, 1970), p. 23.

6. Charles Singer, *A Short History of Scientific Ideas to 1900* (London: Oxford University Press, 1962), p. 226.

7. Descartes, *Discourse,* p. 10.

8. Ibid., p. 12.

9. Ibid., p. 15.

10. René Descartes, *Treatise of Man,* trans. Thomas Steele Hall (Cambridge, Massachusetts: Harvard University Press, 1972), p. 113.

11. Ibid., p. 21.

12. Jaynes, "Problem of Animate Motion," p. 171.

13. Descartes, *Treatise of Man,* p. 106.

14. Quoted in John Morris, *Descartes Dictionary* (New York: Philosophical Library, 1971), p. 15.

15. Descartes, *Discourse,* p. 24.

16. Ibid., p. 25.

17. René Descartes, *Passions of the Soul,* as excerpted in *Descartes: Philosophical Writings,* trans. Norman Kemp Smith (New York: Modern Library, 1958), pp. 275–276.

18. Adapted from Descartes, *Treatise of Man,* p. 84.

19. Descartes, *Passions of the Soul,* pp. 283–284.

Chapter 2. The Physiology of the Mind

1. Quoted in Robert M. Young, *Mind, Brain and Adaptation in the Nineteenth Century* (Oxford: Clarendon Press, 1970), p. 10.

2. Ibid., p. 136.

3. Adapted from C. Morgan, *Phrenology and How to Use It in Analyzing Character* (London: Longmans, 1871), pp. xiv–xv.

4. Quoted in Richard J. Herrnstein and Edwin G. Boring, eds., *A Source Book in the History of Psychology* (Cambridge, Mass.: Harvard University Press, 1965), p. 212.

5. Ibid., p. 213.

6. Ibid.

7. Quoted in J. M. D. Olmsted, "Pierre Flourens." In E. A. Underwood, ed., *Science, Medicine, and History* (New York: Oxford University Press, 1953), Vol. 2, 290–302, p. 296.

8. Ibid., p. 293.

9. Quoted in Young, *Mind, Brain and Adaptation,* p. 61.

10. Walther Riese, "Auto-observation of Aphasia Reported by an Eminent Nineteenth Century Medical Scientist." *Bulletin of the Institute of the History of Medicine (28:* 237–242, 1954), p. 241.

11. Ibid., p. 237.

12. Quoted in Byron Stookey, "A Note on the Early History of Cerebral Localization." *Bulletin of the New York Academy of Medicine (30:* 559–578, 1954), p. 571.

13. Quoted in Howard Gardner, *The Shattered Mind* (New York: Knopf, 1975), p. 68.

14. Adapted from Karl Lashley, *Brain Mechanisms and Intelligence* (Chicago: University of Chicago Press, 1929), p. 74.

15. Ibid., pp. 24–25.

16. Quoted in Keith Oatley, *Brain Mechanisms and Mind* (London: Thames and Hudson, 1972), p. 145.

17. Roberts Bartholow, "Experimental Investigations into the Functions of the Human Brain." *The American Journal of the Medical Sciences (67:* 305–313, 1874), p. 309.

18. Ibid., p. 311.

19. Ibid., p. 312.

20. Quoted in Peter Nathan, *The Nervous System* (Harmondsworth, England: Penguin Books, 1969), p. 241.

21. Ibid., p. 239.

Notes

22. Wilder Penfield and Lamar Roberts, *Speech and Brain-Mechanisms* (Princeton: Princeton University Press, 1959), pp. 45–47.

Chapter 3. The Sensing and Perceiving Mind

1. Quoted in J. Bronowski and Bruce Mazlish, *The Western Intellectual Tradition* (New York: Harper and Row, 1920), p. 474.

2. Quoted in Siegfried Bernfeld, "Freud's Scientific Beginnings." *American Imago (6:* 163–196, 1949), p. 171.

3. Quoted in Leo Koenigsberger, *Hermann von Helmholtz,* trans. Frances A. Welby (New York: Dover, 1965), pp. 64 and 73.

4. Ibid., p. 90.

5. Hermann von Helmholtz, "Recent Progress in the Theory of Vision," in Russell Kahl, ed., *Selected Writings of Hermann von Helmholtz* (Middletown, Connecticut: Wesleyan University Press, 1971), p. 192.

6. Quoted in Nicholas Pastore, "Re-evaluation of Boring on Kantian Influence, Nineteenth Century Nativism, Gestalt Psychology and Helmholtz," *Journal of the History of the Behavioral Sciences (10:* 375–390, 1974), p. 387.

7. Hermann von Helmholtz, "The Facts of Perception," in Kahl, ed., *Selected Writings of Helmholtz,* p. 381.

8. Quoted in Kahl, Introduction to *Selected Writings of Helmholtz,* p. xii.

9. Wolfgang Köhler, *The Task of Gestalt Psychology* (Princeton, New Jersey: Princeton University Press, 1969), p. 60.

10. Ibid., p. 66.

Chapter 4. Psychology in the University

1. Quoted in Duane Schultz, *A History of Modern Psychology,* 2nd ed. (New York: Academic Press, 1975), p. 53.

2. Quoted in Arthur L. Blumenthal, *Language and Psychology: Historical Aspects of Psycholinguistics* (New York: Wiley, 1970), p. 238.

3. William James, *The Principles of Psychology,* 2 Vols. (New York: Dover, 1950), Vol. I, pp. 192–193.

4. Henry James, ed., *The Letters of William James,* 2 Vols. (Boston: Atlantic Monthly Press, 1920), Vol. I, pp. 263–264.

5. Ibid., p. 263.

6. Ibid., pp. 118–119.

7. Ibid., p. 215.

8. "In Memory of Wilhelm Wundt, by his American Students." *The Psychological Review,* (*28:* 153–188, 1921), pp. 162–163.

9. Ibid., p. 185.

10. Quoted in Blumenthal, *Language and Psychology,* p. 21.

11. Erwin A. Esper, *A History of Psychology* (Philadelphia: Saunders, 1964), p. vi.

12. F. O. Matthiessen, *The James Family: Including Selections from the Writings of Henry James, Senior, William, Henry, & Alice James* (New York: Knopf, 1961), p. 161.

13. Gay Wilson Allen, *William James: A Biography* (New York: Viking, 1967), p. 67.

14. James, *Letters,* I, p. 58.

15. William James, *The Varieties of Religious Experience* (New York: Collier Books, 1961), p. 138.

16. James, *Letters,* I, pp. 147–148.

17. Quoted in Ibid., II, p. 16.

18. Quoted in Allen, *William James,* p. 305.

19. James, *Letters,* I, p. 293.

20. Ibid., p. 294.

21. James, *Principles of Psychology,* I, p. 104.

22. Ibid., p. 121.

23. Ibid., p. 127.

24. Ibid., pp. 123–126.

25. Ibid., p. 127.

26. Ibid., pp. 237–238.

27. Ibid., p. 244.

28. Ibid., II, p. 449–450.

29. Ibid., p. 463.

30. Ibid., pp. 561–562.

31. Ibid., pp. 573–574.

32. Ibid., pp. 576–577.

33. Ibid., p. 576.

34. James, *Letters,* II, pp. 2–3.

35. Ibid., pp. 327–328.

36. Allen, *William James,* p. 493.

Notes

Chapter 5. Early Hypnotists

1. Quoted in Frank Pattie, "A Brief History of Hypnotism." In Jesse E. Gordon, ed., *Handbook of Clinical and Experimental Hypnosis* (New York: Macmillan, 1967), p. 13.

2. Ibid., p. 21.

3. G. H. Estabrooks, *Hypnotism* (New York: Dutton, 1957), p. 13.

4. Gregory Zilboorg, *A History of Medical Psychology* (New York: Norton, 1967), p. 352.

5. Ibid.

6. Edwin G. Boring, *A History of Experimental Psychology*, 2nd Edition (New York: Appleton-Century-Crofts, 1957), p. 121.

7. Quoted in Zilboorg, *History of Medical Psychology*, p. 353.

8. Henri F. Ellenberger, *The Discovery of the Unconscious* (New York: Basic Books, 1970), p. 87.

9. Sigmund Freud, "Charcot." In James Strachey, ed., *The Standard Edition of the Complete Psychological Works of Sigmund Freud*, 24 Vols. (London: Hogarth, 1953–1974), Vol. III, p. 12.

10. Ibid., p. 13.

11. Gustave Le Bon, *The Crowd* (New York: Viking, 1960), p. 29.

12. Ibid., pp. 35–36.

13. Ibid., p. 34.

14. Ibid., pp. 31–32.

15. Ibid., pp. 118–119.

16. Ibid., p. 125.

Chapter 6. Man in Conflict

1. Sigmund Freud and Joseph Breuer, *Studies on Hysteria*, in James Strachey, ed., *The Standard Edition of the Complete Psychological Works of Sigmund Freud*, 24 Vols. (London: Hogarth, 1953–1974), Vol. II, p. 108.

2. Ibid., p. 7.

3. Sigmund Freud, *The Origins of Psycho-Analysis* (New York: Basic Books, 1954), p. 170.

4. Sigmund Freud, *The Interpretation of Dreams*, in *Standard Edition*, Vol. IV, p. xxvi.

5. Ibid., Vol. V, p. 583.

6. Freud, *Origins of Psycho-Analysis,* p. 325.

7. Sigmund Freud, "Fragment of an Analysis of a Case of Hysteria," in *Standard Edition,* Vol. VII, p. 64.

8. Ibid., p. 86.

9. Sigmund Freud, *Civilization and Its Discontents,* in *Standard Edition,* Vol. XXI, p. 145.

Chapter 7. The Measurement of Mind

1. Francis Galton, *Memories of My Life* (London: Methuen, 1908), p. 245.

2. Ibid., p. 246.

3. Francis Galton, *Inquiries into Human Faculty and Its Development* (London: J. M. Dent, 1907), p. 19.

4. Ibid., pp. 19–20.

5. Ibid., p. 21.

6. Galton, *Memories,* p. 21.

7. Ibid., p. 24.

8. Ibid., p. 35.

9. Quoted in Karl Pearson, *The Life, Letters and Labours of Francis Galton,* 3 Vols. (Cambridge, England: The University Press, 1914–1930), Vol. I, p. 102.

10. Galton, *Memories,* p. 37.

11. Ibid., p. 79.

12. Ibid., p. 80.

13. Ibid., p. 82.

14. Quoted in Pearson, *Life of Galton,* Vol. I, p. 232.

15. Ibid., Vol. II, Plate XVIII (The letter is reproduced in facsimile.)

16. Francis Galton, *Hereditary Genius* (Gloucester, Mass.: Peter Smith, 1972), p. 45.

17. Ibid., pp. 56–57.

18. Ibid., p. 124.

19. Quoted in Galton, *Memories,* p. 290.

20. Galton, *Human Faculty,* p. 17n.

21. Francis Galton, "Hereditary Talent and Character." *Macmillan's Magazine* (*12:* 157–166, 318–327, 1865), p. 165.

22. Galton, *Memories,* p. 287.

23. Galton, *Hereditary Genius,* p. 411.

24. Ibid., p. 79.

25. Pearson, *Life of Galton,* Vol. II, pp. 135–136.

26. Quoted in Ibid., pp. 136–137 (translated from the French by the author).

27. Francis Galton, *English Men of Science* (London: Frank Cass & Co., 1970), pp. 149–150, 148, 162.

28. Ibid., p. 12.

29. Galton, *Human Faculty,* p. 1.

30. Ibid., pp. 26–27.

31. Ibid., p. 28.

32. Ibid., p. 59.

33. Ibid., pp. 62–63.

34. Adapted from Ibid., pp. 83–84.

35. Ibid., pp. 89–90.

36. Ibid., p. 172.

37. Ibid., p. 134.

38. Ibid., p. 135.

39. Ibid., p. 138.

40. Ibid., p. 145.

41. Ibid.

42. Adapted from a Table in Pearson, *Life of Galton,* Vol. III, p. 14.

Chapter 8. Psychology as the Science of Behavior

1. Ivan P. Pavlov, *Conditioned Reflexes: An Investigation of the Physiological Activity of the Cerebral Cortex* (New York: Dover, 1960), p. 3.

2. Quoted in B. P. Babkin, *Pavlov: A Biography* (Chicago: University of Chicago Press, 1949), p. 214.

3. Ibid., p. 37.

4. Ibid., p. 110.

5. Ibid., p. 94.

6. George A. Miller and Robert Buckhout, *Psychology: The Science of Mental Life,* 2nd Edition (New York: Harper & Row, 1973), p. 231.

7. W. Horsley Gantt, Introduction to I. P. Pavlov, *Conditioned Reflexes and Psychiatry* (New York: International Publishers, 1941), p. 35.

8. John Broadus Watson, Autobiography in Carl Murchison, ed., *A History of Psychology in Autobiography,* Vol. III (Worcester, Mass.: Clark University Press, 1936), p. 272.

9. Ibid., p. 274.

10. Paul G. Creelan, "Watsonian Behaviorism and the Calvinist Conscience." *Journal of the History of the Behavioral Sciences (10:* 95–118, 1974), p. 101.

11. Watson, Autobiography, p. 276.

12. John B. Watson, "Psychology as the Behaviorist Views It." *The Psychological Review (20:* 158–177, 1913), p. 159.

13. Ibid., p. 158.

14. Watson, Autobiography, p. 278.

15. Ibid., p. 280.

16. Quoted in Richard J. Herrnstein, Introduction to John B. Watson, *Behavior: An Introduction to Comparative Psychology* (New York: Holt, Rinehart and Winston, 1967), p. xxii.

17. Watson, *Behavior,* p. 146.

18. Ibid., p. 18.

19. Ibid., pp. 313, 316.

20. John B. Watson, "The Place of the Conditioned Reflex in Psychology." *The Psychological Review (23:* 89–116, 1916), p. 89.

21. John B. Watson, *Psychology from the Standpoint of a Behaviorist* (Philadelphia: J. B. Lippincott, 1919), p. 1.

22. Ibid., p. 200.

23. Ibid.

24. Ibid.

25. Ibid., p. 201.

26. Ibid., p. 214.

27. John B. Watson and Rosalie Rayner, "Conditioned Emotional Reactions." *Journal of Experimental Psychology (3:* 1–14, 1920), p. 4.

28. Ibid., p. 5.

29. Ibid., p. 7.

30. Ibid., pp. 12–13.

31. Ibid., p. 14.

32. Herrnstein, Introduction to *Behavior,* p. xxvii.

33. John B. Watson, *Behaviorism* (New York: Norton, 1970), p. 94.

34. Ibid., p. 104.

35. John B. Watson, *Psychological Care of Infant and Child* (New York: Norton, 1928), pp. 40–41.

36. Ibid., p. 82.
37. Ibid., pp. 81–82.
38. Watson, Autobiography, p. 281.

Chapter 9. Modern Pioneers

1. "Jean Piaget, An Autobiography," in Richard I. Evans, *Jean Piaget: The Man and His Ideas* (New York: Dutton, 1973), 105–143, p. 138n.
2. Ibid., p. 111.
3. Ibid.
4. Ibid., pp. 118–119.
5. Jean Piaget, *Genetic Epistemology* (New York: Norton, 1970), p. 15.
6. Quoted in Evans, *Jean Piaget*, p. 53.
7. B. F. Skinner, Autobiography in E. G. Boring & Gardner Lindzey, eds., *A History of Psychology in Autobiography*, Vol. V (New York: Appleton-Century-Crofts, 1967), p. 407.
8. Ibid., p. 396.
9. B. F. Skinner, *Particulars of My Life* (New York: McGraw-Hill, 1976), p. 237.
10. Ibid., p. 249.
11. Ibid., p. 264.
12. Quoted in Ibid., p. 298.
13. B. F. Skinner, "A Case History in Scientific Method," in Sigmund Koch, ed., *Psychology: A Study of a Science*, Vol. II (New York: McGraw-Hill, 1959).
14. Ibid., p. 362.
15. Adapted from F. S. Keller and W. N. Schoenfeld, *Principles of Psychology* (New York: Appleton-Century-Crofts, 1950), p. 45.
16. B. F. Skinner, *Walden Two* (New York: Macmillan, 1962), p. 264.
17. B. F. Skinner, *Beyond Freedom and Dignity* (New York: Bantam/Vintage Books, 1971), p. 76.
18. Norman Guttman, "On Skinner and Hull: A Reminiscence and Projection." *American Psychologist* (32: 321–328, 1977).
19. Skinner, Autobiography, p. 412.

Index